Early Christians Speak

FAITH AND LIFE IN THE FIRST THREE CENTURIES

EVERETT FERGUSON

3rd Edition

DICK WEBER

A·C·U
PRESS

Early Christians Speak: Faith and Life in the First Three Centuries
Third Edition

A·C·U
PRESS

ACU Station, Box 29138
Abilene, TX 79699

Cover design and typesetting by Tigris Creative Studios, LLC, Fort Worth, Texas.

Acknowledgment
The Plates are used by permission of the
Pontificia Commissione di Archeologia Sacra, Rome.

Original edition ©1981, Biblical Research Press. Assigned 1984 to ACU Press. Revised Edition ©1987 ACU Press.

Third Edition ©1999 Everett Ferguson.

Printed in the United States of America

ISBN 0-89112-045-9

Library of Congress Card Number **99-62814**

1,2,3,4,5

TO MY PARENTS

IN THE FLESH AND IN THE FAITH,

THE AUTHOR'S AUTHORS

Table of Contents

A Word to the Reader

These studies in early church history cover various aspects of the church life of early Christians. They focus on the second century. During that period there was much in the practice and teaching of the church which corresponds to what is found in the New Testament, and during that time many new features developed which were to be characteristic of the later history of the church. Some later material which bears on the second century or which serves to complete the account of a development is brought into these studies. Some New Testament texts bearing on the topic are listed at the beginning of each chapter. There is, thus, a stress on historical continuity. We are talking about the same community of people, the same church, as existed in the New Testament. We are tracing out some features of its historical development through the second century.

An illustration may convey some sense of the time span involved: at the beginning of the 2000s the American Civil War (1861-65) is about as distant as the Fall of Jerusalem (A.D. 70) and the death of most of the apostles was at the beginning of the third century. This shows the distance, but it shows also the living memories and continuing effects of certain events.

The concern in these studies is with the Christian community itself—"church life." After the first chapter, which sketches the historical framework, the following studies fall into certain groups. Chapters II–V summarize the Christian proclamation and consider baptism in its doctrine and practice as the means of admission to the church. Chapters VI–XIII consider the community at worship, with special attention to the Lord's Supper. Chapters XIV–XV take up the organization and discipline of the church. Chapters XVI–XIX look at certain aspects of the Christian style of life. By the middle of the second century the church was turning outwards to the pagan world. Its literature reflects this added dimension, which was not prominent in the New Testament. We have selected from a literature dealing with wider interests passages which bear on matters of internal concern to the church, only occasionally in the later chapters reflecting this wider interest in pagan-Christian relations.

The selectivity in the treatment goes further. This book does not attempt a full description of church life in the second century. I have tried not to distort what is included, but there is a certain distortion from omission. The gathering of many texts with limited comments may leave a false impression of homogeneity. Sometimes even when texts seem to agree, the different contexts from which they come may show a diversity in doctrinal viewpoint. In particular, I have largely left aside passages from those groups which came to be regarded as heretical. A fuller treatment of them would have carried us away from our purpose but would have provided a more accurate picture of the diversity in second-century Christianity.

These studies are written especially for those who know the early church only from the New Testament. It is hoped that the book will enable them to break into the New Testament from a new perspective, and so give them a fresh look at early Christianity. Every time the New Testament is seen against a new background, its meaning becomes fresher and sharper.

All who strive to be New Testament Christians in the present age are in a way second-century Christians. Not that we have, consciously or unconsciously, followed the second-century church or taken it as an authority. But, at best, we stand in relation to the first-century Christians as did the second-century Christians. We can never hope to reproduce the circumstances of the first century with its living apostolic witness, miraculous works of the Spirit, and specific historical setting. Apart from the second century's geographical and chronological proximity to the first century, we stand in the same relation to the first century as did the second century. Our faith is dependent on the first-century testimony, and we try to carry that faith over into a new setting. So, we can hope to be, in a sense, only "second-century Christians." Therefore, it is of value to see what that second-century church was–what was its life, what were its successes and failures. That will say something to us about our efforts in our derivative and secondary situation to be faithful to the first-century message.

The effort has been to make the sources available, to let the early Christians themselves speak. Hence, each chapter begins with a selection of the relevant texts. It should not be thought that all the references on a topic are given, but enough are given to be representative and to allow readers to form some conclusions of their own. The translations have been made afresh by the author (except where noted), but with an eye on existing standard translations where these are available. Each text translated at the beginning of a chapter is given a number in the margin–Roman numeral for the number of the chapter and Arabic numeral for the number of the selection within the chapter. Each text will be referred to by this combined Roman and Arabic number (separated by a period) for the sake of ease of reference. In order to make the use of the original sources as meaningful as possible to those unfamiliar with the second century, and in order to avoid constant repetition about date and locality, an appendix gives an alphabetical listing of all the authors and anonymous documents cited in the various studies along with minimal identifying information. The first chapter gives a classification of the writers and writings employed in the following chapters so that the reader can see them in relation to one another. The chronological chart at the back will help in establishing temporal relationships.

Following the quoted sources there is an interpretive commentary and discussion. The bibliography with each chapter is only to indicate some of the principal secondary studies available. A few foreign titles are included where I have been especially indebted to a particular work or where there is a study for which there is nothing comparable in English. The notes at the end of each chapter represent only a very small acknowledgment to the labors of others in the areas of study. The glossary at the end is designed to assist the reader uninitiated in the terminology of early church history. The notes and the indexes will be of special benefit to the student who wishes to pursue these studies further but of less value to the general reader, whose interests have been kept in mind in the explanatory discussions.

Given a historical continuity between the first and second centuries, then certain conclusions follow. If beliefs or practices existed in the first-century church, there should be some trace of them later. Conversely, if they are not found in the early centuries, a serious question is raised about their presence in the New Testament unless there is explicit and unequivocal evidence in confirmation. In the same way, what existed later (even if not in accord with the New Testament teaching) must be derivable in some way from the New Testament situation.

I

The Setting and Sources
for Our Study

"Bring the Books"

WAYS OF OUTLINING EARLY CHURCH HISTORY

Various outlines may be given in order to present an overall view of the church's history in its first three centuries. We offer here some sketches of important developments in order to provide a framework for the more detailed studies in the second century which will follow. This preliminary survey is necessary to give perspective, but naturally the main interest attaches to the more original studies in the succeeding chapters.

Geographical Expansion

First-Century Centers. The church began at Jerusalem, spread to Syria, Asia Minor, and then to Greece and Italy. The New Testament itself, and principally the book of Acts, tells us most of what we know of this expansion. The main centers were the principal cities–Antioch, Ephesus, Corinth, Rome. At the end of the first century Ephesus and the Roman province of Asia were the center of the numerical strength of the church.

The Second Century. By the end of the second century Rome had replaced Ephesus as the strongest and most influential church, although Asia and adjoining provinces continued to be the area where the largest concentration of Christians was. The growth of the church in Alexandria heralded the future importance of this city and of Egyptian Christianity in the church's history. Latin and Syriac versions of the Bible marked the spread of Christianity in North Africa and the interior regions of Syria. Gaul, Spain, the frontier provinces, and lands to the East outside the Roman Empire were outposts of the Christian mission.

The Third Century. There are no accurate figures, only estimates, but it seems that by the end of the third century Christianity composed a sizable minority of the Empire's population. Moreover, interior Asia Minor and Mesopotamia were effectively penetrated, and the kingdom of

Armenia officially accepted the Christian faith. The church spread among the native population of Egypt. North Africa became one of the strong numerical centers. The church began to expand in Spain, became settled on the frontiers of the Empire, and reached Britain.

The expansion into all segments of society matched the geographical expansion and prepared for the official recognition of Christianity by the Roman Empire in the fourth century.

Relations with the Empire

A Part of Judaism. Roman officials treated the church during the first generation of its existence as part of the Jewish religion, which had official recognition as the ancient national religion of a people which made up part of the Empire; hence Roman officials took no notice of the arguments between Jews and Christians, as such, and intervened only to keep the peace.

Early Conflicts: Nero and Domitian. Several factors perhaps contributed to making Rome aware that the church was something more than a branch of Judaism: the number of Gentile converts, the insistence by the Jews that Christians were different, the Jewish revolt of 66-73 in Palestine. At any rate, the first indication of a separate treatment for Christians came when Nero needed a scapegoat for the great fire of Rome in A.D. 64. He settled on the Christians in Rome. This local outburst of persecution began the era of conflict between the church and the Empire. Under Domitian at the end of the first century the Christian community in Rome and Christians in Asia and Palestine experienced distress.

Sporadic Persecutions. Christianity lacked legal recognition and protection, but there was no general proscription of Christianity. Christians, by virtue of being such, were assumed to be guilty of certain crimes which went with profession of the Name. Christian abstention from elements of community life tinged with idolatry and from the forms of the imperial religion caused suspicion and distrust. As a result, there were many outbreaks of sporadic persecution. Generally mob action was responsible for bringing Christians to trial before provincial governors. The Christian refusal to sacrifice to the Emperor was taken as a sign of disloyalty. Although the emperors Trajan and Hadrian took steps to regularize the legal proceedings, Christians were always in danger from jealous Jews, suspicious pagans, and unscrupulous officials. Still it must be remembered that the early persecutions were local and sporadic.

Empire-wide Persecution. The first general, concerted attack against the church came under Decius in 249-251. There were anticipations of his policy in the attitudes of earlier emperors. The threat from barbarians on the frontier, economic chaos in the Empire, and the revival of Roman nationalism in the celebration of the thousandth anniversary of the founding of Rome contributed to Decius' vigorous action. To rally the

Empire to an expression of unity, he ordered everyone in the Empire to offer sacrifices to the traditional gods. Punishment awaited those who refused.

Decius' death brought a reprieve to the church; the revival of the policy of persecution under Valerian (253-260) was equally shortlived. The church had another long period of peace, but the worst was yet to come. During the rule of Diocletian (285-305) there was launched the most vigorous assault on the church that it had sustained. But the Empire had waited too long. The church was now too strong and the policy of persecution could not succeed.

Alliance with the State. Constantine declared his support for the church and granted toleration with the "Edict of Milan" in 313. Imperial patronage of the church was climaxed when Theodosius (379-395) made Christianity the official religion of the state.

Organizational Development

Plurality of Elder-Bishops. The later books of the New Testament and the earliest post-apostolic writings indicate that at the end of the first century the general pattern of church organization was for local churches to be presided over by a plurality of elders, also called bishops, who were assisted by deacons.

A Singular Bishop. The writings of Ignatius of Antioch to the churches of Asia Minor early in the second century describe a three-fold ministry of one bishop, a plurality of elders, and deacons in the churches. The emergence of one bishop at the head of the local church seems to be a fact for Asia and Antioch at the beginning of the second century. This development appears not to have occurred at this early a date in Greece and the West. By the second half of the second century the Ignatian type of church organization was generally accepted.

Councils and Dioceses. We first hear of the bishops from local congregations in the same province meeting for consultation in the second half of the second century in connection with the problem posed by Montanism (for which see below). These meetings were first held in connection with common problems but became regular gatherings.

As churches in the large cities grew, presbyters (elders) were assigned to particular assemblies within the city. Earlier all congregational functions had been under the supervision of the bishop. Increasingly these had to be assigned to the presbyters. Christians living in outlying areas would not have their own bishop but would look to the city church for leadership. Thus the basis was laid for the bishop to preside over several assemblies, although in theory all remained one church. The territory presided over by a bishop is today called a diocese.

Metropolitans and Patriarchs. The bishop of the capital city of a province (the metropolis) or of another principal city began in the third century to assume a leading position among the bishops of the province. He presided at the provincial councils, gave his approval for the ordination of bishops, and often was the principal ordainer himself when a new bishop was installed. The metropolitan bishops of the ancient church were forerunners of the medieval archbishops in the western church.

The idea of councils of bishops led to the calling of ecumenical councils (world wide) to represent the whole church, the first of which was summoned by the emperor Constantine for Nicaea in 325. The council at Nicaea recognized the churches at Rome, Alexandria, and Antioch as having jurisdictional authority extending beyond the usual provincial limits. This was the germ of the patriarchal system. Eventually five patriarchs were recognized–the bishops of the above three churches and Constantinople and Jerusalem. When the division between the Greek (or Eastern) churches and the Latin (or Western) churches occurred, the Greek Church continued to hold to the patriarchal theory of church organization, whereas the Latin Church had recognized the bishop of Rome as the single pope thus giving it a monarchial organization.

Doctrinal Controversies

The Gospel and the Law of Moses. The relation of Gentile converts to the law of Moses was the first great doctrinal controversy in the young church. The apostle Paul successfully waged the battle for the freedom of Gentile Christians from the regulations of the Old Testament law. The outcome resulted in separating the church from Judaism, but there remained a continuing problem in the second century of the place of the Old Testament in the church.

God and the World. The first serious doctrinal threat to the church, once it was separated from Judaism, came from heretical teaching about the nature of God and the world. Roots of this heresy were already being combated in the New Testament writings. The heresy is now commonly known by the name Gnosticism. It was the major issue before the second-century church. Developed Gnosticism generally looked upon the material world as evil. Various errors went with this pessimistic viewpoint. The Father of Jesus Christ, the Redeemer God, is not the Creator God, because the Father could not be responsible for the evil of creation. Jesus Christ was not fully human but only had the appearance of a human body (the view known as Docetism, meaning "appearance"), because he could not be corrupted by association with a fleshly body. There is no resurrection of the body, because the spirit alone is good and capable of salvation. Moral conduct may be either ascetic (the more common conclusion) or licentious, depending on whether one sought to deny or discipline his bodily existence or indulge it as religiously irrelevant.

Basilides was an early second-century Gnostic teacher in Alexandria. The best religious thinker among the Gnostics was Valentinus, who flourished in the mid-second century. Related to the Gnostics in many aspects of his thought was Marcion, who after his disfellowshipping by the church at Rome in 144 became the most powerful antagonist of orthodox Christianity in the second century.

Part of the reaction against Gnosticism is represented by the schismatic movement led by Montanus in the second half of the second century. Montanus claimed to inaugurate a new age of the Holy Spirit in which there was a rebirth of the gift of prophecy. A significant part of Montanism's appeal was its rigorous Christian ethic.

The Nature of Christ. If the God of Creation and the God of Redemption are one, where does Christ fit in? Christians affirmed "one God," in keeping with their Jewish heritage, and the deity of Christ, in keeping with their own experience of salvation. The Christological controversies of the late second and early third century were thus a part of the internal dialectic of Christian faith.

The principal alternatives proposed were Adoptionism, Modalism, and the Logos Christology. According to Adoptionism, Jesus was a good man whom God adopted as his Son. According to Modalism, Jesus was the same being or person as God, who manifested himself in a different mode at different periods. The majority of Christians were satisfied with neither of these options which rationalized away the paradoxes of Christian faith. The orthodox solution was to affirm at the same time the oneness of God, the deity of Christ, and the distinction of the Son from the Father. Many prominent thinkers offered the explanation that as a person's reason (*logos*) was part of his nature but could become distinct in the spoken word, so Christ was divine but distinct from God. Such efforts to explain and harmonize the basic Christian affirmations led to the Trinitarian controversies of the fourth century.

The Church and Repentance. The third century saw controversy and schism develop over the nature of the church and its life. Under the impact of persecution from the state, the church had to define what was going to be its relation to society and what was going to be its attitude to its members who did not live up to its ideals. Rigorists such as Hippolytus and Novatian said that the church is to be a community of the elite pure and cannot grant forgiveness to its members who fall into serious sins. Such sinful Christians may be forgiven by God at the Judgment if they are truly penitent, but the church is not to readmit them to its communion. Hippolytus and Novatian led successive schisms in the Roman church against bishops Callistus and Cornelius, who saw the church in more comprehensive terms as having a place for weak members who could be forgiven and aided by the church in their search for salvation. It was this comprehensive tendency which prevailed in the Catholic Church, but the sectarian spirit continued to arise, both within the Catholic Church (as in monasticism) and without (as in the fourth-century Donatists).

LITERATURE

Perhaps the most helpful approach to the reader will be a literary history of early Christianity. There follows a classification of the major works of early church literature outside the New Testament. The authors quoted in the following studies are provided with chronological and geographical identifications in the alphabetical listing at the end of the book. A few other writers and documents are included here for the sake of completeness.

A. Apostolic Fathers–the writings nearest in time to the New Testament.

> *Didache*.
> Clement of Rome, letter to the church at Corinth.
> *II Clement*.
> *Barnabas*, or *Pseudo-Barnabas* (if the ascription is made to the New Testament Barnabas).
> Hermas, *Shepherd* (or *Pastor*).
> Papias, known only from later quotations.
> Polycarp, *Epistle to the Philippians*. *The Martyrdom of Polycarp* was written shortly after his death by the church at Smyrna.
> Ignatius, Seven genuine *Epistles*.

B. Apologists–defenders of the Christian faith, especially to the Roman government. The second-century apologists are:

> Aristides, *Apology*.
> *Epistle to Diognetus*.
> Justin Martyr, *Apology I* and *II*; *Dialogue with Trypho*, a Jew.
> Tatian, *Oration Against the Greeks* and *Diatessaron* (a harmony of the Gospels).
> Athenagoras, *Plea for the Christians* and *On the Resurrection* (authorship questioned).
> Theophilus, *To Autolycus*.
> Melito, *On the Passover* (a sermon); his *Apology* is known only from later brief quotations.
> Minucius Felix, *Octavius*, a Latin apology in dialogue form of uncertain date.

C. Apocryphal New Testament–Later works imitating the canonical New Testament writings. Second-century representatives include:

> *Gospel of Peter*, a passion Gospel.
> *Gospel of Thomas*–two works go under this name, a later infancy Gospel and a second-century collection of sayings ascribed to Jesus (found in a library of mostly "Gnostic" writings at Nag Hammadi, Egypt), sometimes referred to as the Coptic

Gospel of Thomas (although most of the sayings are also extant in Greek).

Protevangelium of James, devoted to the life of Mary.

Acts of John.

Acts of Paul.

Acts of Peter.

Epistle of the Apostles, really a post-resurrection revelation.

Apocalypse of Peter, visions of the beauty of heaven and the torments of hell.

D. Theologians–Major writers on Christian doctrine.

Irenaeus, *Against Heresies* and *Proof of the Apostolic Preaching*.

Hippolytus (perhaps more than one author's works are attributed to him), *Apostolic Tradition; Refutation of All Heresies; Commentary on Daniel; Against Noetus;* numerous other works.

Tertullian, *Apology; Against Marcion; Prescription of Heretics; Against Praxeas; On Baptism;* many others.

Cyprian, *Epistles* and several treatises, doctrinally the most important of which is *On the Unity of the Church*.

Clement of Alexandria, *Exhortation to the Greeks; Instructor; Miscellanies; Who Is the Rich Man that is Saved?*

Origen, *On First Principles; Against Celsus; On Prayer;* many homilies and commentaries.

E. Others.

There also survive from the second century Acts of the Martyrs, some poems and hymns, a few heretical writings, and some miscellaneous works.

Eusebius of Caesarea, church historian and theologian from the early fourth century, deserves special mention because he quotes so much earlier material now lost except for what he tells us.

BIBLIOGRAPHY

Church History Surveys

Chadwick, Henry. *The Early Church*. "Pelican History of the Church." Baltimore: Penguin Books, 1993. Paperback.

Comby, J. *How to Read Church History*, Vol. 1. New York: Crossroad, 1985.

Ferguson, Everett. *Church History, Ancient and Medieval*. "The Way of Life." Abilene, Texas: Biblical Research Press, 1966. Paperback. Reprint, ACU Press.

Frend, W. H. C. *The Rise of Christianity*. Philadelphia: Fortress, 1984.

Hall, Stuart G. *Doctrine and Practice in the Early Church*. Grand Rapids: Eerdmans, 1991. Paperback.

Guides to Christian Literature

Hamman, Adalbert. *How to Read the Church Fathers*. New York: Crossroad, 1993. Paperback.

Quasten, Johannes. *Patrology*. 4 vols. Westminster, MD: Christian Classics, 1953-1986.

Ramsey, Boniface. *How to Read the Fathers*. New York: Paulist Press, 1985. Paperback. (Topical.)

Collections of Translations

Ancient Christian Writers. New York: Paulist Press, 1946–.

Ante-Nicene Fathers. Buffalo: Christian Literature, 1885-1896; repr. Grand Rapids: Eerdmans, 1950; Peabody: Hendrickson, 1994.

Fathers of the Church. Washington: Catholic University of America Press, 1947–.

Library of Christian Classics. Vols. 1-9, 12. Philadelphia: Westminster, 1953-58.

Nicene and Post-Nicene Fathers. New York: Christian Literature, 1887-1894; repr. Grand Rapids: Eerdmans, 1952; Peabody: Hendrickson, 1994.

Oxford Early Christian Texts. Oxford: Clarendon, 1970–.

Lightfoot, J. B. *The Apostolic Fathers*. Ed. J. R. Harmer, Second edition. Grand Rapids: Baker, 1998.

Stevenson, J. and W. H. C. Frend. *A New Eusebius*, Revised edition. London: S.P.C.K., 1987. Paperback.

General Reference

Bercot, David W., ed. *A Dictionary of Early Christian Beliefs: A Reference Guide to More Than 700 Topics Discussed by the Early Church Fathers*. Peabody: Hendrickson, 1998.

Cross, F. L and E. A. Livingstone, *Oxford Dictionary of the Christian Church*, third edition. Oxford: Oxford University Press, 1997.

Ferguson, Everett, with Michael P. McHugh and Frederick W. Norris. *Encyclopedia of Early Christianity*, second edition. 2 vols. New York: Garland, 1997. Paperback, 1 vol., 1998.

Kelly, Joseph F. *The Concise Dictionary of Early Christianity*. Collegeville: Liturgical Press, 1992.

II

The Faith Preached and Believed

"The gospel which I preached, which also you received"

Some New Testament Texts: Acts 10:36-43; Romans 1:3f.;
1 Corinthians 15: 1-11; I Timothy 3:16; 1 Peter 3:18-22; 1 Corinthians
8:6; Matthew 28:19; 2 Corinthians 13:13; Ephesians 4:4-6.

SOURCES

HERMAS, *SHEPHERD:* First of all believe that God is one, who   II.1
created, fashioned, and made all things to exist out of nothing and who
contains all things and is himself alone uncontained. Believe then in him
and reverence him. (*Mandate* 1.1-2=26. 1-2)

IGNATIUS: For our God Jesus Christ was conceived by Mary   2
according to God's plan of the seed of David and of the Holy Spirit,who
was born and was baptized in order that he might purify the water by his
passion. (*Ephesians* 18.2)

Be deaf whenever anyone speaks to you apart from Jesus Christ, who   3
was of the race of David, who was from Mary, who was truly born, both
ate and drank, was truly persecuted under Pontius Pilate, was truly
crucified and died, with beings heavenly, earthly, and under the earth
looking on, who also was truly raised from the dead, his Father raising
him. (*Trallians* 9)

JUSTIN: In the books of the prophets we found proclaimed   4
beforehand that Jesus our Christ would come, would be born through the
virgin, become man and heal every sickness and disease, raise the dead,
be hated and unrecognized, be crucified, die, and be raised again, and
ascend into heaven, who is and is called the Son of God, and that certain
men would be sent by him to every race of men to preach these things.
(*Apology* I, 31.7)

II.5   In the water there is named over the one who chooses to be born again and who repents of his sins the name of God the Lord and Father of all, he who leads the one being washed to the water using only this description of God . . . . The one who is enlightened is washed also in the name of Jesus Christ who was crucified under Pontius Pilate and in the name of the Holy Spirit who through the prophets foretold everything concerning Jesus. (*Apology* I, 61.10,13)

6   IRENAEUS: And this is the drawing-up of our faith, the foundation of the building, and the consolidation of a way of life. God, the Father, uncreated, beyond grasp, invisible, one God the maker of all; this is the first and foremost article of our faith. But the second article is the Word of God, the Son of God, Christ Jesus our Lord, who was shown forth by the prophets according to the design of their prophecy and according to the manner in which the Father disposed; and through Him were made all things whatsoever. He also, in the end of times, for the recapitulation of all things, is become a man among men, visible and tangible, in order to abolish death and bring to light life, and bring about the communion of God and man. And the third article is the Holy Spirit, through whom the prophets prophesied and the patriarchs were taught about God and the just were led in the path of justice, and who in the end of times has been poured forth in a new manner upon humanity over all the earth renewing man to God. (*Proof of the Apostolic Preaching* 6)[1]

7   For the church, although dispersed throughout the whole world as far as the ends of the earth, received from the apostles and their disciples the faith in one God the Father Almighty, who has made the heaven, the earth, the seas, and all things in them; and in one Christ Jesus the Son of God, who was made flesh for our salvation; and in the Holy Spirit, who has proclaimed through the prophets the plans of God and the comings of Christ, both the birth from the virgin, the passion, the rising from the dead, and the bodily ascension into heaven of the beloved Christ Jesus our Lord, and the manifestation in the glory of the Father for the summing up of all things and the raising in the flesh of all humanity, . . . in order that he might make a just judgment on all, that he might send the spiritual hosts of wickedness, the angels who transgressed and went into apostasy, and the impious, unjust, lawless, and blasphemers among human beings into the eternal fire, but might grant incorruptible life and eternal glory to those who are righteous, holy, and keep his commandments, and who persevere in his love either from the beginning or by repentance. (*Against Heresies* 1.10.1)

8   *EPISTLE OF THE APOSTLES:* They [the five loaves] are a picture of our faith concerning the great Christianity; and that is in the Father, the ruler of the entire world, and in Jesus Christ our Saviour, and in the Holy Spirit, the Paraclete, and in the holy Church and in the forgiveness of sins. (5)[2]

DER BALYZEH PAPYRUS: One confesses the faith thus: I believe   II.9
in one God the Father Almighty and in his only Son our Lord Jesus
Christ and in the Holy Spirit and in the resurrection of the flesh and the
holy catholic church.[3]

PRESBYTERS OF SMYRNA: We also truly know one God; we   10
know the Christ; we know the Son who suffered as he [the Christ]
suffered, died as he died, and rose again on the third day, and is on the
Father's right hand, and will come to judge the living and the dead.
(Quoted by Hippolytus, *Against Noetus* 1)

TERTULLIAN: The rule of faith which is believed: there is but   11
one God, and he alone is the creator of the world, who by the sending
forth of his Word in the beginning brought the universe into being out of
nothing; and this Word, called his Son, was seen in various ways in the
name of God by the patriarchs, was heard always in the prophets, and last
of all was brought down into the virgin Mary by the spirit and power of
God the Father, was made flesh in her womb and was born from her as
Jesus Christ; thereafter he proclaimed a new law and a new promise of the
kingdom of heaven, worked miracles, was nailed to the cross, was
resurrected on the third day, was taken up to heaven to sit at the Father's
right hand and to send in his place the power of the Holy Spirit to guide
believers, and will come again in glory to take the saints into the
enjoyment of life eternal and the heavenly promises, and to condemn the
impious to everlasting fire, both parties being raised from the dead and
having their flesh restored. (*Prescription of Heretics* 13)

HIPPOLYTUS: And when he who is to be baptised goes down to the   12
water, let him who baptises lay hand on him saying thus:
Dost thou believe in God the Father Almighty?
And he who is being baptised shall say: I believe.
Let him forthwith baptise him once, having his hand laid upon his
head.
And after this let him say:
Dost thou believe in Christ Jesus, the Son of God, Who was born of
the Holy Spirit and the Virgin Mary, Who was crucified in the days of
Pontius Pilate, and died, [and was buried,] and rose the third day living
from the dead and ascended in the heavens and sat down at the right
hand of the Father, and will come to judge the living and the dead?
And when he says: I believe, let him baptise him the second time.
And again let him say:
Dost thou believe in the Holy Spirit in the Holy Church, [and the
resurrection of the flesh]?
And he who is being baptised shall say: I believe. And so let him
baptize him the third time. (*Apostolic Tradition* 21.12-18)[4]

II.13   OLD ROMAN SYMBOL:[5] I believe in God [the Father] Almighty; and in Christ Jesus, his only Son, our Lord, who was born from the Holy Spirit and the virgin Mary, who under Pontius Pilate was crucified and buried and on the third day rose again from the dead, ascended into heaven, and sits at the right hand of the Father, whence he is coming to judge the living and the dead; and in the Holy Spirit, the holy church, forgiveness of sins, the resurrection of the flesh, *life eternal.*

DISCUSSION

The above excerpts represent the efforts of early Christians to formulate the essentials of their faith. Numerous other, but very similar, quotations could be added. The impression given is one of a fidelity to the biblical facts of the Gospel, a "history of salvation" view. The Christian faith centered in Christ and what God did through him. But this was prepared for in the Old Testament revelation. The statements quoted show how second-century Christians tried to state the central core of the biblical faith.

The early Christians have left us little about the subjective side of faith, but they said much about the objective content of their faith. The above quoted passages give some of their summaries of belief, some of their confessions of faith. As in the New Testament, there was no fixed formulation of the faith, but a multiplicity of ways of stating the "one faith," "once for all delivered." There was no "creed," in the sense of a formal or official statement which was used as a test of fellowship. (There were certainly doctrinal truths which had to be affirmed in order to remain in the fellowship of the church–e.g., the incarnation in 1 John 4:2-6–but these were not reduced to a fixed wording.) This was no less true of the second century than of the first. But the church did have a clearly defined set of beliefs which it preached and confessed from its beginning. "Creeds," in the sense of confessions of faith, are abundant in the New Testament and in later Christian literature. We have cited some examples from this abundance of confessional material. Although there is no fixity of wording, the quotations are striking for their similarities. A common faith, in continuity with the New Testament proclamation, is testified to.

The New Testament contains summaries of the faith consisting of one-member (about Christ–1 Corinthians 15:1-8; Romans 1:3-4; 1 Peter 3:18-22), two members, (about God and Christ–1 Corinthians 8:6; 1 Timothy 2:5-6; 6:13-14), or three members (about God, Christ, and the Holy Spirit–Matthew 28:19; 2 Corinthians 13:13). Creedal or creed-like statements constructed on the same patterns continue to appear in the second century.

Examples of one-member Christ proclamations are given in selections II.2, 3, and 4.[6] Declarations about Christ are the most fully developed elements in the confessional statements of the early church. Affirmations about Christ are also the most frequently occurring form of confessional statement in the second century. Selection II.1 is exceptional in that it is about God, as would be typical of Jewish statements; the author is probably referring to a traditional sequence ("first") which he then does not continue.

There are a few two-membered statements, as selection II.10.[7] This was a confession used by the presbyters at Smyrna about 190 when they examined Noetus, who carried the faith in one God to a denial of the distinction between the Father and the Son (Modalism). The result was to make the one who suffered on the cross the same as the Father, or else to say that only the humanity suffered. His opponents stressed that it is the divine Son who suffered.

Three-membered or Trinitarian declarations become more common in the second century, as the selections we have quoted go to show. The baptismal "formula" of Matthew 28:19 was of decisive influence here, and many of the passages are in a baptismal context (as II.5 and 12; see further ch. III). But the pattern of "Father, Son, and Holy Spirit" was rather deeply implanted in the structure of Christian faith and in the early church's worship life (chs. XII and XIII).

The currently accepted explanation is that the later expanded confessional statements (II.6, 11, 12, 13) arose from combining longer Christological proclamations (the facts about Christ, such as II.4) with shorter, balanced Trinitarian statements (such as II.5). This combination was made in order to give a fuller statement of Christian belief and perhaps in order to make explicit the church's rejection of certain heretical doctrines. There were various ways of including the items which were thought to be essential to a summary of Christian doctrine. The facts about Christ might be added to the third article as part of the Spirit's predictions through the prophets (II.7). It was more customary, however, to expand the second section about Christ (II.6, 11).[8] Some items might simply be added on at the end (II.8, 9), although there is good reason to see these additions (church, forgiveness of sins, resurrection) as related to the work of the Spirit. The end result (II.12, 13) was to upset the neat Trinitarian balance with the enlarged second article and with other items loosely strung on at the end after the mention of the Spirit.

The earliest detailed descriptions of baptism show the candidate confessing his or her faith in response to questions (II.12). It has, indeed, been argued that this is what was meant by "baptism in the name of the Father, Son, and Holy Spirit." No "formula" was pronounced by the administrator. He asked the questions, and baptism "in the name" was baptism administered at the candidate's response (confession) to the interrogation about the name. This might be confirmed by the fact that the earliest known baptismal creed (as a fixed wording which was confessed at baptism) is the interrogatory creed of Hippolytus' *Apostolic*

Tradition (II.12). Declaratory creeds, in which the candidate repeated a set formula, first appear in the baptismal liturgy of the fourth century. (Voluntary professions by the candidate may be distinguished, for Acts 8:37 is as old as the second century, if not original.) Whether all the statements about baptism in the triune name (see Ch. III) can be explained in this way is another matter. Be that as it may, the Trinitarian interrogations at baptism provided a suitable outline for framing summaries of essential Christian belief, especially in the instruction of those preparing for baptism.

Baptism and instruction for baptism were not the only occasions for the use of confessional material. Among other circumstances where we find creedal summaries are worship (especially benedictions), correspondence, and exorcism (the casting out of demons "in the name of Jesus, who was crucified under Pontius Pilate").[9] Naturally, what was believed and confessed was what had been preached. In preaching, especially in polemics against false doctrine, appeal was made to summaries of the faith (II.6, 7, 11).

When Christians opposed false teaching, they pointed to the facts of the preaching as it had come down to them. Ignatius (II.3) opposed the Docetists who denied the bodily reality of the coming of Christ. He reinforced the traditional summary of Christian teaching which he cites by the insertion of "truly."

Irenaeus and Tertullian, in opposing heretical teaching, call their summaries of Christian teaching the "canon of truth," or "rule of faith."[10] Formerly, it was thought that by these terms they were referring to creeds, which they then paraphrased. Others have seen the terms as a reference to a body of tradition coming down from the apostles alongside the Scriptures. It now seems clear that, for Irenaeus in particular, the "canon of truth" is the truth itself, the main content of the Scriptures.[11] For Tertullian the "rule" more nearly approximates a set form of words, but for him too the reference is to a summary of apostolic teaching.

The summaries which these writers give under the heading of the rule of truth or of faith closely resemble the *kerygma*, or preaching, which modern scholars find in the proclamations of the gospel in the Acts and Epistles of the New Testament.[12] The wording was variable, but of course the basic facts and convictions were consistent, and these writers were talking about the central affirmations of Christianity.

The relationship between the rules of faith (II.6, 7, 11) and the creeds (II.12, 13) was that the former were summaries of the preaching and teaching (hence the fluidity in wording but similar content) and the latter were the confessions made in response to the preaching when it was received and believed (and so tended toward fixity of wording). Obviously there was a correlation between the teaching given and the faith professed, but the context for each differed. Rules of faith were summaries of the teaching given to new converts and then could be used to oppose false teaching; confessions of faith were made principally at baptism, but confessional statements occurred in other settings as well.

From the end of the second century the fluidity which characterized the external expressions of Christian faith and worship began to be replaced by a greater standardization of forms. The Roman church appears to have been the pioneer in the production of crystallized, creedal forms, as it was in other like developments. Its tendency was to reduce the area of allowable variety. Hippolytus' *Apostolic Tradition* provides set forms of written prayers in the worship, but expressly provides that these exact words need not be used but that each may pray according to his ability provided his prayer is orthodox (VIII.5). But the tendency was there.

The confession known as the "Old Roman Symbol," or Creed, likely goes back to Hippolytus' time, with whose baptismal interrogations it has striking similarities. Indeed, the Old Roman Symbol is achieved, with few modifications, simply by turning Hippolytus' questions into statements. This creed was the declaratory baptismal confession in Rome in the fourth century. It was delivered to the candidates during their preparation for baptism, and they recited it verbatim before their baptism. Whether it was contemporary with or (but this is unlikely) even older than Hippolytus, or derived from the interrogations he records, the Old Roman Symbol is the first known creedal form to achieve relative fixity of wording and official sanction. One of its descendants is known as the "Apostles' Creed" and is still recited in many churches today. The name was in use in the fourth century, as was the legend that it had been delivered to the churches by the apostles personally. One form of the legend attributed the composition of each section of the creed to a separate apostle. The present form of the "Apostles' Creed" is first found in a manuscript of the eighth century, but the variations from the Old Roman Symbol are not major, and there is a direct line of descent. But the creed, and the legend about it, was unknown in the Greek churches of the East, and so its popularity in Western Christendom is due to Rome's influence and is not representative of the whole of Christendom.

Creeds were commonly called "symbols" in the ancient church. The reason is not altogether clear. The meaning may be a "pact" or "covenant." Or, if the basic meaning of the word is adhered to, the creed was a token or sign, pointing to the reality of the faith which was confessed by the words.

The *Der Balyzeh Papyrus*, dating from the sixth-seventh century, has sometimes been claimed as containing a creed as old as the second century (II.9). Hence, it is included here, and there is nothing in it that could not come from that early date. But the latest critical edition posits a baptismal setting for the creed, and unless Egyptian usage (which the liturgy in the rest of the papyrus reflects) differed from what is known elsewhere, such a declaratory creed is unlikely at this early date.

The *Epistle of the Apostles* is one second-century document with what appears to be a positive creed (II.8). Its community clearly had a set confession of five points, so that an allegorical significance could be seen in the five loaves of the Gospel miracle of the multiplication of the loaves and fish. The setting in which the confession was used unfortunately is not known, and the details of the wording vary considerably in the existing (Ethiopic) manuscripts.

All of these early confessional formulas and creedal forms lack the philosophical or metaphysical concerns of the later (fourth century, especially Eastern) creeds. The concern is with history, with the primitive proclamation about Christ. That provides a clear point of continuity between the New Testament and the second-century church. It is interesting that the confessions from the New Testament are largely in settings that originally have to do with Christian experience rather than theology–acceptance of preaching, baptism, benedictions, hymns. The second century confessions are becoming more doctrinal but are still functional rather than ontological in their content. The conviction was that God who made all things had entered the world and history in the person of Jesus Christ and the effects of that visitation remained in the Holy Spirit, the church, and forgiveness of sins. The situation was not the same, but the faith was still essentially the same.

The items appended to the end of the confessional formulas after the Holy Spirit are probably not to be thought of as separate objects of faith. Perhaps what is confessed is the Holy Spirit (or all three divine Persons) in the church and the other items, or the working of the Holy Spirit in these ways. Since the confessions are so often connected with baptism, the items mentioned (membership in the church, remission of sins, and resurrection) may originally have gained admission to the confessional statements as gifts conferred in baptism. The description of the church as "catholic" is to be understood in the early sense of the word as "universal." The catholicity of the church, in contrast to local assemblies, was stressed increasingly during the second century in opposition to the heresies which arose later and were geographically more limited than the great church.

BIBLIOGRAPHY

Barr, O. S. *From the Apostles' Faith to the Apostles' Creed.* New York: Oxford University Press, 1964.

Crehan, Joseph. *Early Christian Baptism and the Creed.* London: Burns Oates & Washbourne, 1950.

Kelly, J. N. D. *Early Christian Creeds.* Third edition. London: Longmans, 1972.

Sider, Robert D. *The Gospel and its Proclamation*. Wilmington: Michael Glazier, 1983.

Young, Frances. *The Making of the Creeds*. Philadelphia: Trinity Press International, 1991.

NOTES

[1] Quoted from the translation of the Armenian by Joseph P. Smith, *St. Irenaeus Proof of the Apostolic Preaching*, Ancient Christian Writers, Vol. 16 (Westminster, Maryland: Newman Press, 1952), p. 51. (Used by permission.) For a close parallel cf. *Against Heresies* 4.33.7.

[2] Quoted from *New Testament Apocrypha*, Volume One, edited by Edgar Hennecke and Wilhelm Schneemelcher. English translation edited by R. McL.Wilson. Published in the U.S.A. by the Westminster Press, 1963. Copyright © 1959, J.C.B. Mohr (Paul Siebeck),Tübingen. English translation © 1963, Lutterworth Press. Used by permission. The same translation is in the revised edition, ed. Wilhelm Schneemelcher (Louisville: Westminster/John Knox, 1991), Vol. I, p. 253.

[3] Translated from the text in C. H. Roberts and B. Capelle, *An Early Euchologium: The Der Balyzeh Papyrus Enlarged and Reedited* (Louvain, 1949). An English translation is also in P. F. Palmer, *Sources of Christian Theology*, Vol. 1: *Sacraments and Worship* (Westminster, Maryland: Newman, 1955), pp. 46f.

[4] Quoted from Gregory Dix, *The Treatise on the Apostolic Tradition of St. Hippolytus of Rome* (Reissued with Corrections; London: S.P.C.K., 1968), pp. 36f. I have consulted the edition of Dom Bernard Botte, *La tradition apostolique de saint Hippolyte: Essai de reconstitution*, "Liturgiewissenschaftliche Quellen und Forschungen," 39 (Muenster, 1963). The first passage marked with brackets is bracketed by Botte, because it occurs in only one witness to the text. The second passage in brackets is omitted by Botte as an interpolation. Geoffrey J. Cuming, *Hippolytus: A Text for Students* (Bramcote: Grove, 1976), p. 19 omits the first bracketed phrase but includes the second.
On the triple immersions, see Chapter III.

[5] There are two fourth-century witnesses to the text, the Greek of Marcellus of Ancyra's profession of faith to bishop Julius of Rome (preserved by Epiphanius, *Panarion* 72.3) and the Latin of Rufinus' *Commentary on the Apostle's Creed*. I translate from the Greek, italicizing what is not represented by the Latin and adding in brackets what is in the Latin but wanting in the Greek.

[6] Justin offers numerous examples: *Apology* I, 21.1; 42.4; 46.5; *Dialogue* 63.1; 85.2; 126.1; 132.1. See also Ignatius, *Smyrnaeans* 1 and Aristides, *Apology* 2 (Syriac) 15 (Greek); Melito, *On The Passover* 104-105.

[7] Other examples are Polycarp, *Philippians* 2; *Acts of Justin* 2; Irenaeus, *Against Heresies* 3.4.2.

[8] Tertullian, *On the Veiling of Virgins* 1 expands the facts about Christ after a reference to faith in the Father; *Against Praxeas* 2 does so within a Trinitarian confession of faith.

[9] Justin, *Apology* II, 6; *Dialogue* 85.2.

[10] Similar language in Clement of Alexandria, *Miscellanies* 6.15.124, 125.

[11] Valdemar Ammundsen, "The Rule of Truth in Irenaeus," *Journal of Theological Studies*, Vol. 13 (1912), pp. 574-80.

[12] C. H. Dodd, *The Apostolic Preaching and its Developments* (New York: Harper, 1944). For other summaries of apostolic preaching cf. *3 Corinthians* and *Acts of Paul*, frg. 10, about the preaching of Paul, and Eusebius, *Church History* 1.13.20-21, about the preaching of Thaddaeus to Abgar in Edessa.

III

Baptism in the Second Century

"He who believes and is baptized will be saved"

Some New Testament Texts: Matthew 28:18-20; John 3:5; Acts 2:38; 18:8; 22:16; 1 Peter 3:21.

SOURCES

BARNABAS: Let us inquire if the Lord was careful to make a revelation in advance concerning the water and the cross. Concerning the water it was written with regard to Israel how they will not receive the baptism which brings forgiveness of sins but will supply another for themselves. . . . Blessed are those who placed their hope in his cross and descended into the water. . . . We descend into the water full of sins and uncleanness, and we ascend bearing reverence in our heart and having hope in Jesus in our spirit. (11.1, 8, 11) III.1

HERMAS, *SHEPHERD:* The tower which you see being built is myself, the church. . . . Hear, then, why the tower has been built on the waters. Your life was saved and will be saved through water. The tower has been founded by the pronouncement of his almighty and glorious Name, and it is supported by the invisible power of the Master. (*Vision* 3.3.3, 5=11.3, 5) 2

"I have heard, Sir, from some teachers that there is no other repentance except that one when we descended into the water and received the forgiveness of our former sins." He said to me, "You heard correctly, for it is so. He who has received forgiveness of sins ought to sin no more but to live in purity." (*Mandate* 4.3.1-2=31.1-2) 3

Therefore these also who have fallen asleep received the seal of the Son of God and "entered into the kingdom of God." For, he said, before a man bears the name of the Son of God he is dead, but whenever he receives 4

III.   the seal, he puts away mortality and receives life. The seal then is the water. They descend then into the water dead and they ascend alive. The seal itself, then, was preached to them also, and they made use of it in order that they might "enter into the kingdom of God." . . . These apostles and teachers who preached the name of the Son of God, when they fell asleep in the power and faith of the Son of God, preached also to those who had fallen asleep before them and gave to them the seal of the preaching. They descended therefore with them into the water and ascended again. The former went down alive and came up alive, but the latter who had fallen asleep previously went down dead but came up alive. (*Similitude* 9.16.3-6=93.3-6)

5   DIDACHE: Concerning baptism, baptize in this way. After you have spoken all these things, "baptize in the name of the Father, and of the Son, and of the Holy Spirit," in running water. If you do not have running water, baptize in other water. If you are not able in cold, then in warm. If you do not have either, pour out water three times on the head "in the name of the Father, and of the Son, and of the Holy Spirit." Before the baptism the one baptizing and the one being baptized are to fast, and any others who are able. Command the one being baptized to fast beforehand a day or two. (7)

6   JUSTIN: We shall explain in what way we dedicated ourselves to God and were made new through Christ lest by omitting this we seem to act improperly in our explanation. As many as are persuaded and believe that the things taught and said by us are true and promise to be able to live accordingly are taught to fast, pray, and ask God for the forgiveness of past sins, while we pray and fast with them. Then they are led by us to where there is water, and in the manner of the new birth by which we ourselves were born again they are born again. For at that time they obtain for themselves the washing in water in the name of God the Master of all and Father, and of our Savior Jesus Christ, and of the Holy Spirit. For Christ also said, "Unless you are born again, you cannot enter the kingdom of heaven." ... Since we have been born without our knowledge or choice at our first birth from the moist seed at the union of our parents and have existed in bad habits and evil conduct, in order that we might not remain children of ignorance and necessity but become children of choice and knowledge and might obtain in the water the forgiveness of past sins, there is called upon the one who chooses to be born again and who repents of his sins the name of God the Master of all and Father. ... This washing is called illumination since they who learn these things are illuminated in their understanding. (*Apology* I, 61)

7   For Christ, being "the firstborn of all creation," became also the beginning again of another race, who were born again by him through water, faith, and wood (that is, the mystery of the cross). (*Dialogue* 138.2)

FRAGMENT OF AN UNCANONICAL GOSPEL: You have washed III.8
in these running waters wherein dogs and swine have been cast night and
day, and you have cleansed and wiped the outside skin which also the
harlots and girls who play the pipe anoint, wash, wipe, and beautify for
the lust of men, but within they are full of scorpions and all wickedness.
But I and my disciples, who you say were not baptized [*baptizō* for
ceremonial purification], have been dipped [*baptō*] in the waters of eternal
life . . . ." (*Oxyrhynchus Papyri* V:840)[1]

PSEUDO-CYPRIAN: It follows therefore that Israel is condemned by 9
the hand thrust toward the baptismal bath, and there it is witnessed what
he believed. And after the reception of the seal, purified by the Spirit, he
prays to receive life through the food of thanksgiving, namely of the
bread which comes from benediction. . . . Those learn who one time
taught, they keep commandments who once commanded, are dipped
(*intingō*) who used to "baptize" (*baptizō*), and are circumcised who used to
circumcise. Thus the Lord wanted the Gentiles to flourish. You see to
what extent Christ has loved you. (*Against the Jews* 10.79-82)[2]

MELITO: Are not gold, silver, copper, and iron, after being fired, 10
baptized with water? One in order that it may be cleansed in appearance,
another in order that it may be strengthened by the dipping. [The author
proceeds with illustrations of baptism from nature and concludes:] Now if
the sun with the stars and moon is washed in the ocean, why is Christ
also not washed in the Jordan? (Fragment of his lost work *On Baptism*)[3]

THEOPHILUS: On the fifth day came into existence the living 11
creatures in the waters, through which the manifold wisdom of God is
made plain. For who would be able to count their multitude and variety?
Moreover, the things which come from the waters were blessed by God,
in order that this might be a sign that men were going to receive
repentance and forgiveness of sins through water and the "washing of
regeneration," namely all those who come to the truth and are born
again, and receive blessing from God. (*To Autolycus* 2.16)

IRENAEUS: Now, this is what faith does for us, as the elders, the 12
disciples of the apostles, have handed down to us. First of all, it
admonishes us to remember that we have received baptism for remission
of sins in the name of God the Father, and in the name of Jesus Christ,
the Son of God, who became incarnate and died and was raised, and in
the Holy Spirit of God; and that this baptism is the seal of eternal life and
is rebirth unto God, that we be no more children of mortal men, but of
the eternal and everlasting God. (*Proof of the Apostolic Preaching* 3)[4]

For so (they said) do the faithful keep when there abides constantly in 13
them the Holy Spirit, who is given by Him in baptism. (*Ibid.* 42)

III.14   CLEMENT OF ALEXANDRIA: Is Christ perfected by the washing and is he sanctified by the descent of the Spirit? It is so. The same thing also takes place in the case of us, for whom the Lord became the pattern. Being baptized we are illuminated, being illuminated we are made children, being made children we are perfected, being perfected we are made immortal. . . . This work is variously called a grace gift, illumination, perfection, washing. It is the washing through which we are cleansed of our sins, the grace gift by which the penalties for our sins are removed, the illumination through which the holy light of salvation is beheld, that is through which the divine is clearly seen. . . . Instruction leads to faith, and faith together with baptism is trained by the Holy Spirit. . . . We who have repented of our sins, renounced our faults, and are purified by baptism run back to the eternal light, children to their father. (Instructor 1.6.25.3–26.2; 30.2; 32.1)

15   TERTULLIAN: We as little fishes, in accordance with our *ichthys*[5] Jesus Christ, are born in water. (*On Baptism* 1)

16   It has assuredly been ordained that no one can attain knowledge of salvation without baptism. This comes especially from the pronouncement of the Lord, who says, "Except one be born of water he does not have life." (Ibid. 12)

DISCUSSION

Baptism was the decisive act of conversion for one who accepted the Christian gospel. It marked the break with the past and the initiation into the church of Christ. The fundamental convictions of the faith that was preached by Christian teachers found expression in the act of baptism. Baptism was an act of faith, and it embodied the faith. The centrality of baptism for the faith of early Christians is testified to in early Christian art.[6]

The reader may notice the following items in the texts: baptism was customarily an immersion in water; it was administered to believing penitents; and it was understood as bringing the forgiveness of sins. All are present in the *Barnabas* passage (III.1). Only a few Gnostics on the remote fringes of Christianity denied water baptism or its necessity for the remission of sins. Subsequent chapters will discuss the practice of pouring as a substitute for immersion and the rise of infant baptism.

The Practice

It may be noted here that the references presuppose immersion as the ordinary manner in which baptism was administered: "We descend into the water . . . and ascend" (III.1); "they descended with them into the water and ascended again" (III.4); "they are led by us to where there is water" (III.6). Melito's illustrations are of a dipping in water (III.10). The word baptism itself means a dipping or plunging and was used by Jews and Christians for a ritual bath involving the dipping of the whole body. The passage from the *Didache* (III.5) permitting pouring will be discussed in the next chapter.

The *Didache* (III.5) and Justin (III.6) tell us what we know about the order of baptism in the early second century. A period of instruction, especially pertaining to the moral implications for the Christian life, preceded the baptism. A preparatory time of prayer and fasting enhanced the seriousness of the occasion. An administrator (self-immersion is not confirmed for Christian baptism, unlike Jewish proselyte baptism) and some witnesses were present, but not necessarily the whole community. Baptism was administered to those who believed Christian teaching and repented of their sins.

All references to a "formula" pronounced at the baptism give the triune name ("Father, Son, and Holy Spirit") as in Matthew 28:19 (III.5, 6, 12).[7] References to baptism "in the name of Christ" characterize the baptism as Christian baptism or refer to the confession of faith made by the candidate at his baptism.[8] The "pronouncement of his almighty and glorious Name" (III.2) would be the name of Christ (cf. "suffer on account of the Name" in *Vis.* 3.3.1=10.1). The words said by the administrator may have been interrogatory (as in II.12) rather than declaratory, but this is not certain. The confession of faith in Christ was an essential feature of the baptism and is intimately bound up with all descriptions of baptism and accounts of the meaning of baptism. The phrase "in" or "into the name" is to be understood as meaning "with reference to," "with regard to," "for the sake of," "for the worship of."

The Recipients

As the confession implies, faith was the necessary prerequisite to baptism. Baptism was administered to those who "are persuaded and believe" (III.6), and they are baptized in a spirit of reverence and trust. "Hope" (III.1) is often used by early Christian writers, especially those of a Jewish background, much as "faith" is used today, bringing out the elements of trust and faithfulness that were in the early Christian understandings of "faith."

Baptism was also viewed as an act of repentance (III.3). It was a turning away from past sins and a "promise to live" according to Christian teaching (III.6).

Doctrinal Meaning

Not only was baptism connected with the faith and repentance of the candidate, but it was also connected with the cross of Jesus (III.1, 7,

II.2).[9] This connection is underscored by the preference for the Passover season as the time for administering baptism.[10] It is this connection which gives baptism its doctrinal meaning and accounts for the claims made for baptism.

Quite impressive is the way all second-century authors speak of the meaning and benefits of baptism. Among the blessings ascribed to baptism in these writers are the following: remission of sins, salvation, illumination, eternal life, new birth or regeneration, and the gift of the Holy Spirit. The idea of sacramental regeneration (regeneration effected *by* the water when properly administered in distinction from a regeneration effected *in* the water) that developed in the ancient church is possible only from a position which relates baptism directly to the procuring of spiritual blessings.[11] Hermas even went so far as to say that the righteous dead before the coming of Christ had to receive baptism in order to obtain life (III.4). Such a view finds no support in the New Testament, but it does testify to the strength of the writer's conviction about the necessity of baptism, which was related to a generalizing of the thought found in John 3:5. The unanimity and vigor of the early second-century statements about baptism are presumptive of a direct relationship between baptism and forgiveness of sins from the early days of the church. The consistency with which second-century authors make the statements which they do would have been impossible if this had not been the common Christian understanding earlier. It is inconceivable that the whole Christian world reversed its understanding of the meaning of its central rite of conversion within fifty years of the lifetime of the apostles.

A common designation for baptism in the early sources was "the seal" (e.g., III.4, 12; *2 Clement* 6.9; 7.6; 8.6), signifying that the person now belonged to the Lord.[11a] When the bestowal of the Holy Spirit was identified with the post-baptismal laying on of hands and anointing, the terminology of the seal was applied to these actions (III.9).

The language of new birth or regeneration appears to have been the favorite conception of the second-century church about baptism. John 3:5, or the language from the same tradition, laid hold on the imagination of the early church and shaped much of its thinking about baptism. There seems to have been no doubt that the text referred to baptism (III.4, 6 [cf. IX.3], 16).[12] Its imagery was everywhere used to describe the meaning of baptism, and its influence helped to determine new practices (ch. V).

The first treatise devoted to baptism of which we know, by Melito of Sardis (III.10), indicates the importance of baptism. In the one passage from the work which survives the author finds all of nature having received a baptism. Hence, it was fitting that the Lord of nature was baptized. Our oldest surviving work on baptism is by Tertullian (III.15, 16). He goes further in finding baptism everywhere he finds a reference to water in scripture.

The benefits conferred by Christian baptism placed it in contrast with the ceremonial washings of the Jews (III.1, 8, 9).[13] This is the chief point in the episode from the otherwise unknown apocryphal gospel preserved in the Oxyrhynchus papyri. This document and Pseudo-Cyprian attest the use of *baptizō* for the Jewish ritual bath by immersion. *Intinguō* (or *intingō*), "to dip, plunge, or dye," was the Latin equivalent of the Greek *baptizō*, which the Latin borrowed and which prevailed over *intinguō* as the Latin term for the Christian ceremony.

The Ceremony

Considerable elaboration in the ceremony of Christian initiation had occurred by the end of the second century. The writings of Tertullian of Carthage and Hippolytus of Rome at the beginning of the third century are in sufficient harmony to indicate a fairly uniform baptismal ceremony in the West by the end of the second century. One can discern through the elaboration the simpler New Testament process of instruction, confession of faith, immersion, and acceptance into Christian fellowship. Many of the elements in the procedure may be seen as a "ritualizing" of the teaching concerning faith and repentance in connection with baptism. Some elements from Jewish and Greek culture were borrowed and used to develop Christian ideas. All added to the solemnity of the occasion.

We follow in the outline below the procedure described in the full account of Hippolytus' *Apostolic Tradition*, with the supporting references from Tertullian added.[14]

A. Preliminaries.

1. Catechumenate (*Apostolic Tradition* 16-19)–Three years were to be spent as "hearers of the word" before baptism, but character and not length of time was the decisive thing. Many occupations and sins were to be rejected before one could be a candidate for baptism.
2. Scrutiny (*Apos. Trad.* 20)–The candidate's life was "examined" and those who brought him testified to his manner of life while a catechumen.
3. Baptismal preparation (*Apos. Trad.* 20; Tertullian, *On Baptism* 20)–On the Thursday before the Sunday of the baptism (Passover and Pentecost were the preferred times according to *On Baptism* 19) the candidate, according to Hippolytus, bathed. He spent Friday and Saturday in fasting, on Saturday was exorcised by the bishop (to drive out any demons), and spent Saturday night in a vigil of Scripture reading and instruction. Tertullian refers to fasting, praying, and confessing one's sins.

B. Pre-Baptismal Liturgy.
1. Blessing the water (*Apos. Trad.* 21; *Bapt.* 4)–Prayer to God brought the sanctifying power of the Holy Spirit upon any waters in order to give them the power to confer spiritual blessings. This practice has plausibly been connected with the change from "running" (literally "living") water, as in the *Didache* (III.5), to cistern water for baptizings.[15]
2. Disrobing (*Apos. Trad.* 21)–The candidates removed their clothes, for they were naked at their baptism. Later writers tell of provisions to preserve modesty.
3. Renunciation of Satan (*Apos. Trad.* 21; Tertullian, *On the Crown* 3 and *On Shows* 4)–The candidate made a verbal repentance before witnesses, "I renounce you Satan, and all your service[16] and all your works" (Hippolytus), "the Devil, his pomp, and his angels" (Tertullian). Later sources balance this with a verbal adherence to God.
4. Anointing with oil of exorcism (*Apos. Trad.* 21)–All evil spirits departed so the candidate was delivered from their power and was ready to be brought into Christ.

C. Baptism Proper.
1. Confession of faith (*Apos. Trad.* 21)–The candidate was asked if he or she believed in Father, Son, and Holy Spirit, and following each affirmation there was an immersion (II.12). The triple confession alternating with immersions may be alluded to by Tertullian (*Bapt.* 6; more clearly in *On the Crown* 3), but another passage seems to imply a profession of faith before the baptism (*On Shows* 4). In other sources later a declaratory recitation of one's faith supplanted (or supplemented) the reply to interrogations. Both procedures may be ancient (cf. the reading of Acts 8:37 in the manuscripts of the "Western" text, represented in the Authorized Version, for the candidate's declaratory confession).
2. Triple immersion (*Apos. Trad.* 21; Tertullian, *On the Crown* 3; *Against Praxeas* 26)–The confession according to Hippolytus is made while the candidate is standing in the water. The administrator's hand rests on his head and after each confession plunges it beneath the water. Tertullian admits that the triple immersion is an "ampler pledge than the Lord appointed in the Gospel." Its origin is obscure. Possible explanations refer to the influence of the triune formula in Matthew, contrast with Jewish proselyte baptism, or controversies in the second-century church over the Trinitarian nature of God.[17] Hippolytus makes no reference to a formula pronounced by the administrator in addition to the interrogations, but Tertullian declares that Christ had delivered the formula in the command to baptize (*Bapt.* 13).

Tertullian allows the baptism to be performed by a bishop, presbyter, deacon, or disciple (*Bapt.* 17), but Hippolytus assigns different functions in the ceremony to each.

3. Anointing with oil of thanksgiving (*Apos. Trad.* 21; Tertullian, *Bapt.* 7)–This was done by a presbyter as soon as the one baptized emerged from the water. The person then dried off, put on clothes, and was led into the assembly.

D. Post-Baptismal Liturgy.

1. Laying on of hands and second anointing (*Apos. Trad.* 22; Tertullian, *Bapt.* 8)–The bishop laid a hand on the newly-baptized person's head, prayed, poured oil on his head, and "signed him." Tertullian mentions only the laying on of the hand at this point and connects the coming of the Holy Spirit with this moment and not with the baptism. This assumes that his reference to anointing in chapter 7 is to be equated with Hippolytus' first anointing. In *On the Resurrection of the Flesh* 8 he puts an anointing, signing, and laying on of the hand together. Tertullian's interpretation is the starting point for treating confirmation as a separate sacrament from baptism.

2. Kiss of peace and baptismal eucharist (*Apos. Trad.* 22-23; Tertullian, *On the Crown* 3)–The kiss was a sign of fellowship and brotherly love. At the new Christian's first communion, which followed immediately on the baptism, there was given along with the bread and wine a cup of water and then milk mixed with honey. This was the food of infants and symbolized entrance into Canaan, the promised land.

The three acts of immersion (symbolizing cleansing and remission), anointing (symbolizing receipt of the Holy Spirit), and taking the eucharist (symbolizing fellowship and the heavenly banquet) were kept together and were regarded as forming the whole of initiation and acceptance into the church. The sermon *Against the Jews* (III.9), preserved among the writings of Cyprian but possibly dating from the end of the second century, alludes to the three acts together, and in so doing pulls together a common conception.[18]

BIBLIOGRAPHY

Benoît, André and Charles Munier. *Le Baptême dans l'Eglise ancienne (Ier-IIIe siècles)*. Traditio Christiana IX. Bern/NewYork: Peter Lang, 1994. [Original Greek and Latin texts with French translations; the German edition has German translations.]

Ferguson, Everett. "Baptismal Motifs in the Ancient Church." *Restoration*

Quarterly. Vol. 7:4 (1963), pp. 202-216.

Ferguson, Everett, ed. *Conversion, Catechumenate, and Baptism in the Early Church.* Studies in Early Christianity, Vol. XI. New York: Garland, 1993.

Finn, Thomas M. *Early Christian Baptism and the Catechumenate: West and East Syria.* Message of the Fathers of the Church 5. *Early Christian Baptism and the Catechumenate: Italy, North Africa, and Egypt.* Message of the Fathers of the Church 6. Collegeville: Liturgical Press, 1992.

Whitaker, E. C. *Documents of the Baptismal Liturgy.* Second edition. London: S.P.C.K., 1970.

Ysebaert, J. *Greek Baptismal Terminology.* Nijmegen, Netherlands: Dekker & Van de Vegt, 1962.

NOTES

[1] The papyrus itself is fourth-century, but the editors (Greenfell and Hunt) assign the original to the second century. Jesus and his disciples have been criticized by a Jewish priest for ceremonial uncleanness. The quotation is from Jesus' reply, partially restored at the end, but the restoration is certain.

[2] I have closely followed the German translation of the Latin original given by Dirk Van Damme, *Pseudo-Cyprian Adversus Iudaeos,* "Paradosis" XXII (Freiburg, 1969).

[3] Translated from E. J. Goodspeed, *Die ältesten Apologeten* (Göttingen, 1914), pp. 310f. Cf. also, R. M. Grant, *Second Century Christianity* (London: S.P.C.K., 1946), pp. 73f.

[4] This and the following passage are quoted from the translation of Joseph P. Smith, *St. Irenaeus Proof of the Apostolic Preaching,* Ancient Christian Writers 16 (New York: Newman, 1952), and are used by permission.

[5] *Ichthys* is the Greek word for fish. Origen, *Commentary On Matthew* 13.10 and the Inscription of Abercius (see ch. XIII.11) refer to Christ as the Fish. Is the "big fish" of the Coptic *Gospel of Thomas* 8 Christ? The classic study of the fish symbolism in early Christianity is F.J. Dölger,

Ichthys: Das Fisch-Symbol in frühchristlicher Zeit (Münster, 1928), 4 vols., the last two of which are plates. Dölger argues that the acrostic on the letters of the Greek word for fish–Jesus Christ, God's Son, Savior–which is found in the *Sibylline Oracles* 8.217-250 is as old as the second century (Vol. 1, pp. 51-68; cf. 153-159). The acrostic poem on "Jesus Christ, God's Son, Savior" in the *Sibylline Oracles* is quoted in Eusebius, *Or. Const.* 18. "Jesus Christ, God's Son, Savior" is a short confessional formula, but it is an open question whether the initial letters of the words in the formula was the start of the fish symbol for Christ or the symbol gave rise to the acrostic. For fishes as a designation of Christians, see J. Daniélou, *Primitive Christian Symbols* (Baltimore: Helicon Press, 1964), pp. 50f. *Piscina* (= fish pond) was a favorite word for baptistery. Note the picture in the Catacomb of Callistus showing the baptism of Christ alongside a fisherman drawing a fish from the water–Plate I of this book, and compare Plate III.

[6] André Grabar, *Christian Iconography* (Princeton, N.J.: Princeton University Press, 1968), *passim*; F. van der Meer and Christine Mohrmann, *Atlas of the Early Christian World* (New York: Nelson, 1958), pp. 42, 125ff.; J. Wilpert, *Die Malereien der Katakomben Roms* (Freiburg, 1903), plates 27, 29, 39, 58, 73, 228, 240. See Plates I and II of this book.

[7] *Acts of Peter* 5; Pseudo-Clement, *Recognitions* 4.32; *Didascalia* 16.

[8] Joseph Crehan, *Early Christian Baptism and the Creed* (London: Burns Oates & Washbourne, 1950).

[9] For the connection of the passion and baptism, see also Justin, *Dialogue* 13 and 86. Ignatius (II.2) expresses the further thought that the baptism of Christ had purified water for the purposes of salvation; cf. Clement of Alexandria, *Selections from the Prophets* 7.

[10] Tertullian, *On Baptism* 19.

[11] The Pseudo-Clementine *Homilies* 11.25ff. strongly stresses the necessity of baptism. This passage is considered to belong to an early stratum of this composite work.

[11a] G. W. H. Lampe, *The Seal of the Spirit*, Second edition (London: S.P.C.K., 1967).

[12] Add also Irenaeus, *Against Heresies* 3.17.1f.; Clement of Alexandria, *Miscellanies* 4.25.

[13] Cf. also Justin, *Dialogue* 14; 19.

[14] The full texts are given in Whitaker (see bibliography), pp. 2-9. See ch. II, note 4 for editions of the *Apostolic Tradition*.

[15] For "living water" see Pseudo-Clement, *Contestatio* 1.2 and the article cited in note 7 to Chapter IV. For the blessing of the water, L. L. Mitchell, "The Thanksgiving over the Water in the Baptismal Rite of the Western Church," in B. D. Spinks, ed., *The Sacrifice of Praise* (Rome: Edizioni Liturgiche, 1981). On artificial collections of water, Timoteo Jose Ofrasio, *The Baptismal Font: A Study of Patristic and Liturgical Texts* (Rome: Pontificio Instituto Liturgico, 1990).

[16] "Pomp" is preferred by Botte, *La tradition apostolique de saint Hippolyte* (Münster, 1963), *ad loc.*, as the Greek word behind the Sahidic for "service."

[17] The comparison of the three immersions to the three days spent by Jesus in the tomb is a symbolic explanation and hardly the cause of the practice–Cyril of Jerusalem, *Lectures on the Mysteries* 2.4 (= Catechetical *Lectures* 20.4). A curious piece of evidence for the practice is the triple immersion of the lion in the name of Jesus Christ in the Coptic fragment of the *Acts of Paul* (Wilhelm Schneemelcher, ed., *New Testament Apocrypha*, rev. ed., Vol. 2 [Louisville: Westminster/John Knox, 1992], p. 264).

[18] *The Acts of Peter* 5 has the sequence of baptism in the triune name, signing, and eucharist.

IV

Alternatives to Immersion

"Buried with Christ by baptism into death"

Some New Testament Texts: Matthew 3:16; John 3:23; Acts 8:
36-39; Romans 6:3-5; Colossians 2:12.

SOURCES

Testimony that Baptism was a Submersion

TERTULLIAN: Baptism itself is a bodily act, because we are immersed   IV.1
in water, but it has a spiritual effect, because we are set free from sins. (*On
Baptism* 7)
    There is no difference whether one is washed in the sea or in a pool, in   2
a river or a fountain, in a reservoir or a tub, nor is there any distinction
between those whom John dipped in the Jordan and those whom Peter
dipped in the Tiber, unless that eunuch whom Philip dipped in the
chance water found on their journey obtained more or less of salvation.
(*Ibid.* 4)

ORIGEN (in commenting on the crossing of the Red Sea speaks of   3
Christian baptism): The evil spirits seek to overtake you, but you descend
into the water and you escape safely; having washed away the filth of
sin, you come up a "new man," ready to sing the "new song." (*Homilies on
Exodus* 5.5)

CYRIL OF JERUSALEM: For as he who plunges into the waters and is   4
baptized is surrounded on all sides by the waters, so were they also
baptized completely by the Spirit. The water, however, flows around the
outside, but the Spirit baptizes also the soul within completely.
(*Catechetical Lectures* 17.14)[1]

IV.5   BASIL OF CAESAREA: How then do we become in the likeness of his death? We were buried with him through baptism. . . . How then do we accomplish the descent into Hades? We imitate the burial of Christ through baptism. For the bodies of those being baptized are as it were buried in water. (*On the Holy Spirit* 15.35)

6   AMBROSE: We discoursed yesterday on the font, the appearance of which in shape is like a tomb,[2] into which we are received, believing in the Father and the Son and the Holy Spirit, and we are plunged and we lift ourselves up, that is we are resurrected. . . .

So therefore also in baptism, since it is a likeness of death, without doubt when you dip and rise up there is made a likeness of the resurrection. (*On the Sacraments* 3.1.1, 2)

7   JOHN CHRYSOSTOM: When the priest pronounces, "So-and-so is baptized into the name of the Father and of the Son and of the Holy Spirit," he three times puts the head down and raises it up, preparing you to receive the descent of the Spirit by this mystical initiation. (*Baptismal Instructions* 2.26)[2a]

8   Exactly as in some tomb, when we sink our heads in water, the old man is buried, and as he is submerged below, he is absolutely and entirely hidden. Then when we lift our heads up, the new man again comes *up*. (*Homilies on John* 25.2, on John 3:5)

Evidence of a Different Practice

9   CYPRIAN: You have asked also, what I thought concerning those who obtain God's grace in sickness and weakness, whether they are to be accounted legitimate Christians, because they are not washed with the water of salvation but have it poured on them. . . . We think that the divine benefits can in no way be mutilated and weakened. . . . In the sacraments of salvation, when necessity compels, and God bestows his mercy, the divine abridgements confer the whole benefit on believers, nor ought any one to be troubled that sick persons seem to be sprinkled or poured upon when they obtain the Lord's grace. . . . Whence it appears that the sprinkling also of water holds equally with the washing of salvation. When this is done in the church, where the faith both of receiver and giver is sound, all things may stand firm and be consummated and perfected by the majesty of the Lord and by the truth of the faith. (*Epistle* 69 [75].12)

10   EUSEBIUS: [Novatian] fell seriously ill and was thought to be about to die. In the bed itself on which he was lying he received grace[3] by water being poured around over him, if it is proper to say that such a one received it. . . . When he believed, he was counted worthy of the office of

presbyter by the favor of the bishop who laid his hand on him for this IV.
rank. The bishop was opposed by all the clergy and many of the laymen, since it was not lawful for someone who had received pouring in bed on account of sickness to become a member of the clergy,[4] but he asked to be allowed to ordain this one alone. (*Church History* 6.43.14, 17, quoting a letter from Cornelius, bishop of Rome, 251-253)

DISCUSSION

Immersion Was Customary

The ordinary practice of baptism in the ancient church was immersion. Such is the consistent testimony of the sources from the New Testament until later times. Chapter III noted the early second-century indications of immersion (III.1, 3, 4, 6, 15) and described the ceremony at the end of the second century according to the reports of Hippolytus and Tertullian.[4a] The sources at the beginning of this chapter (IV.1-8) give a sampling of representative texts from the third and fourth centuries. These writers clearly describe or allude to a total submersion of the body. They are representative, authoritative church leaders from both the Greek and Latin speaking branches of the church.

Immersion has remained the practice of the Greek and other Eastern Churches until this day. The exceptions came to prevail in the medieval Western Church, and from that development most Protestant churches used mainly sprinkling or pouring, but immersion is becoming more common even in churches (both Catholic and Protestant) that have not traditionally used it.

The Didache's Exception

The earliest reference to a substitute for immersion, and the only one before the third century, is found in the *Didache* (III.5). It may be noted that in this document "baptize" (*baptizō*) still means "immerse," and to describe another action another word was used. The document reveals many Jewish affinities, and the preferences for the kind of water for baptism may go back to Jewish preferences. The word for "running" water is "living." Motion was a characteristic of "life" in ancient thought and made such water more appropriate for a "life-giving" ordinance. "Still" water that had been collected in a pool or cistern was subject to impurities. Natural sources of water supplied the locations for baptism in the earliest times (IV.2) before specially designed structures were built. It was in the absence of such natural sources or of water in sufficient depth for immersion that the compiler of the *Didache* permitted pouring. And that is clearly a last resort.

According to the *Didache* a copious amount of water could be poured three times on the head. The three times may have been due to the Trinitarian formula; trine immersion was customary by the end of the second century (Chapter III). The head, as the most important part, perhaps represented the whole body.

One of the leading modern students of the *Didache*, the Roman Catholic scholar J. P. Audet, has concluded that the section after the command to immerse in the triune name in running water is an interpolation into the original document.[5] Audet's elaborate analysis of the document is not at all convincing. Nevertheless, there is good evidence that the present form of the *Didache* has undergone several stages of compilation. It is a characteristic of the church order literature, of which this is the earliest representative, to bring the instructions "up-to-date" by including later practices alongside earlier material. There are grammatical changes in the text at the point where Audet marks the interpolation. The unusual, not to say exceptional, nature of the *Didache's* instructions about pouring could be explained as an interpolation made somewhere in the transmission of this composite document. On the other hand, since I would accept such hypotheses only if other explanations fail, I would propose a way in which the passage as it stands can be accepted and placed in the line of development.

Didache 7 may be describing in its later part a "partial immersion," and not a simple pouring. According to a partial immersion the candidate stands in as much water as the font will hold and water is poured over the head three times in sufficient amount to run down over the remainder of the body and wet the whole person.[6] The intention may have been to give the effect of running water covering the person. Such a "partial immersion" is permitted as an alternative to a submersion in modern Orthodox Churches and is found by some scholars in the archaeological evidence. It is possible that the *Didache is* saying, "If you do not have either cold water (in a natural pool or fountain) or warm water (in an artificial container) in sufficient amount to duck the head into it, pour out water three times on the head."

The substitution of pouring perhaps came through Jewish influence with the different types of purifications under the Law. The Jewish "flavor" of the *Didache* has already been noted, and "Jewish" influence was stronger in the Western Church, which took the Old Testament more literally, than in the Greek Church. A triple lustration was known in paganism, and if this passage is early, the analogy of pouring may have led to the three immersions. Another possibility, especially applicable to the baptisteries mentioned below, was the desire to reproduce "living water" where cistern water was used.[7] In the present state of knowledge we are reduced to speculation.

Other Possible Exceptions

Tertullian, *Baptism* 12, allows that some call a baptism the overwhelming of the apostles in the boat during a storm (Matt. 8:24), but he denies that this was Christian baptism.[8] His statement in *On Repentance* 6, "Who will grant a man of such faithless repentance a single sprinkling of any water," means that an impenitent person would not be given even a sprinkling much less an immersion. The apocryphal second-century *Epistle of the Apostles* has been thought by some to refer to pouring,[9] but the words about the hand of the administrator do not necessarily imply affusion: "I [Jesus is speaking] have given them the right hand of the baptism of life and forgiveness" (27).[10] The work survives only in late Coptic and Ethiopic manuscripts. If the latter translation is more literal, the reference could be to the hand of the administrator and imply nothing about affusion. There is a reference to pouring and sprinkling water in the Christian *Sibylline Oracles* 7.74-91, but what is being described in the ceremony, which draws on the imagery of pagan sacrificial ritual, is obscure and offers no clear evidence for normal church practice.[11]

Evidence from Archaeology

Natural supplies of water or already existing structures built for the collecting and storing of water supplied the first sites for baptism. Tertullian's listing of sources in pairs of running versus still water (IV.2)[12] may be to quiet reservations about the propriety of using stored water. For Tertullian the validity of any water depends on the coming of the Holy Spirit upon it.

The earliest specially designed baptisteries which have been identified and dated do not go behind the third century.[13] These early baptisteries are too large, and indeed unnecessary, for an affusion. But it has been contended that some are not large enough or deep enough for submersion. It is possible that some of these were constructed for the partial immersions described above. Where the dimensions (about a yard in length) would seem to rule out a horizontal immersion (but with the shorter stature of ancient peoples this would not be the case as often as might be supposed), a vertical immersion (the administrator's hand ducking or bending the upper part of the body under the water) would be possible. Literary texts (II.12; IV. 6, 7, and 8) and pictures showing the administrator's hand on the head of the candidate[14] indicate that this was the normal mode of immersion. Such a procedure does not require the size baptistery that laying the body out (in imitation of modern burial practice) does. Some existing fonts or basins are reported to be too shallow even for this (sunk a foot or less below floor level).[15] But it is not clear that there were never walls built up around the depression. Walls extending at least to waist height occur commonly in fourth-century and later baptismal fonts.

Lack of space precludes the examination of individual baptisteries that a full study would require, but their later date gives them only secondary value for a study of the second-century practice. One of the famous finds of Christian archaeology is the house at Dura Europos remodeled as a place of Christian meeting after 232 and destroyed before 256. One room was designed for the performance of baptism and paintings were executed on the walls. At one end of the room was placed a basin under a canopy. The dimensions of the basin are a length of five feet four inches by a width which varies from three feet to three feet four inches by a depth of three feet one inch. A step or ledge on the inside aided entry and could have been used for a person to sit on and have the upper part of his body lowered beneath the water, submerging the whole.[16]

Some of the Christian catacomb paintings have in the past been dated to the second century, but the current conclusion is that there is no Christian art before about 200.[17] Some of the earliest paintings from the Catacombs depict a baptism. Indeed a baptism (especially the baptism of Christ) was one of the more popular scenes on wall paintings in the Catacombs and in sculpture on sarcophagi.[18]

Certain characteristic features in the portrayal of baptismal scenes argue for an immersion. The candidate is normally naked, as for the baths. He stands in water or (in sculpture) the water is piled up behind him. The administrator's hand rests on the head of the candidate, ready to guide the head down. No early picture shows the administrator pouring or sprinkling water. Where, in later pictures, something comes from the beak of the dove, we should likely think of the anointing oil which symbolized the Holy Spirit given after baptism (see Ch. III), inasmuch as the dove symbolized the Holy Spirit. Since the nakedness and the hand on the head are mentioned in the literary texts (II.12; IV.7), the artist was giving a realistic portrayal, whatever symbolic meaning was present (nakedness–new birth; hand on the head–blessing). Since immersion is a continuous act, it cannot be portrayed in a still picture as easily as a pouring or sprinkling could be shown. A particular moment has to be selected. What is shown is consistent with an immersion and contains details inappropriate, unnecessary, or contradictory to some other method of administering baptism. The low level of water in some pictures, particularly in the sculptures on sarcophagi, is to allude to the presence of water rather than to give a realistic picture.

There is some evidence for streams of water coming into some of the fonts, and some of the sculpture may indicate that the head was pushed into the stream of water or that the water was guided over the head of the one being baptized. Such might be an indication of partial immersion, but such representations are later and are not necessarily exceptions to submersion.[19] Pictures of an undoubted sprinkling do not come until the late Middle Ages in the West.[20] Even after infant baptism (Ch. V) became the rule, immersion was the usual practice, as shown by both art and the baptisteries.

Clinical Baptism

The *Didache* is the only indication before the middle of the third century of the use of anything but immersion, even in case of emergency. In the third century there is evidence for pouring as a substitute for dipping in the cases of infirm or sick persons. Since it was given to persons confined to their beds (*klinē* in Greek), it was called clinical baptism. Initially the practice seems to have sought to duplicate the normal rite as much as possible by wetting the whole person.

Cyprian (IV.9) is the first writer to give a systematic defense of such a practice. Apparently there were those who had doubts about its efficacy. Cyprian recognizes that it is an "abridgement" or "accommodation." He is careful to insist that everything else must be in order, but when it is, he considers sick-bed pouring equally effective with the normal practice. It may be noted that his language contrasts "wash" with "pour." "Wash" in itself said nothing about the manner of the application of water, but the word was used by Christians for the baptismal immersion bath (perhaps in part from the influence of Greco-Roman bathing establishments). Cyprian's terminology reflects Christian word usage.

The clinical baptism of Novatian (IV.10) provided an interesting case. We know the circumstances from his opponent, Cornelius, who was elected bishop of Rome in A.D. 251. Novatian set himself up as a rival bishop, receiving ordination from three Italian bishops. Cornelius had every interest in discrediting his rival, and the report reflects this. The opposition to the validity of Novatian's ordination rested as much on the fact of his receiving sick-bed baptism as on the way it was administered, but doubts about the latter were part of the misgivings about the former.[21] There was a feeling that those who received baptism in these circumstances were not fully converted and submitted to baptism only as a safety precaution in view of impending death. The question of the sincerity of Novatian's conversion was groundless, but the reservations attaching to the practice continued in the feeling that such individuals should not be recognized in the clergy.

The Reasoning Behind the Substitution

The origin of alternative practices was in emergencies—either shortage of water or the circumstances of the candidate. What made the change justifiable was the importance attached to baptismal grace. Cyprian calls baptism "receiving God's grace." Because baptism was so important, a substitute in the mode was considered better than missing out on the act altogether. There would not have been a substitution, if baptism had not been considered essential for one's salvation.

By the mid-third century the water plus the Trinitarian formula had become all-important for the validity of baptism. Conscious faith, the command of Christ, and exact obedience were not in the forefront of thinking. If water worked the cleansing, could the amount of water or the manner of its application be essential? This emphasis on the water, *per se*, apart from faith and the meaning of the act may be related to the "sanctification of the water," which Chapter III showed to have become a part of the baptismal ceremony. This can more properly be called "water salvation" than can the New Testament teaching.

BIBLIOGRAPHY

Conant, T. J. *The Meaning and Use of* Baptizein. New York: American Bible Union, 1861.

Khatchatrian, A. *Les baptistéres paléochrétiens*. Paris, 1962.

Stauffer, S. Anita. *On Baptismal Fonts: Ancient and Modern*. Bramcote: Grove, 1994.

NOTES

[1] Cf. his *Lectures on the Mysteries* 2.4 (=*Catechetical Lectures* 20.4), which some scholars ascribe to his successor John of Jerusalem.

[2] For archaeological confirmation on this point, see J. G. Davies, *The Architectural Setting of Baptism* (London: Barrie and Rockliff, 1962), pp. 14ff. and references there. See also W. M. Bedard, *The Symbolism of the Baptismal Font in Early Christian Thought* (Washington, 1951), chapter II.

[2a] The numbering is that of Paul W. Harkins, *St. John Chrysostom: Baptismal Instructions*, Ancient Christian Writers 31 (New York: Paulist, 1963).

[3] The Greek reads, "received," and the object must be supplied: "baptism," or better "grace." Note Cyprian's phrase (IV.9) and the same usage in inscriptions (V.19-21, 23, 27). The following phrase "by water being poured around over him" is a paraphrase to bring out the force of a single Greek word which suggests an abundance of water being spread over an object.

[4] Such a regulation is found in Canon 12 approved by the Council of Neo-Caesarea in the early fourth century.

4a Acts of Peter 5 and Acts of Paul and Thecla 34 are other early evidence.

5 J. P. Audet, La Didache (Paris, 1958), pp. 105-110, 365-67. When the fourth-century compiler of the Apostolic Constitutions (7.2.22) used the Didache's instructions on baptism he did not include the part on pouring; he either did not find it in his text, considered the exception no longer relevant (in an age of artificial baptisteries), or objected to it. W. Rordorf and A. Tuillier, La Doctrine des Douze Apôtres, Sources Chrétiennes 248 (Paris: Cerf, 1978), p. 36, and Kurt Niederwimmer, The Didache: A Commentary, Hermeneia (Minneapolis: Fortress, 1998), pp. 125-129, speak of the redactor rather than an interpolator adding the passage and place his work quite early.

6 Gregory of Nyssa, Catechetical Oration 35 has been thought to refer to a partial immersion: "having the water three times poured over us (epicheamenoi) and ascending again from the water." Gregory certainly intends the water to cover completely (see in the same chapter, "immersed himself in death as we in water," and "to be three times in the water"), so he may refer to the water pouring over the body as it goes under rather than to an administrator pouring the water on the body. Cf. his On the Baptism of Christ where he speaks of "three plungings" (kataduseis) and "hidden in the water as the Savior was in the earth."

7 Theodore Klauser, "Taufet in lebendigen Wasser!" Pisciculi, ed. T. Klauser and A. Ruecker (Münster, 1939), pp. 163f.

8 The Ante-Nicene Fathers translation of On Baptism 2, "A man is dipped in water and amid the utterance of some few words is sprinkled," should be changed to, "A man is sent down into the water and between a few words is dipped." The first verb refers to the descent into the baptistery; the second is tingo ("to dye, wet, bathe, dip") and is Tertullian's usual word to translate the Greek "baptize."

9 M.R. James, The Apocryphal New Testament (Oxford: Clarendon Press, 1953), p. 494. The revision by J. K. Elliot (Oxford: Clarendon, 1993) drops James' translation, "I poured out upon them" in chapter 27 and reads instead, "having given them the right hand of the baptism of life and forgiveness" (p. 573); chapter 42 reads similarly (p. 583).

10 New Testament Apocrypha, revised edition, Vol. I, p. 265 [See Ch. II, note 2.] Chapter 42 in the Ethiopic version is clearer, "They will receive by my hand through you the baptism of life and forgiveness of their sins" (p. 273). J. Daniélou, Theology of Jewish Christianity (Philadelphia: Westminster, 1964), p. 239 translates, "With my right hand I gave them

the baptism of life."

[11] Introduction and translation by J. J. Collins in James H. Charlesworth, *The Old Testament Pseudepigrapha*, Vol. 1 (Garden City: Doubleday, 1983), p. 412.

[12] Pseudo-Clement, *Recognitions* 4.32 speaks of "sins washed away with the water of the fountain, river, or even sea." The *Acts of Thomas* record baptisms in public baths (26), a river (49), and in vessels for the storage of water in a private home (132); but the former two are mentioned only in the revised Syriac text and not in the Greek-both texts are printed in Whitaker, *Documents of the Baptismal Liturgy* (London: S.P.C.K., 1960), pp. 10ff.

[13] Davies, *op. cit.*, p. 2.

[14] L. de Bruyne, "L'imposition des mains dans l'art chrétien ancien," *Rivista di archeologia Christiana* XX (1943), 212-246, has assembled the evidence, but I differ with his interpretation that the hand on the head represents the conferring of the Holy Spirit in confirmation following the baptism. The *Apostolic Tradition* (II.12) shows that the hand on the head refers to the moment of the baptismal confession. For the Catacomb pictures, see J. Wilpert, *Die Malereien der Katakomben Roms* (Freiburg, 1903), plates 27, 39, 58, 73, 228, 240; for art in general Gunter Ristow, *The Baptism of Christ*, "Library of Eastern Church Art" (Recklinghausen: Aurel Bongers, 1967). See Plates I and II of this book, and note in the latter that the body of the one being baptized is inclined forward.

[15] Davies, *op. cit.*, pp. 23ff.

[16] Carl H. Kraeling, *The Christian Building, The Excavations at Dura Europos*, Final Report VIII, II (New Haven, 1967), Part I, Section III on the Structure.

[17] André Grabar, *Christian Iconography: A Study of Its Origins* (Princeton, N.J.: Princeton University Press), p. 7, and *The Beginnings of Christian Art*, "The Arts of Mankind" (London: Thames and Hudson, 1967), p. 82; Paul Corby Finney, *The Invisible God: The Earliest Christians on Art* (New York/Oxford: Oxford University Press, 1994), p. 99 and passim.

[18] Walter Lowrie, *Art in the Early Church* (N.Y.: Pantheon Books, 1947), p. 78.

[19] C. F. Rogers, *Baptism and Christian Archaeology, Studia Biblica et*

Ecclesiastica Vol. V (1903), p. 274. Rogers argues that affusion was the normal practice. I question his conclusion, but the work, pp. 239-358, represents a still valuable collection of evidence. See also his articles in *Journal of Theological Studies*, Vol. 6 (1905), pp. 107-110 and Vol. 12 (1911), pp. 437-445. The reply by I. Abrahams, "How Did the Jews Baptize," *Journal of Theological Studies*, Vol. 12 (1911), pp. 609-612 proves immersion among the Jews; his evidence about the amount of water required for Jewish baptism may be relevant for the *Didache's* exception. See the Mishnah tractate *Mikwaoth* ("Immersion-Pools"), especially 1.6-8; 2.1-10; 5.6.

[20] The picture of the baptism of Christ in the dome of the Cathedral Baptistery (Baptistery of the Orthodox) at Ravenna (fifth century) is often reproduced as an example of pouring: the naked Christ is waist deep in water while John pours water from a vessel above his head. However, the part with John's arm and the pouring is a nineteenth-century restoration; in the original the hand of John would have rested on Jesus' head, as in the nearly contemporary picture in the Arian Baptistery at Ravenna. Spiro K. Kostof, *The Orthodox Baptistery of Ravenna* (New Haven: Yale University Press, 1965), pp. 86-87.

[21] A negative attitude toward clinical or death-bed baptism continued in the fourth century; see my "Exhortations to Baptism in the Cappadocians," *Studia Patristica*, Vol. XXXIII (1997), pp. 121-129, esp. 123-125.

V

The Beginning of Infant Baptism

*"Unless you turn and become like children you will
never enter the kingdom of heaven"*

Some New Testament Texts: Matthew 18:1-4; 19:13-15; Mark
10:13-16; 1 Corinthians 7:14; Ephesians 6:1-4.

SOURCES

Innocence of Infants

HERMAS: Those who believed are such as these: They are like   V.1
innocent infants, in whose heart no wickedness enters and who do not
know what evil is but always remain in innocence. Such as these will
undoubtedly live in the kingdom of God, because in no way did they
defile the commandments of God but innocently remained in the same
frame of mind all the days of their life. As many of you then who will
continue and be as infants, with no wickedness, will be more honored
than all others, for all infants are honored before God and are in the first
rank before him. Blessed are all of you, therefore, who remove evil from
yourselves and put on guiltlessness. (*Similitudes* 9.29.1-3=106.1-3)

I, the angel of repentance, judge all of you to be blessed who are as   2
innocent as infants, because your part is good and honorable before God.
(*Ibid.* 9.31.3=108.3)

Have sincerity and be innocent, and you shall be as children, who do   3
not know the evil which destroys the life of men. (*Mandate* 2.1=27.1)

BARNABAS: Since he renewed us in the forgiveness of sins, he made   4
us into another image, so as to have the soul of children, as if he were
indeed refashioning us. (6.11)

ARISTIDES: And when a child has been born to one of them   5

V.   [Christians], they give thanks to God; and if it should die as an infant, they give thanks the more, because it has departed life sinless. (*Apology* 15.11)[1]

6   ATHENAGORAS: Although all human beings who die are resurrected, not all those resurrected are judged. If justice in the judgment were the only cause of the resurrection, it would follow, of course, that those who have not sinned nor done good, namely quite young children, would not be resurrected. (*On the Resurrection* 14)

7   CLEMENT OF ALEXANDRIA: We have shown that not only are all of us called children by Scripture, but also that we who have followed Christ are figuratively spoken of as babes. (*Instructor* 1.7.53.1)[2]

8   And if there should be one fishing, it will remind you of the apostle and the children drawn out of the water. (*Ibid.* 3.11.59.2)[3]

9   [After quoting Job 1:21] Not naked of possessions (for this is a trivial and common thing), but, as a just man, he departs naked of evil and sin. . . . For this was what was said . . . [Matthew 18:3] pure in flesh, holy in soul by abstinence from evil deeds; God shows that he would have us to be such as he has generated us from our mother, the water. (*Miscellanies* 4.25.160.1-2)

10   IRENAEUS: Who were those who were saved and received the inheritance? Those, obviously, who believed in God and kept their love for him, such as Caleb son of Jephunneh and Joshua son of Nun, and innocent children, who have no sense of evil. Who are those now who are saved and receive eternal life? Is it not those who love God and believe his promises and "in malice have become little children"? (*Against Heresies* 4.28.3)

Evidence for Baptism of Children

11   IRENAEUS: For he came to save all by means of himself–all, I say, who by him are born again to God–infants, children, adolescents, young people, and old people. (*Against Heresies* 2.22.4)

12   TERTULLIAN: According to the circumstances and nature, and also age, of each person, the delay of baptism is more suitable, especially in the case of small children. What is the necessity, if there is no such necessity, for the sponsors as well to be brought into danger, since they may fail to keep their promises by reason of death or be deceived by an evil disposition which grows up in the child? The Lord indeed says, "Do not forbid them to come to me." Let them "come" then while they are growing up, while they are learning, while they are instructed why they are coming. Let them become Christians when they are able to know

Christ. In what respect does the innocent period of life hasten to the V.
remission of sins? Should we act more cautiously in worldly matters, so
that divine things are given to those to whom earthly property is not
given? Let them learn to ask for salvation so that you may be seen to have
given "to him who asks." (*On Baptism* 18)

HIPPOLYTUS: And they shall baptise the little children first. And if 13
they can answer for themselves, let them answer. But if they cannot, let
their parents answer or someone from their family. And next they shall
baptise the grown men; and last the women. (*Apostolic Tradition* 21.3-5)[4]

ORIGEN: I take this occasion to discuss something which our brothers 14
often inquire about. Infants are baptized for the remission of sins. Of what
kinds? Or when did they sin? But since "No one is exempt from stain,"
one removes the stain by the mystery of baptism. For this reason infants
also are baptized. For "Unless one is born of water and the Spirit he
cannot enter the kingdom of heaven." (*Homily on Luke* 14.5)

[After quoting Psalm 51:5 and Job 14:4] These verses may be adduced 15
when it is asked why, since the baptism of the church is given for the
remission of sins, baptism according to the practice of the church is given
even to infants; since indeed if there is in infants nothing which ought to
pertain to forgiveness and mercy, the grace of baptism would be
superfluous. (*Homily on Leviticus* 8.3)

[After quoting Leviticus 12:8 and Psalm 51:5] For this also the church 16
had a tradition from the apostles, to give baptism even to infants. For
they to whom the secrets of the divine mysteries were given knew that
there is in all persons the natural stains of sin which must be washed away
by the water and the Spirit. On account of these stains the body itself is
called the body of sin. (*Commentary on Romans* 5.19)

CYPRIAN: If, when they afterwards come to believe, forgiveness of sins 17
is granted even to the worst transgressors and to those who have
previously sinned much against God, and if no one is held back from
baptism and grace; how much less ought an infant to be held back, who
having been born recently has not sinned, except in that being born
physically according to Adam, the infant has contracted the contagion of
the ancient death by its first birth. The infant approaches that much
more easily to the reception of the forgiveness of sins because the sins
remitted to it are not its own, but those of another. (*Epistle* 64 [58])

Some Inscriptions

Eusebius, an infant, going to the place of the saints, being without sin 18
through his age, rests in peace.[5]

V.19   Sweet Tyche lived one year, ten months, fifteen days, Received [grace] on the eighth day before the Kalends. Gave up [her soul] on the same day. (*Inscriptiones latinae christianae veteres*, Vol. I, number 1531)[6]

20   Postumius Eutenion, a believer, who obtained holy grace the day before his birthday at a very late hour and died. He lived six years and was buried on the fifth of Ides of July on the day of Jupiter on which he was born. His soul is with the saints in peace. Felicissimus, Eutheria, and Festa his grandmother to their worthy son Postumius. (ILCV I:1524, from the early fourth century)

21   Irene who lived with her parents ten months and six days received [grace] seven days before the Ides of April and gave up [her soul] on the Ides of April. (ILCV I:1532)

22   To the sacred divine dead. Florentius made this monument to his worthy son Appronianus, who lived one year, nine months, and five days. Since he was dearly loved by his grandmother, and she saw that he was going to die, she asked from the church that he might depart from the world a believer. (ILCV I:1343, from the third century)

23   Pastor, Titiana, Marciana, and Chreste made this for Marcianus, their worthy son in Christ, who lived twelve years, two months, and . . . days, who received [grace] on the twelfth day before the Kalends of October, Marianus and Paternus the second time being consuls, and gave up [his soul] on the eleventh day before the Kalends. Live among the saints in eternity. (ILCV II:3315, dated A.D. 268)

24   Innocent, the neophyte, lived twenty-three years. (ILCV I:1484)

25   To Paulinus, the neophyte, in peace, who lived eight years. (ILCV I:1484 B)

26   To Proiecto, neophyte infant, who lived two years seven months. (ILCV I:1484 C)

27   To the worthy Antonia Cyriaceti who lived nineteen years, two months, twenty-six days. Received the grace of God and died a virgin on the fourth day. Julius Benedictus her father set this up for his most sweet and incomparable daughter. Twelfth of Kalends of December. (ILCV I:1529, dated A.D. 363)

DISCUSSION

Innocence of Infants

The early Christian feeling about the innocence of infants finds clear expression in second-century authors and in the writer who makes the first explicit reference to infant baptism in Christian history, Tertullian (V.1-10, 12).[7] Innocence here meant sinlessness, or at least guiltlessness. The author who is the clearest is the apologist Aristides (V.5); therefore his testimony has been much discussed. The presence of this passage in fourth-century Greek papyri testifies to its genuineness. The phrase about "passed through the world without sins" suggests that the child entered the world without sin and departed in the same condition. There is no suggestion of baptism as the reason for this sinless condition. Indeed elsewhere Aristides (*Apology* 15.6) speaks of the Christians using persuasion in making disciples of children:

> If they should have bondmen and bondwomen or children,they persuade them to become Christians in order that they might be friends, and when they have become such, they call them brethren without distinction.

In the other passages the baby is the standard of purity and innocence. The whole language of "rebirth" in connection with baptism implies the guiltlessness of the infant.[8] The idea is the return to an original purity that would be meaningless if the child were thought of as sinful. If the saved were compared to infants, then surely infants were considered saved. Early Christian art often depicts the one being baptized as a naked child (or more accurately a diminutive adult), not because he is in fact a child (Christ is himself so shown) but because of the new birth symbolism.[9] As in early Christian art in general the meaning more than the actual event is being portrayed. Clement of Alexandria goes behind the infant and declares that "even the seed of the sanctified is holy."[10]

This feeling plus the stress on baptism for the remission of sins explains why there is no early reference to infant baptism. It was actually the growth of the practice of infant baptism which led to a changed view of the spiritual condition of the infant. We seek in this chapter the evidence in regard to infant, and not just child baptism.

Baptism of Infants

The earliest plausible reference to infant baptism is to be found in Irenaeus (V.11). Earlier passages have been appealed to: Polycarp declared at his trial, "Eighty-six years have I served my king."[11] Justin speaks of "many men and women of the age of sixty and seventy years who have been disciples of Christ from childhood."[12] These passages imply nothing about the age of baptism and are as easily explained from the believers' baptism standpoint as from a pedobaptist standpoint. With Irenaeus the situation appears to be different. The context of Irenaeus' statement is his doctrine of recapitulation according to which Christ summed up all of humanity in himself. Involved in this conception for Irenaeus was the idea that Jesus passed through all the ages of life, sanctifying each. There is, again, nothing specifically about baptism, but "born again" makes one think of baptism. "Regeneration," a different word from what is used in the passage under consideration, regularly means baptism for Irenaeus.[13] "Born again" may refer to Christ's renewing work and not specifically to baptism. Even if it does mean the same as "regeneration" does elsewhere in Irenaeus, this passage may be rhetorical and not imply that infants actually received baptism. Nevertheless, the practice of baptizing infants must have begun about Irenaeus' time, and this passage has the best claim to be the first reference to the practice.

The first unambiguous reference is to be found in Tertullian (V.12), and he was opposed to the practice. Tertullian was not talking about a tendency or a hypothetical situation. The practice was present and had its defenders. On the other hand, Tertullian was enough of a traditionalist in his early career that it hardly seems likely that he would oppose a practice of long standing or general acceptance. He seems to be stating, as elsewhere in his treatise *On Baptism* (which has an anti-heretical thrust), the common position of the church. He does not sound like an innovator fighting an established custom. North Africa continued to be the place where infant baptism had its strongest support, and it may be that this was the region where it began.

Hippolytus in the *Apostolic Tradition* (V.13) tells us how baptism was administered in the early third century, and presumably he is describing practices which in their main outlines if not in all details reach back into the second century. His baptismal ceremony is clearly designed for those of responsible age, who can pass through a catechumenate, fast, renounce the Devil, confess their faith, and join in the communion.[14] This description, as all the other ancient liturgies of baptism, clearly presupposes those of accountable age, and the provision for sponsors was an awkward adjustment for those who could not answer for themselves. The confession of faith was considered so integral to the baptismal act that it could not be dispensed with even for those unable to make their own confession.

The writings of Origen provide the first claim that infant baptism was an apostolic custom delivered to the church (V. 16). We do not know on what basis this assertion is made, but it may be an inference from John 3:5, the importance of which in the development of infant baptism will be noted further below, or from the interpretation of Matthew 19:14, which was already being cited in Tertullian's time in defense of the practice. Of the passages from Origen on infant baptism only the one from *Homilies on Luke* (V. 14) survives in Greek, and his Latin translators were not always faithful. Origen did refer to infant baptism, but perhaps full confidence cannot be put in every phrase found only in the Latin.

Origen affords evidence that the practice preceded the theological justification (V.14, 15). The sequence was infant baptisms then the doctrine of infant sinfulness, and not a doctrine of original sin leading to the practice of infant baptism. The reasons for baptizing a child were being discussed. The child did not have sins of his own. Origen's answer was that a stain attaches to birth. This is not yet a doctrine of original sin (that is, the inheritance of the guilt of Adam's transgression), for Origen in the *Homily on Luke* 14.3 contrasts sin and stain and says the latter attached to Jesus by reason of his taking a human body (and so the necessity of purification in Luke 2:22).

The same relationship between infant baptism and infant sin appears in the writings of Cyprian (V.17). He is the first clear theological exponent of the baptism of new-born babes. His letter conveys the answer of the North African bishops to an inquiry whether infant baptism should be given on the eighth day. The answer allows for the immediate baptism after birth. The unanimous reply indicates a long-standing and generally accepted practice. Cyprian is consistent and speaks of infant communion too. Tertullian's opposition had been put down. Cyprian's argument is that if baptism is effective in the case of hardened sinners, then how much more is it a means of grace to one whose only stain comes from another (Adam). Ceremonial uncleanness from the Old Testament has a definite connection with the development of the doctrine of original sin in the speculations of the first theologians to suggest this view of the infant–Origen and Cyprian. They were both reasoning from the practice to the doctrine, offering a theological justification for a practice that had come to be accepted. They were responding to questions raised by the anomaly of baptizing infants, since infants had no sins.

As infant baptism became even more general, and since baptism was uniformly regarded as administered "for the forgiveness of sins,"[15] the practice of infant baptism became a decisive argument for the doctrine of original sin. Such is the case in the Pelagian controversy at the beginning of the fifth century when Augustine, bishop of Hippo in North Africa, secured the triumph of the doctrine of original sin. One of his main arguments was from infant baptism,[16] which had become such an established thing that Pelagius, who denied original sin, could not deny the appropriateness of baptizing children.

Infant baptism did not immediately after its introduction become the uniform practice. There are many instances where children in Christian homes in the fourth century were not baptized until their mature years.

Such great leaders of the fourth-century church as Ambrose, Gregory of Nazianzus, Basil of Caesarea, Jerome, and many others were grown before they were baptized.[17] In fact, in the fourth century the delay of baptism became a problem. The feeling developed that such a powerful sacrament which brought forgiveness of all sins should not be utilized too early but reserved until a time when the maximum benefits could be secured. This was, of course, a one-sided and distorted understanding of the doctrine of baptism, and church leaders protested against this delay.[18] But this misunderstanding is hardly the reason that sons of bishops, such as Gregory of Nazianzus, or children from the homes with the longest Christian heritage and deepest spiritual piety, such as that from which Basil came, were not baptized as infants. The extraordinary delay of baptism was a perversion of the usual practice of allowing children to reach a responsible age before being baptized rather than a revolutionary phenomenon.

The Testimony of the Inscriptions

Early Christian inscriptions, which in the largest numbers come from the environs of Rome, furnish some instances of child and infant baptism for the third century. Inscriptions which can be identified as Christian begin in the late second century, but only in the third century is the number of dated inscriptions significant.[19] Nearly all of the early Christian inscriptions are epitaphs. A considerable number of these are for the graves of children. The vast majority give no indication whether the child was baptized or not.[20] Presence in a Christian catacomb or the use of phrases like *in pace* ("in peace") do not furnish evidence of baptism. Nor may it safely be concluded that absence of an explicit statement implies that the child was not baptized. Yet, those inscriptions making specific reference to baptism create a presumption against its presence where it is not mentioned.

Actually, the word "baptism" is seldom used. The idea is expressed by "received grace," "made a believer," or "neophyte" ("newly planted" used to mean "newly baptized"). The earliest Christian art and inscriptions were reticent about explicit reference to things Christian.

Children of various ages, from a few months to twelve years, are spoken of as receiving baptism a short time before their death. These were cases of "emergency baptism" where parents did not want them to die unbaptized. Nearly all of the cases of infant or child baptism noted in the inscriptions fall into this category. Parents wanted it known that their child died baptized. Perhaps it is unsafe to generalize from what may be exceptional cases. In the nature of the case we are not told when a person who lived a normal Christian life was baptized; only an emergency situation caused the baptism and the death to be noted together. But in the cases recorded the child received baptism only because of the imminent approach of death, and these children at least had not been baptized immediately or shortly after birth. The implication would seem to be that baptism was not routinely administered in infancy, and only the prospect of death caused it to be performed when it was.

The circumstance of emergency baptism may provide the clue for the actual origin of infant baptism.[21] Having rejected the doctrine of original sin as the cause of the practice, we are obligated to seek another explanation. Here may be the real contribution of the inscriptions to the study of infant baptism, for they show us popular Christian thinking. The children referred to in the inscriptions were baptized shortly before their death. As we have indicated, this must have been the occasion for the baptism. Since these inscriptions are at burial sites, the fact of baptism must have been significant as a preparation for the afterlife. The Appronianus inscription (V.22) explicitly says that the grandmother wanted the child to be baptized before his death. Tertullian himself perhaps allows the propriety of such emergency baptisms (V.12), but his phrase is ambiguous. The request for baptism was natural enough in itself, and once made would be hard to refuse. The request was reinforced by the influence of John 3:5, "Unless one be born of water and the Spirit he cannot enter the kingdom of heaven," the importance of which in the second century was noted in Chapter III. Once that statement was detached from the total theological framework of baptism, it would be a strong proof-text for the necessity for every individual to receive baptism. The Old Testament analogy of circumcision would have contributed its part.[22] The strong emphasis on the necessity of baptism and "outside the church there is no salvation" confirmed the tendency. Once the practice began, it was natural to extend the precaution before there was illness. So infant baptism spread. On the other hand, the thought of baptism on the point of death could be extended in the other direction to the end of life, as was done in the fourth century.

Conclusion

The matter of the age of baptism appears to have been left to parental or individual choice in the early centuries. The first ecclesiastical command to baptize infants is contained in the fourth-century *Apostolic Constitutions* 6.15:

> Do you also baptize your infants, and bring them up
> in the nurture and admonition of God. For he says,
> "Suffer the little children to come unto me, and forbid
> them not."[23]

In the fifth century infant baptism became a general practice. The number of large baptisteries that were built in the fifth and sixth centuries, if not simply the continuation of a traditional architecture that was now outmoded, indicates that immersion of adults was still common.

BIBLIOGRAPHY

Aland, Kurt. *Did the Early Church Baptize Infants?* Philadelphia: Westminster, 1963.

_____. *Die Stellung der Kinder in den frühen christlichen Gemeinden–und ihre Taufe.* Munich: Kaiser, 1967.

Ferguson, Everett. "Inscriptions and the Origin of Infant Baptism." *Journal of Theological Studies.* New Series, Vol. 30 (1979), pp. 37-46. Repr. in Everett Ferguson, ed. *Conversion, Catechumenate, and Baptism in the Early Church.* Studies in Early Christianity, Vol. X1. New York: Garland, 1993. Pp. 391-400.

Jeremias, Joachim. *Infant Baptism in the First Four Centuries.* Philadelphia: Westminster, 1960.

_____. *The Origins of Infant Baptism.* "Studies in Historical Theology," 1. Naperville, Illinois: Allenson, 1963.

Wright, David F. "The Origins of Infant Baptism–Child Believers' Baptism?" *Scottish Journal of Theology,* Vol. 40 (1987), pp. 1-23.

NOTES

[1] The Apology of Aristides exists complete only in a Syriac translation and in a late Greek adaptation of the original. The passage quoted here and the one on p. 58 are found in a papyrus fragment preserving the original Greek of 15.6–16.1; see H.J.M. Milne, "A New Fragment of the Apology of Aristides," *Journal of Theological Studies,* Vol. 25 (1924), pp. 73-77.

[2] *Instructor* 1.5-6, devoted to the theme that Christians are called children, provides the setting for this summary statement.

[3] Clement has in mind the imagery of Christians as fish drawn out of the waters of baptism–see Chapter III, note 5 and III.15.

[4] Quoted from Gregory Dix, *The Treatise on the Apostolic Tradition of St. Hippolytus of Rome* (Reissued with Corrections; London: S.P.C.K., 1968). The section on baptism is present in all the eastern versions of the document, and although the Latin is truncated at this point, the agreement of the witnesses in the other line of transmission seems to guarantee the authenticity of the quoted passage.

[5] Quoted from H. P. V. Nunn, *Christian Inscriptions* (Eton: Savile Press, 1952), p. 36, and used by permission of The Provost and Fellows of Eton College.

[6] Edited by E. Diehl (second edition; Berlin, 1961). Henceforth abbreviated ILCV.

[7] Fragment VIII of the apostolic father Papias says, "They used to call those who practiced godly guilelessness 'children.'" See also Minucius Felix 2.1; Origen, *Commentary on Matthew* 13.16. For Adam in infant innocence before his sin: Irenaeus, *Proof of the Apostolic Preaching* 12; 14; Theophilus, *To Autolycus* 2.25. The theme is studied against its philosophical background in Hans Herter, "Das Unschuldige Kind," *Jahrbuch für Antike und Christentum*, Vol. 4 (1961), pp. 146-162.

[8] In addition to the passages noted in Chapter III at note 12 about the use of John 3:5, see on baptism as a new birth *Barnabas* 16.8; Justin, *Apology* I, 61; 66; *Dialogue* 138.2; Tatian, *Oration* 5; Theophilus, *To Autolycus* 2.16.

[9] Gunter Ristow, *The Baptism of Christ*, "Library of Eastern Church Art" (Rechlinghausen: Aurel Bongers, 1967), p. 13; L. Hertling and E. Kirschbaum, *The Roman Catacombs* (London: Darton, Longman & Todd, 1960), p. 236; F. van der Meer and C. Mohrmann, *Atlas of the Early Christian World* (New York: Nelson, 1958), p. 127. Plates I and II of this book.

[10] *Miscellanies* 3.6.46.5.

[11] *Martyrdom of Polycarp* 9.3. The legendary *Life of Polycarp* does not mention his baptism, but by its account of his purchase while a boy by a Christian woman who reared him, it leaves the implication that he was not baptized as an infant.

[12] *Apology* I, 15.6. See XVI.5 for the context.

[13] The noun *regenerationis* means baptism in *Against Heresies* 1.21.1 (*anagennesis*, "rebirth" in the Greek, which is preserved for this passage); 3.17.1; 5.15.3. The verb *renascor* is used in the passage quoted, but the use of "regeneration" for the Greek "rebirth" in 1.21.1 may mean that there is no significance in the Latin translator using a verb form from a different root in 2.22.4.

[14] See Chapter III for details of the baptismal liturgy. E. C. Whitaker's *Documents of the Baptismal Liturgy* (London: S.P.C.K., 1960) shows the

situation described continuing in the later liturgies.

[15] John Chrysostom in the East defended the baptism of sinless infants on the basis of other benefits conferred–*Baptismal Instructions* 3.6.

[16] *On the Merits and Forgiveness of Sins, and on the Baptism of Infants* 1.23, 28, 39; 3.2, 7.

[17] Joachim Jeremias, *Infant Baptism in the First Four Centuries*, p. 88; David F. Wright, "At What Ages Were People Baptized in the Early Centuries?" *Studia Patristica*, Vol. XXX (1997), pp. 389-394.

[18] Basil, Homily 13, "Exhortation to Holy Baptism"; Gregory of Nazianzus, *Oration* 40; Gregory Nyssa, *Against Those Who Defer Baptism*. Studied in my "Exhortations to Baptism in the Cappadocians," *Studia Patristica*, Vol. XXXIII (1997), pp. 121-129.

[19] W. M. Calder, ed., *Monumenta Asiae Minoris Antiqua*, Vol. I (Manchester University Press, 1928), Introduction; Michael McHugh, "Inscriptions," in Everett Ferguson, ed., *Encyclopedia of Early Christianity*, second edition (New York: Garland, 1997), Vol. 1, pp. 574-576.

[20] See the collection by F. Cabrol and H. Leclercq, *Monumenta ecclesiae liturgica*, Vol. I (Paris, 1900–1902), p. clii and pp. 19-68, 154-176.

[21] Everett Ferguson, "Inscriptions and the Origin of Infant Baptism," *Journal of Theological Studies*, New Series, Vol. 30 (1979), pp. 37-46.

[22] It should be noted, however, that the earliest Christian sources identify the gift of the Holy Spirit, not baptism, as the new covenant's counterpart to circumcision–Everett Ferguson, "Spiritual Circumcision in Early Christianity," *Scottish Journal of Theology*, Vol. 41 (1988), pp. 485-497.

[23] It should be noted that the first six books of the *Apostolic Constitutions* is a rewriting of the third-century *Didascalia*, which does not contain this command.

VI
Christian Assemblies

"In the spirit on the Lord's day"

Some New Testament Texts: Acts 20:7; 1 Corinthians 16:1f.;
Revelation 1:10; Luke 24:1-35; John 20:1-29; Hebrews 10:25.

SOURCES

The Day of Christian Assembly

DIDACHE: Having earlier confessed your sins so that your sacrifice   VI.1
may be pure, come together each Lord's day of the Lord, break bread, and
give thanks. (14.1)

IGNATIUS: If therefore those who lived according to the old practices   2
came to the new hope, no longer observing the Sabbath but living
according to the Lord's day, in which also our life arose through him and
his death (which some deny), through which mystery we received faith,
and on account of which we suffer in order that we may be found disciples
of Jesus Christ our only teacher, how shall we be able to live apart from
him for whom even the prophets were looking as their teacher since they
were his disciples in the spirit? (*Magnesians* 9)

BARNABAS: Moreover God says to the Jews, "Your new moons and   3
Sabbaths I cannot endure." You see how he says, "The present Sabbaths
are not acceptable to me, but the Sabbath which I have made in which,
when I have rested from all things, I will make the beginning of the
eighth day which is the beginning of another world." Wherefore, we
[Christians] keep the eighth day for joy, on which also Jesus arose from
the dead and when he appeared ascended into heaven. (15.8-9)

VI.4   JUSTIN: We are always together with one another. And for all the things with which we are supplied we bless the Maker of all through his Son Jesus Christ and through his Holy Spirit. And on the day called Sunday there is a gathering together in the same place of all who live in a city or a rural district. [There follows an account of a Christian worship service, which is quoted in VII.2.] We all make our assembly in common on the day of the Sun, since it is the first day, on which God changed the darkness and matter and made the world, and Jesus Christ our Savior arose from the dead on the same day. For they crucified him on the day before Saturn's day, and on the day after (which is the day of the Sun) he appeared to his apostles and taught his disciples these things. (*Apology* I, 67.1-3, 7)

5   There is no other thing for which you blame us, my friends, is there than this? That we do not live according to the Law, nor are we circumcised in the flesh as your forefathers, nor do we observe the Sabbath as you do. (*Dialogue with Trypho* 10.1. In verse 3 the Jew Trypho acknowledges that Christians "do not keep the Sabbath.")

6   The commandment of circumcision, requiring them always to circumcise the children on the eighth day, was a type of the true circumcision by which we are circumcised from error and evil through the resurrection from the dead on the first day of the week of Jesus Christ our Lord. For the first day of the week, although it is the first of all days, yet according to the number of the days in a cycle is called the eighth (while still remaining the first). (*Dialogue* 41.4)

7   *EPISTLE OF THE APOSTLES*: I [Christ] have come into being on the eighth day which is the day of the Lord. (18)[1]

8   *GOSPEL OF PETER*: Early in the morning when the Sabbath dawned, a multitude from Jerusalem and the surrounding country came to see the sealed sepulchre. In the night in which the Lord's day dawned, while the soldiers in pairs for each watch were keeping guard, a great voice came from heaven. [There follows an account of the resurrection.] Early in the morning of the Lord's day Mary Magdalene, a disciple of the Lord ... came to the sepulchre. (9.34-35; 12.50-51) [Cf. Selection VII. 7.]

9   *ACTS OF PETER*: Paul had often contended with the Jewish teachers and had confuted them, saying, "It is Christ on whom your fathers laid hands. He abolished their sabbath and fasts and festivals and circumcision." (1.1)[2] [Cf. chap. 7; 29; 30; and the fragment in Schneemelcher, *New Testament Apocrypha*, Revised Edition, Vol. II (1992), p. 285, "On the first day of the week, which is the Lord's day."]

10   CLEMENT OF ALEXANDRIA: Plato prophetically speaks of the Lord's day in the tenth book of the *Republic*, in these words: "And when

seven days have passed to each of them in the meadow, on the eighth   VI.
they must go on." (*Miscellanies* 5.14.106.2)

[In commenting on each of the Ten Commandments and their   11
Christian meaning:] The seventh day is proclaimed a day of rest,
preparing by abstention from evil for the Primal day, our true rest. (*Ibid.*
6.16.138.1)

He does the commandment according to the Gospel and keeps the   12
Lord's day, whenever he puts away an evil mind . . . glorifying the Lord's
resurrection in himself. (*Ibid.* 7.12.76.4)

TERTULLIAN: Others . . . suppose that the sun is the god of the   13
Christians, because it is well-known that. . .we regard Sunday as a day of
joy. (*To the Nations* 1.13)[3]

To us Sabbaths are foreign. (*On Idolatry* 14.6)[4]   14

Let him who contends that the Sabbath is still to be observed as a balm   15
of salvation, and circumcision on the eighth day because of the threat of
death, teach us that in earliest times righteous men kept the Sabbath or
practised circumcision, and so were made friends of God. . . . It follows,
accordingly, that, inasmuch as the abolition of carnal circumcision and of
the old law is demonstrated as having been consummated in its own
times, so also the observance of the Sabbath is demonstrated to have
been temporary. (*An Answer to the Jews* 2.10; 4.1)

BARDESANES: Wherever we are, we are all called after the one name   16
of Christ–Christians. On one day, the first of the week, we assemble
ourselves together....(*On Fate*)[5]

EUSEBIUS: [The Ebionites] were accustomed to observe the Sabbath   17
and other Jewish customs but on the Lord's days to celebrate the same
practices as we in remembrance of the resurrection of the Savior. (*Church
History* 3.27.5)

Exhortations to Assemble Together

DIDACHE: You shall seek daily the faces of the saints in order that you   18
may rest content with their words. You shall not make a schism, but you
shall make peace between those who are fighting. (4.2-3)

You shall come together more frequently and seek the things beneficial   19
for your souls. (16.2)

BARNABAS: You are not to retire by yourself and live alone as if you   20
were already righteous, but you are to come together in one place and
seek the common good. (4.10)

Remember the day of judgment night and day, and you are to seek daily   21
the faces of the saints, either laboring through word and going about to

VI. exhort and taking care to save your soul by word or working with your hands for the ransom of your sins. (19.10)[6]

22 IGNATIUS: Let no one be deceived: Unless one is within the place of sacrifice he is deprived of the bread of God. For if the prayer of one or two has such great strength, how much more the prayer of the bishop with the whole church? Therefore, he who does not come to the assembly is already puffed up and has passed judgment on himself. (*Ephesians* 5.2)

23 Give diligence therefore to come together more frequently for thanksgiving and glory to God, for when you are frequently together in one place, the powers of Satan are destroyed and his destructiveness is nullified by the concord of your faith. (*Ibid.* 13)

24 Let assemblies be held more frequently; seek all by name. (*Polycarp* 4.2)

25 SECOND CLEMENT: Let us not seem merely to believe and give attention now while we are being admonished by the elders, but also when we have gone home let us remember the commandments of the Lord and not be drawn away by worldly desires. Rather let us come together more frequently and try to make progress in the commandments of the Lord in order that we may all be of the same mind and may be gathered together unto life. (17.3)

26 HIPPOLYTUS: And let every faithful man and woman when they arise from sleep at dawn before they undertake any work wash their hands and pray to God, and so let them go to their work. But if there should be an instruction in the word let each one prefer to go thither, considering that it is God whom he hears speaking by the mouth of him who instructs. For having prayed with the Church he will be able to avoid all the evils of that day. The God-fearing man should consider it a great loss if he does not go to the place in which they give instruction, and especially if he knows how to read. If there is a teacher there, let none of you be late in arriving at the assembly at the place where they give instruction. Then indeed it shall be given to him who speaks to utter things which are profitable to all, and thou shalt be profited by the things which the Holy Spirit will give to thee by him who instructs and so thy faith will be established by what thou hearest. And further he shall tell thee there what thou oughtest to do in thine own house. And therefore let each one be careful to go to the assembly to the place where the Holy Spirit abounds. And if there is a day on which there is no instruction let each one at home take a holy book and read it sufficiently what seems profitable. (*Apostolic Tradition* 35)[7]

DISCUSSION

The Day of Christian Assembly

The evidence for the early Christians' day of assembly is clear and unmistakable. They did not observe the seventh day, the Sabbath, as the Jews, but they assembled on the first day of the week, the day of the resurrection of Christ. A rest day and a day for the worship assembly of the whole congregation were united in Judaism and in much modern Christian practice, but the two are distinct matters and were distinct in the early church. Christians kept no day as a rest day, neither Saturday nor Sunday, until the civil legislation of Constantine in the fourth century made Sunday a legal holiday for many occupations. An exception was furnished by certain Jewish Christians who continued to keep the law and so had Saturday as a rest day and Sunday as their day of Christian worship (VI.17 and below). Christians had to work, and their meetings were before dawn or at night when they could get together (VII.1). The time of evening meetings would have been determined by whether Jewish time reckoning (which began the day at sunset) or Roman (which began it at midnight) was being followed. Regardless, the day for the common assembly of the church was still the first day of the week. The Lord's supper was not celebrated on Saturday in earliest times, and only later did liturgical practice reach back to Saturday with special preparatory services. The references are numerous, unanimous, and unambiguous. Those that pertain to the second century are given above in approximate chronological order.

The term Sunday, or "day of the Sun," was the pagan designation, and it appears in the writings of the Christian apologists who were addressing pagan audiences (VI.4, 13). The phrase "first day of the week" (literally "first of the Sabbaths"–the first day between the Sabbaths) was a Jewish expression based on the practice of designating the days of the week by their number leading up to the sixth (the Preparation) and the seventh (the Sabbath). This was the common terminology of the New Testament and of early Christian writers from a Semitic background (as the Syrian Bardesanes, VI.16, or Justin in addressing a Jew, VI.6). "Lord's day" and "eighth day" were distinctive Christian names and will be discussed further.

Lord's day is used by Christians with reference to the day of Christ's resurrection, and the term is consciously distinguished from the Sabbath day (VI.2, 8, 17).[8] The Sabbath is never referred to as *kuriakē*, "Lord's," or "lordly." It became common to omit the word "day" after *kuriakē*, leaving the adjective alone with the noun to be understood. (Revelation 1:10 reflects the earliest usage in giving the full phrase.) Thus in modern Greek the word for Sunday or the first day of the week is *kuriakē*. This usage was well established at an early date, for in Christian Latin the word for Sunday was *dominica*, the exact translation of the Greek, "Lord's." The word for Sunday in modern Romance languages is derived from this usage—*domenica* (Italian), *domingo* (Spanish), and *dimanche* (French).

Early Christian sources repeatedly connect the first day of the week with the resurrection (VI.2, 3, 4, 8, 17). It is clear that it was this decisive event in salvation history which made that day the "Lord's day." The resurrection of Christ and his meeting with his disciples on this day provided the basis for Christians to assemble on the first day of the week. At that time the risen Christ was preeminently present with his followers. This connection with the resurrection may have some relevance to the partaking of the Lord's supper at dawn (Ch. VII).

The *Didache* (VI.1) contains a curious double expression "Lord's day of the Lord." The adjective *kuriakē* is used with the noun "day" understood according to the usage described above. It is a descriptive adjective meaning "pertaining to, belonging to the Lord." Then comes the noun "Lord," in the genitive case, which is used for possession. It is the word appearing in the biblical phrase "day of the Lord," which especially refers to the Lord's visitation at the end of time and is a distinct expression from the term for the first day of the week. Various explanations for the double expression may be offered ranging from confusion in the transmission of the text,[9] to the author's attempt to distinguish the Christian usage from pagan usage of *kuriakē* for things associated with the emperor ("imperial"),[10] to a reference to Easter,[11] to an effort to give an eschatological reference to the day of worship. If we are to keep the text as it is, perhaps the simplest explanation is to see the phrase as a counterpart to the Old Testament and Jewish phrase, "the Sabbath of the Lord" (cf. Leviticus 23:38), meaning the Sabbath is the Lord's.[11a] *Kuriakē* would already have been for the author the name of a particular day of the week. It belongs to the Lord (Christ now and not God), as well as bearing his name. It is "the Lord's Sunday," or, "the Lordly day of the Lord."

The passage from Ignatius (VI.2) contains a textual problem. The text we have followed employs *kuriakē* without a noun, whereas other manuscripts contain the noun "life" after the adjective, giving the reading "living according to the Lord's life." The latter possibly is original. Christian sources consistently contrast the Sabbath with the Lord's day and that contrast may have been made more explicit by scribes who dropped the word "life." The contrast, however, is still in the passage, and the reading we have followed is correct for the import of the passage. The Christians' life comes from the resurrection of Christ, and there is a clear allusion to this in the language of "arising." Jewish converts now lived according to the resurrection and not according to the Sabbath. Ignatius was opposing Judaizing influences and implies the Sabbath–Lord's day contrast even if that is not what he explicitly said.

The anti-Judaic literature of the early church everywhere distinguishes Christian and Jewish practice (VI.3, 5, 15).[12]

Since the Lord's day was the day of the resurrection, Christian sources often identify it as a day of joy (VI.3, 13).[13] This was a pervasive note in contrast to the Sabbath. The rabbis stressed joy in connection with the Sabbath, but the Jewish customs for the Sabbath seemed somber to outside observers.

The designation of the Lord's day as the eighth day (VI.3, 6, 7, 10) derives from the Jewish custom of numbering the days of the week. Justin Martyr explains that the eighth day is the same as the first day (VI.6), and he and Barnabas (VI.3) identify this day as the day of the resurrection (cf. VI.7). The resurrection and meetings of Jesus with his disciples were on the eighth day in contrast to the seventh (John 20:1, 19, 26). The Christians wanted to avoid the idea that the Sabbath was the climax of the week, so they continued the count.

Jewish apocalyptic literature seems to provide the basis for the Christian adoption of the eighth day terminology. On the basis that a day with the Lord is as a thousand years (Psalm 90:4; 2 Peter 3:8), according to one scheme the world will last for six thousand years (according to the six days of creation) and be followed by the Messianic age. Christian premillennialists took this over in the form of six thousand years for life as it is now, followed by the millennial reign of Christ on earth, and then followed by the heavenly world (which would be an eighth age).[14] Another scheme in apocalyptic literature, however, made seven thousand years stand for the complete time of this age, with the number eight as the end of the world.[15] Nonmillennialists could see the seventh age as the whole Christian age, to be followed by the eighth as the world to come. This may be in the background of those authors who interpret the Sabbath commandment as meaning that Christians always keep Sabbath (every day) in abstaining from evil and devoting every day to God.[16] Barnabas may have a 6-1-1 sequence in mind (in the rest of his chapter on the Sabbath), but he seems to blend two schemes with the symbolism at one time of seven and at another of eight as referring to the new world.[16a] At any rate, in Christian usage the number eight served as a symbol of regeneration, new creation, and the world to come. The resurrection day of Christ which inaugurated these things was appropriately the eighth day.

God had created the world in six days, rested on the seventh, and on the eighth had continued his work with a new creation. Thus much could be made of the eight saved in the ark of Noah (cf. the context of III.7) and circumcision on the eighth day (VI.6). Baptisteries later were commonly in the shape of an octagon because of this symbolism of resurrection and a new beginning associated with the number eight.[17] Some of the number speculations by Greek philosophers may have had their influence too (cf. VI.10), but it seems that when one wanted to stress the new creation for pagans the language of the first day served (VI.4). The world to come would be the Christians' true rest, as Hebrews 4 had already indicated (VI.3).

The Sabbath was related to both the creation and the deliverance of Israel from Egypt by the Old Testament (Exodus 20: 8ff.; Deuteronomy 5:12ff.). Justin (VI.4) similarly connects the first day of the week with both creation and redemption. It was the beginning of God's creative activity and the beginning of the new creation through the resurrection of Christ. In keeping with this thought Christians made much of Christ as the Sun, the true light of men. In other respects Justin sums up the central Christian affirmations about Sunday.

The New Testament apocryphal literature is almost worthless for information about New Testament times, but it is quite valuable as evidence for the beliefs and practices of the authors who wrote and those for whom they wrote. As such we find it confirming the linguistic usage of the second-century church–eighth day as the Lord's day (VI.7), the Lord's day as the day of the resurrection (VI.8), the first day of the week as the Lord's day (VI.9), Sunday as the day of meeting (VII.7), and the Christian rejection of the Sabbath (VI.9).

The Christian authors at the turn of the second to the third century summarize the points which we have found in writers from the early and middle of the century, giving a consistent witness spanning the whole century and all parts of the Christian world. Clement of Alexandria's comments are incidental while discussing other things. They are all the more valuable because of the allusiveness, for this shows what was taken for granted. The eighth day is the Lord's day (VI.10), the Lord's day is the day of the resurrection and is best kept abstaining from evil (VI.12), and the Sabbath is interpreted allegorically as an anticipation of the new creation, the true first day (VI.11). Clement's reference to Plato (VI.10) is part of a collection of Greek testimonies to Christian doctrines and practices. Of course Plato had no such idea as the Lord's day in mind; Clement has simply picked up the number eight as symbolically important. Clement's effort to give a Christian interpretation to the Old Testament Sabbath command (VI.11) becomes complicated, but his praise of the first day in the context leaves no doubt of the important day for Christians, in spite of his extended discussion of the seven-day cycle. He plays on the fact that the letter used for the numeral six in Greek had dropped out of the alphabet, so that if one counted the letters in actual use the numeral eight was the seventh letter, thus giving a basis for applying the command about the seventh day to the first day.[17a] There was, however, no thought by Clement of Christians keeping Sunday as a literal rest day. He spiritualizes the meaning of keeping the Lord's day (VI.12) in the same manner as he gives in the same chapter a spiritual interpretation of prayer and fasting. Clement does not reject outward observances, but he constantly points to the moral and spiritual meaning.

The true way to remember the Lord's resurrection is by living the life of the new age, abstaining from evil.

Eusebius' description (VI.17) of those Jewish Christians known as Ebionites, who added a belief in Jesus as the Messiah and certain Christian features to their basically Jewish religious life, offers an explanation for some of the alleged evidence for Christian observance of the Sabbath.[18] There were some who continued to follow the law, but these were not Gentiles and this was not the prevailing Christian pattern of life.

Exhortations to Assemble Together

In addition to the regular first day of the week meeting for common worship (Chapter VII gives a description), Christians met together at other times. The encouragements to meet together "in one place" (e.g. VI.20, 23) show the recognition by early Christians of the social dimension of their faith and the need to be together frequently.[18a] It is impossible to determine how many of these statements apply to the Lord's day assembly, but most seem to have in mind other assemblies as well (VI.24), it being taken for granted that one would be in the assembly on Sunday if possible. In spite of the threat of persecution Christians did not give up their corporate assemblies.

Part of the concern was with the danger posed by schismatic assemblies which did not hold to the one faith (VI.18, 22, 23), part was with the danger of the spiritual pride or simply negligence in doing the Lord's will which would result from absence (VI.20, 25). Quite striking, however, is the way nearly all of these statements occur in contexts referring to the end time. The universal church found only partial expression in the present through the gatherings of limited numbers of believers in one place, but when the Lord came again there would be a true assembly of the whole church (see VIII.3). The assemblies now were with a view toward this eschatological gathering together. According to some sources, not only had the Lord appeared on the first day of the week, but he had ascended on this day too (VI.3).[19] This found expression later in the idea that the Lord would return on a first day of the week.[20] In this naive speculation may be found a yet profound thought which unites the concerns expressed in both sets of quotations given in this chapter.

Where Christians Met

Separate structures built by Christians specifically as meeting places belong primarily outside our chronological limits.[20a] The first references to church buildings are sometimes found in Clement of Alexandria, but there seems no reason to take *ekklēsia* in other than its common meaning of assembly without any reference to a building, although the passage clearly implies a recognized building where the assembly occurred.[21] Having a better claim, if the sources are reliable, are the *Chronicle of Arbela* (compiled about 550 but based here on a second-century record) which reports that bishop Isaac (123-136) was responsible for building a church and the *Chronicle of Edessa* which says that a building of the Christians was destroyed in a flood in 202, both of which are Syriac sources.[22] There is no way of knowing whether these buildings differed in any way from domestic structures. Architecturally speaking, before the Constantinian peace virtually all church buildings that are known were houses or commercial buildings modified for church use.

Outdoor meetings were known (VII.1). More commonly a wealthy Christian made a room in his house available for Christian meetings.[23] This room or a complex of rooms then might be reserved for Christian use (this was the case with the fourth-century Roman villa at Lullingstone in Kent). At the next stage a house would be acquired and remodeled as a church building (this stage is represented by the third-century Christian building at Dura Europos, the earliest identified Christian meeting house). Then house complexes would come into Christian possession. Not until the age of Constantine do we find specially constructed buildings, at first simple halls and then the Constantinian basilicas. Any space where an assembly was permitted was a possible site for Christian gatherings.

BIBLIOGRAPHY

Carson, D.A., ed. *From Sabbath to Lord's Day*. Grand Rapids: Zondervan, 1982.

Ferguson, Everett. "Sabbath: Saturday or Sunday? A Review Article." *Restoration Quarterly*. Vol. 23:4 (1980), pp. 172-181. [Review of Samuele Bacchiocchi, *From Sabbath to Sunday: A Historical Investigation of the Rise of Sunday Observance in Early Christianity* (Rome: Pontifical Gregorian University Press, 1977) and Roger T. Beckwith and Wilfrid Stott, *This is the Day: The Biblical Doctrine of the Christian Sunday* (Greenwood, SC: Attic Press, 1978).]

Rordorf, Willy. *Sunday*. Philadelphia: Westminster, 1968.

_____. *Sabbat und Sonntag in der alten Kirche*. Traditio Christiana II. Zurich: Theologischer, 1972. [Original Greek and Latin texts with German translation; there is also a French edition–*Sabbat et dimanche* (Neuchâtel: Delachaux & Niestlé).]

White, L. Michael. *The Social Origins of Christian Architecture*. 2 vols. Valley Forge: Trinity Press International, 1997.

NOTES

[1] Translation from the Coptic text in *New Testament Apocrypha*, Volume One, edited by Edgar Hennecke and Wilhelm Schneemelcher. English translation edited by R. McL. Wilson. Published in the U.S.A. by the Westminster Press, 1963. Copyright © 1959, J.C.B. Mohr (Paul Siebeck), Tübingen. English translation © 1963, Lutterworth Press. Used by permission. "I came into being" in the revised edition, ed. Wilhelm Schneemelcher (Louisville: Westminster/John Knox, 1991), Vol. I, p. 259. Cf. Clement of Alexandria, *Excerpts from Theodotus* 63 for Lord's day=ogdoad.

[2] *Ibid.*, Vol. II (©1966), pp. 279f.; revised edition, Vol. II (1992), p. 288.

[3] Cf. his *Apology* 16, "If we devote the day of the sun to rejoicing, it is for a far different reason than worship of the sun."

[4] He proceeds to indicate that Christians have a festive day every eighth day.

[5] This dialogue, also known as *Book of the Laws of Divers Countries*, was put in literary form by Bardesanes' disciple Philip. The translation is that of B. P. Pratten printed in *Ante-Nicene Fathers* (American Reprint edition; Grand Rapids: Wm. B. Eerdmans, 1951; Peabody: Hendrickson, 1994), Vol. VIII, p. 733.

[6] The reader will notice the similarities of VI.18 to 21 and 19 to 20. The former pair derive from a common "Two Ways" tradition of instruction which was probably Jewish before being adapted by Christian authors, and the latter pair from an eschatological exhortation which may have been part of the same tradition. To VI.20 compare Hermas, *Similitudes* 9.26.3=103.3.

[7] Translation from Gregory Dix, *The Treatise on the Apostolic Tradition of St. Hippolytus of Rome* (Reissued with Corrections; London: S.P.C.K., 1968).

[8] Cf. *Acts of Paul* 7, "And Paul cried out to God on the Sabbath as the Lord's day approached." Tertullian, *Fasting* 15 lists them as two different days of the week.

[9] J. P. Audet, *La Didache* (Paris, 1958), pp. 72-73, 460. P. 46 omits *kuriakē* with the Georgian version and on the basis of his conjecture that it was missing from the text used by the compiler of *Apostolic Constitutions*

7.30.1 ("Come together without fail on the day of the resurrection of the Lord, we say the Lord's day [kuriakē]"). The awkwardness may not be the compiler's but something he was trying to explain. Since "day of the Lord" had a special eschatological meaning not likely to lend itself to use for the day of worship in the early period, one might think that it is more likely that we should omit the phrase "of the Lord" as an interpolation occurring after its specific meaning was not so clear and after kuriakē became simply a name for a day in the week. One must then reckon with the changes in the external witnesses.

[10] S. Vernon McCasland, "The Origin of the Lord's Day," *Journal of Biblical Literature*, Vol. 49 (1930), 65-82, suggests kuriakē had a use in Mithraism as the designation for Sunday; the Didache had to use the double expression because there was a kuriakē other than that of the Lord.

[11] C. W. Dugmore, "Lord's Day and Easter," *Neotestamentica et Patristica*, Supplements to *Novum Testamentum* VI (Leiden: Brill, 1962), pp. 272-81, says the *Didache's* phrase would mean "*the* Sunday of the Lord," that is Easter, and he suggests "Lord's day" primarily meant the annual rather than the weekly day. Origen, *Against Celsus* 8.22, appears to use the term "Lord's day" for Easter. On the other hand, the weekly pattern seems so deeply ingrained in the early church that the weekly usage should be regarded as primary.

[11a] *Barnabas* 15.1 provides a contemporary use of "Sabbath of the Lord." Cf. C.H. Turner, *Studies in Early Church History* (Oxford, 1912), p. 8 and W. Telfer, "The *Didache* and the Apostolic Synod of Antioch," *Journal of Theological Studies*, Vol. 40 (1939), p. 141. Kurt Niederwimmer, *The Didache: A Commentary*, Hermeneia (Minneapolis: Fortress, 1998), pp. 194-195, approves of this possibility.

[12] Christian writers frequently reproach Jews for keeping the Sabbath: Aristides, *Apology* 14 (Syriac text); *Epistle to Diognetus* 4.5. They argued that the Sabbath was not kept before Moses and therefore was not part of the permanent will of God: Tertullian, *An Answer to the Jews* 2-4; Justin, *Dialogue with Trypho* 19.2; 21.1 and frequently; Irenaeus, *Against Heresies* 4.16.2.

[13] Hence, on Sunday one was not to fast, kneel for prayer at worship, or engage in an activity which caused anxiety–Tertullian, *On the Crown* 3; *On Prayer* 23 (which should be translated, "We ought to avoid every appearance and duty which causes anxiety" on the day of the Lord's resurrection).

[14] Justin, *Dialogue with Trypho* 81.4; Irenaeus, *Against Heresies* 5.28.3.

[15] *Second Enoch* 33:2.

[16] Cf. VI.11, 12; Justin, *Dialogue with Trypho* 12.3; Irenaeus, *Proof of the Apostolic Preaching* 96. The Coptic *Gospel of Thomas* 27 (Nag Hammadi Codex II, 38, 19-20), "If you keep not the Sabbath as Sabbath you will not see the Father," is to be understood of such a spiritual Sabbath observance, for the same saying interprets fasting as a "fast from the world." A. Guillaumont, *et al.*, *The Gospel According to Thomas* (Leiden: E.J. Brill, 1959), p. 19. The saying is also in Greek–P. *Oxyr.* 1.2. In the same vein the second-century Gnostic Ptolemy in his *Letter to Flora* 3 (Epiphanius, *Against Heresies* 33.5) understands the Sabbath law as typical or allegorical of keeping away from evil deeds. Cf. Justin, *Dial.* 12.3; Clement of Alexandria, *Misc.* 3.99.4; Tertullian, *Against the Jews* 4.

[16a] Everett Ferguson, "Was *Barnabas* a Chiliast? An Example of Hellenistic Number Symbolism in *Barnabas* and Clement of Alexandria," in David Balch, *et al.*, eds., *Greeks, Romans, and Christians: Essays in Honor of Abraham J. Malherbe* (Minneapolis: Fortress, 1990), pp. 157-167.

[17] F. J. Dölger, "Zur Symbolik des altchristlichen Taufhauses," *Antike und Christentum*, Vol. 4 (1934), pp. 153-189. Cf. J. G. Davies, *The Architectural Setting of Baptism* (London: Barrie and Rockliff, 1962), p. 16.

[17a] Clement's introduction of the number 8 contrasts with Philo's praise of 7, although Clement otherwise borrows much from Philo's arithmology–*On the Creation of the World* 89-128; *Allegorical Laws* 1.2-20. Cf. what the Jewish author Aristobulus does with these numbers–Martin Hengel, *Judaism and Hellenism* (Philadelphia: Fortress, 1974), p. 166.

[18] Cf. Origen, *Homilies on Leviticus* 5.8. Justin, *Dialogue with Trypho* 47.2 allows fellowship with Jewish Christians who keep the Sabbath provided they do not impose their custom on others. Irenaeus, *Against Heresies* 1.26.2, in describing the practices of the Ebionites, does not specifically mention their keeping the Sabbath but such would be implicit in what he does say. The late apocryphal *Passion of the Holy Apostles Peter and Paul* 2 allows that the Sabbath was not abolished for Jews.

C. W. Dugmore, *The Influence of the Synagogue upon the Divine Office* (Westminster: Faith Press, 1966), pp. 29-36, argues from the slender evidence and from presumption for a continued special regard for the Sabbath as well as the first day by orthodox Christians in the early centuries. This I do not find extending to "Sabbath-keeping," except in regard to the aforementioned Jewish Christians. Robert A. Kraft, "Some Notes on Sabbath Observance in Early Christianity," *Andrews University Seminary Studies*, Vol. 3 (1965), pp. 18-33, argues that some Christian communities in the second century kept the Sabbath, but the evidence is weak.

[18a] Everett Ferguson, "'When You Come Together': *Epi To Auto* in Early Christian Literature," *Restoration Quarterly*, Vol. 16 (1973), pp. 202-208. To the passages studied there, add *Acts of Justin* 3.1 (Rec. B); Origen, *On Prayer* 31.5.

[19] The ascension appears to be put on the day of the resurrection in *Gospel of Peter* 13.56.

[20] Origen, *Commentary on John* 10.35(20) calls the general resurrection "the great Lord's day."

[20a] Cf. the *Acts of Paul* and other apocrypha for meetings in homes, hired halls, etc.

[21] *Instructor* 3.11.79.3 and *Miscellanies* 3.18.108.2. Even in *Miscellanies* 7.5.29.4, "I do not now call the place but ... the elect the church," the context is that of the church as a spiritual temple so may not imply the use of "church" for a building. *Misc.* 5.6 is more likely a reference to a building. "The church in the house of Onesiphorus" in *Acts of Paul and Thecla* 7 is again the people. Pseudo-Clement, *Recognitions* 10.71 is more likely a reference to a house as a church. Origen, *Against Celsus* 6.77, uses *ekklēsia* for a building.

[22] J. G. Davies, *The Origin and Development of Early Christian Church Architecture* (New York: Philosophical Library, 1953), p. 14. Davies appears a bit optimistic in finding references to buildings.

[23] *Acts of Justin* 2 mentions private property as a site of a Christian meeting in Rome. L. Michael White, *The Social Origins of Christian Architecture* (Valley Forge: Trinity Press International, 1997), Vol. 2, pp. 33-257 presents a comprehensive survey of the literary and archaeological evidence for Christian meeting places until the time of Constantine.

VII

Early Worship Services

*"Devoted themselves to the apostles' teaching and fellowship,
to the breaking of bread and the prayers"*

Some New Testament Texts: Acts 2:42; 20:7-11; 1 Corinthians 14;
16:1-2; 1 Thessalonians 5:25-27; 1 Timothy 4:13; Luke 4:16-22; Acts
13:14-16.

SOURCES

PLINY: [The former Christians] affirmed, however, the whole of their   VII.1
guilt, or their error, was, that they were in the habit of meeting on a
certain fixed day before it was light, when they sang in alternate verses a
hymn to Christ, as to a god, and bound themselves by a solemn oath, not
to any wicked deeds, but never to commit any fraud, theft or adultery,
never to falsify their word, nor deny a trust when they should be called
upon to deliver it up; after which it was their custom to separate, and
then reassemble to partake of food-but food of an ordinary and innocent
kind. Even this practice, however, they had abandoned after the
publication of my edict, by which, according to your orders, I had
forbidden political associations. I judged it so much the more necessary
to extract the real truth, with the assistance of torture, from two female
slaves, who were styled deaconesses; but I could discover nothing more
than depraved and excessive superstition. (*Letters* Book 10.96, addressed
to the Emperor Trajan)[1]

JUSTIN: We always remind one another of these things [our   2
teachings]. Those with possessions provide for all those in want. [Next
two sentences are the first two in VI.4] And on the day called Sunday
there is a gathering together in the same place of all who live in a city or
a rural district. The memoirs of the apostles or the writings of the
prophets are read, as long as time permits. Then when the reader ceases,
the president in a discourse admonishes and urges the imitation of these

VII.   good things. Next we all rise together and send up prayers. And, as I said before, when we cease from our prayer, bread is presented and wine and water. The president in the same manner sends up prayers and thanksgivings according to his ability, and the people sing out their assent saying the "Amen." A distribution and participation of the elements for which thanks have been given is made to each person, and to those who are not present it is sent by the deacons. Those who have means and are willing, each according to his own choice, gives what he wills, and what is collected is deposited with the president. He provides for the orphans and widows, those who are in want on account of sickness or some other causes, those who are in bonds and strangers who are sojourning, and in a word he becomes the protector of all who are in need. (*Apology* I, 67)[2]

3   TERTULLIAN: We are a body with a common feeling of religion, a unity of discipline, and a covenant of hope. We meet together in an assembly and congregation so that praying to God we may win him over by the strength of our prayers. This kind of force is pleasing to God. We pray also for emperors, for their servants and those in authority, for the order of the world, for peaceful circumstances, for the delay of the end. We meet together in order to read the sacred texts, if the nature of the times compels us to warn about or recognize anything present. In any case, with the holy words we feed our faith, we arouse our hope, we confirm our confidence. We strengthen the instruction of the precepts no less by inculcations; in the same place there are also exhortations, rebukes, and divine censures. For judgment is administered with great authority, as among those in the presence of God, and it is the supreme anticipation of the judgment to come if any has so sinned that he is banished from participation in our prayer, our gatherings, and all holy fellowship.[3] Elders who are proved men preside over us, having attained that honor not by purchase but by attestation. For not anything of God's is determined by purchase. Although we have a kind of money chest, it is not gathered from the fees of our leaders as if religion were a matter of purchase. Every individual puts in a small contribution on the monthly day, or when he wishes and only if he wishes and is able. For no one is compelled, but he contributes voluntarily. These contributions are trust funds of piety. (*Apology* 39.1-5)[4]

4   There is among us a sister whose lot it has been to have gifts of revelation, which she experiences by ecstacy in the Spirit during the regular services of the Lord's day in the church. . . . Whether it is when the Scriptures are read, or the psalms are chanted, or sermons are preached, or prayers arc sent up, all such occasions are supplied with visions. (*On theSoul* 9.4)[5]

5   CLEMENT OF ALEXANDRIA: Always giving thanks in all things to God through righteous hearing and divine reading, true inquiry, holy

oblation, blessed prayer, praising, hymning, blessing, singing, such a soul   VII.
is never separated from God at any time. (*Miscellanies* 6.14.113.3)

   Those who gave reverence to the discourse about God leave inside what   6
they heard and outside lounge idly with the atheists. . . . Those who sing
such and sing in response are those who before hymned immortality.
(*Instructor* 3.11.80.4)

ACTS OF JOHN: On the next day, since it was the Lord's day and all   7
the brethren were assembled, John began to say to them. . . .
   And having spoken these things to them, he prayed thus: [the prayer is
addressed to Jesus Christ] . . . .
   And he asked for bread and gave thanks thus: [again addressed to
Christ] . . . .
   And he broke bread and gave to us all, praying for each of the brethren
to be worthy of the Lord's grace of the most holy eucharist. When he
himself likewise tasted of it he said, "May I have a part with you, and
peace be with you, beloved." (106-110)

[Chapter 46 has the same order of preaching, prayer, eucharist, and
blessing. Cf. *Acts of Paul* 5, "bowing of knees, breaking of bread, and the
word of God"; frg. 9 mentions singing and the contribution.]

DISCUSSION

Our earliest description of Christian worship outside the New
Testament comes from a non-Christian source. Pliny, in reporting to the
emperor Trajan on his investigations of Christians, spoke of their
assemblies (VII.1). The value of this early testimony is offset by its
limitations. Pliny's information comes largely from Christians who have
apostatized or have lapsed back into the world. Their conceptions or
their memory may have been imperfect. Pliny himself had certain
interests, which did not extend to the total conduct of the worship, and
he necessarily saw the reports which he received in terms of his own
experience.

The "fixed" or stated day for the common assembly would have been
Sunday, according to the evidence assembled in Chapter VI. The
pre-dawn gathering would have been necessitated by the social
circumstances of the Christians: as slaves and workmen they could get
away for their meetings only at such a time. Nearly a century later
Tertullian listed among the Christian customs: "We take the sacrament
of the eucharist, which was commanded by the Lord at meal time and for
all alike, in congregations before daybreak and from the hand of none but
the presidents."[6]

Hymns to Christ as divine were the most striking thing to Pliny about
Christian gatherings. Another interpretation of the phrase translated

"sang . . . a hymn" is possible. The phrase may be rendered "recite a form of words among themselves." In keeping with this rendering a baptismal interpretation of this passage has been proposed.[7] The words spoken alternately would be the interrogations and responses of the baptismal confession of faith (see Ch. III). This interpretation has not won a majority, and the Latin usage of the phrase argues for the common translation "to sing a hymn" or "to chant verses."[8] The translation "alternate verses" should not be understood as "antiphonally." What can be deduced from Jewish influence on Christian practice suggests congregational responses to what is recited by the leader.[9] It does coincide with what we know of early hymnic material (for which see Ch. XIII) to see the deity of Christ as the central content, for the early hymns were principally confessions of faith.

Private associations of the Hellenistic and Roman world required an oath (to observe the statutes of the club) as part of the entrance ceremony for new members. Pliny, concerned about the potential threat to the State of secret associations, was naturally interested in the content of the Christian's membership oath. What he learned has given some support to the baptismal interpretation of the gathering he was describing, for moral teaching was an important part of the preparation for baptism. The word for oath is *sacramentum*, from which "sacrament" is derived. Since *sacramentum* was used later by Tertullian with the Christian sense of sacrament, and in particular reference to such ceremonies as the Lord's supper (as well as baptism), it is possible that Pliny's informants spoke of this ceremony and Pliny gave to the word the more familiar meaning of "oath" and added what he had learned about Christian moral teaching. Or, the word may be a non-technical reference to the conduct inculcated in Christian assemblies. In this connection some have seen from the items listed an indication of the use of the Ten Commandments in Christian services.

The gathering later in the day, presumably in the evening, was for dinner. This meal was likely the "love feast" (or *agapē*, Jude 12) which was observed in the evening at the time of the main meal of the day (ch. XI). It does not seem possible that Christians would have abandoned the Lord's supper even for an imperial edict, but they could have suspended their fellowship meals.

In spite of the problematic features of this text, it does call attention to some important features of Christian divine service: the Christ-centered nature of Christian worship, the intimate connection of worship and life in nurturing moral earnestness, and the corporate nature of the Christian faith which brought Christians together regularly as a community.

Justin Martyr (VII.2) gives the fullest and most circumstantial account of a second-century worship service. The extent of Justin's acquaintance and the circumstances of his *Apology* argue that his description is fully representative of Christian practice at the mid-second century. Justin's account follows immediately on his discussion of Christian initiation and so is intended as a description of church life following on baptism. Justin does not refer in the passage quoted to singing hymns, which so impressed Pliny. At another place he refers to hymns in such close association with prayers that one may think he included hymns in his reference to the general prayer of the congregation:

> We praise [the Maker of the universe] as much as we are able by the word of prayer and thanksgiving for all the things with which we are supplied, since we have learned that the only honor worthy of him is not to consume with fire the things made by him for our sustenance but to use them for ourselves and those in need and, being thankful in word, to send up to him honors and hymns for our creation, all the means of health, the various qualities of the different classes of things, the changes of the seasons, while making petitions for our coming into existence again in incorruption by reason of faith in him. (*Apology* I, 13)

Tertullian shows the same apologetic interests as Justin: rational nature of Christian worship, morally circumspect character of these gatherings, and good deeds done by Christians. He is more rhetorical, however, and he shows the reticence characteristic of the third century to speak about the Lord's supper to pagans. The chapter giving an extended description of Christian assemblies (VII.3) concludes with an account of a "love feast." There is no place for the Lord's supper in the context of this meal, and Tertullian's other evidence is against the Lord's supper still being a part of the fellowship meal at this time. Apparently he has deliberately omitted it from his account.

Other references from the second century give only a summary report of some of the acts of worship (VII.4-7). It is characteristic of Clement of Alexandria to weave together texts about religious worship with his discussion of daily activities. These summaries are of value for what stood out in the author's mind. They do point to the basic components of Christian Sunday assemblies.

What was done, and the order, constitutes the study of liturgy. The word is derived from the Greek *leitourgia*, which means "public service" and was used in the Greek Old Testament for sacrificial service. It came to be used by Christians for the public ministry to God. As presently used, liturgy is confined to services of worship. It would be the equivalent of the religious use of the word "services" in reference to gatherings for divine worship.

From the surviving accounts we find the following acts in early Christian worship: Scripture reading, preaching, [singing,] praying, partaking of the Lord's supper, and giving. The order of listing follows Justin (VII.2), for he seems to be stating the elements of worship in sequence and one passage from Tertullian (VII.4) agrees.

The prevailing theory of the early history of the Christian liturgy is that the Christian order of worship was built up from the Jewish synagogue service of scripture teaching and prayer with the addition of the distinctively Christian rite of the Lord's supper. The latter, too, has antecedents in the Jewish Passover meal and table prayers, but these were family or home observances in Judaism. The meal became a part of the community assembly of Christians. These two basic parts of Christian worship have received various names: the liturgy of the word and the liturgy of the table (or of the upper room), synaxis (assembly) and eucharist (next chapter), proanaphora and anaphora (literally "offering up" with special reference to the great eucharistic prayer), fore-Mass and Mass (after this terminology, which is the current Roman Catholic terminology, came into use), Mass of the catechumens and Mass of the faithful (on the basis that the unbaptized and those under discipline were dismissed after the first part of the service so that only the faithful remained for the Lord's supper), the Office and the Mass.

The liturgy of the word might occur daily, and Hippolytus, *Apostolic Tradition* 35 (VI.26) provides for daily periods of instruction and prayer. The Lord's supper was celebrated only on Sunday as far as our second-century sources go. Tertullian perhaps refers to the different kinds of gatherings when he mentions what occasions a Christian woman might have for appearing in public: "Either some one of the brothers who is sick is visited, or the sacrifice is offered, or the word of God is dispensed" (*On the Apparel of Women* 2.11). (Sacrificial language for the Lord's supper is considered in Ch. X.) The synagogue-type service and the Lord's supper are fused in a united whole in Justin's account.

The synagogue service included Scripture readings, interspersed with Psalm chants, a sermon, prayers, and almsgiving. The rabbinic sources for these elements of synagogue services are later than the second century, but we find these same elements in the early accounts of Christian worship: readings, singing, preaching, praying, and giving.[10] The Lord's supper had its own prayers, Scriptures, and formulae. The same components of the service and basically the same order, with considerable elaboration, formed the basis of the written liturgies which were produced in the fourth and fifth centuries.

Succeeding chapters will give special discussion to the Lord's supper, the prayers, and the hymns of the early church. Hence, more attention will be given in the following paragraphs to Scripture reading, preaching, and the contribution.

The Scripture readings (the lections) were taken from both the Old and New Testaments. Justin refers to the "writings of the prophets": early Christian authors use "prophets" as a general designation for the entire

Old Testament. The "memoirs of the apostles" would be specifically the Gospels. Other New Testament writings were also read. The synagogue employed regular cycles of reading, and the later lectionary texts of the New Testament suggest that Christians from an early date did the same. Tertullian (VII.3) gives an indication of the importance of the Scriptures to the religious life of the early Christians. Many of the scenes in early Christian art are taken from biblical history.[11] It must be remembered that the principal opportunity for most Christians to become acquainted with the Scriptures was through hearing them read in church. Therefore, the regular, consecutive reading of the Bible occupied a principal place in the service.

Other Christian literature and communications between churches might also be read at the Sunday gatherings. Thus Dionysius of Corinth writing to Soter, bishop of Rome, about 170 refers to a letter received from Rome and an earlier one which survives as Clement's *Letter to the Corinthians*:

> Today we celebrated the holy Lord's day and we read your letter which we shall have always to be admonished by when we read it from time to time as also we read the former letter to us written by Clement.[12]

The preaching was based on the Scriptures read in the assembly (VII.2, 3, 4).[13] Synagogue preaching was either expository or took the reading of the day as a basis for a topical address. Early Christian preaching seems to have been predominantly expository. Thus the surviving homilies of Origen are expository in nature. So are most of the sermons from some of the great fourth- and fifth-century preachers–John Chrysostom and Augustine. It so happens that the few surviving second-century sermons are more topical in nature, but they are still closely based on the Scripture reading.

Our oldest complete Christian sermon, *Second Clement*, deals with repentance. The author states:

> Brothers and sisters, after the God of truth, I am reading to you an exhortation to give attention to the things written, in order that you may save yourselves and the one reading among you. (19.1; cf. VI.25)

The contents would seem to fit Justin's description of a sermon.[14] Clement of Alexandria's *Who is the Rich Man that Is Saved?* is an interpretation of Mark 10:17-31, which he quotes, applied to Clement's wealthy church members. The spiritual interpretation, directing the text against attachment to wealth but not against the possession of wealth, has a surprisingly modern ring. Melito of Sardis' homily *On the Passover*[15] opens with a reference to the preceding Scripture reading, "The Scripture of the Hebrew Exodus has been read and the words of the mystery explained," and proceeds to give a typological interpretation of the Passover as fulfilled in the death of Christ. Here is a clear instance of the Bible reading serving as the point of departure for a message of instruction. Having literary affinities with Melito's sermon is the Pseudo-Cyprian sermon *Against the Jews*.[16] It opens with comments on the parables of the wicked husbandmen and the wedding feast, which may have been read before the sermon, and develops the point that the Old Testament has been replaced by the New. Another sermon which was ascribed to a third-century author has also been claimed for the second century–the Pseudo-Hippolytus *Homily on the Passover*.[17] It, too, is a Christian interpretation of the Passover.

The congregation's offerings might be made in produce,[18] out of which the bread and wine for the communion was taken, but the sources quoted above refer to monetary contributions. This was a part of the service, and later sources describe the formal offering by the faithful of their gifts at the table where the eucharist was spread. Tithing was not practiced, being suspended with the end of the Old Testament.[19] Justin makes the act of giving a regular feature of the weekly assembly. Tertullian says the donation was put in "on the monthly day" or whenever one wished, perhaps indicating whenever he received income. In Tertullian's time or congregation there may have been a change in practice from the weekly offering. Another possibility, however, is to be considered. The private clubs and associations of the Roman world commonly had monthly dues and generally might meet only once a month. It is possible that Tertullian is describing Christian practice according to what was known in the pagan world and is identifying the church in the minds of his readers with the legal associations of their experience. The Christian sources stress the voluntary nature of the giving, in contrast to the subscriptions of associations, whose activities (as noted by Pliny) Rome was careful to regulate. The reference to a "small contribution," which was used for charitable work, was to allay governmental fears of this secret organization accumulating vast sums of money which might be used for subversive purposes.

Other noteworthy points in the texts will be covered in later chapters. But note may be taken of Tertullian's statement that the elders preside over the assembly. Notice of the elders may be due to the prominence which Tertullian gives to discipline, and the exercise of discipline was one of their principal functions (ch. XV). Justin refers to the "president" of the brethren. He employs, a non-technical term for the benefit of his readers, but by his time the person referred to was the "bishop" (ch. XIV), a kind of presiding or chief elder.

BIBLIOGRAPHY

Bradshaw, Paul F. *The Search for the Origins of Christian Worship: Sources and Methods for the Study of Early Liturgy*. New York: Oxford University Press, 1993. Paperback.

_____. *Early Christian Worship: A Basic Introduction to Ideas and Practice*. London: S.P.C.K., 1996. Paperback.

Carroll, T. K. and T. Halton. *Liturgical Practice in the Fathers*. Collegeville: Liturgical Press, 1988. Paperback.

Dugmore, C. W. *The Influence of the Synagogue upon the Divine Office*. Westminster: Faith Press, 1966.

Ferguson, Everett, ed. *Worship in Early Christianity*. Studies in Early Christianity, Vol. XV. New York: Garland, 1993.

Jones, Cheslyn *et al.*, eds. *The Study of the Liturgy*. Revised edition. New York: Oxford University Press, 1992.

Jungmann, Josef A. *The Early Liturgy*. London: Darton, Longman, and Todd, 1960.

NOTES

[1] The translation is that of William Melmoth in the Loeb Classical Library (Cambridge, Mass.: Harvard University Press, 1915).

[2] The following sentence is quoted in VI.4. A parallel description of the Lord's supper is quoted VIII.4. The present passage is studied in my "Justin Martyr and the Liturgy," *Restoration Quarterly*, Vol. 36 (1994), pp. 267-278.

[3] Church discipline, when called for, was administered in the context of the congregational assembly. See Chapter XV.

[4] Tertullian, as Justin, proceeds with a description of the benevolent use to which church funds were put (XVII.16).

[5] This passage was written after Tertullian left the great church and became a Montanist. The Montanists were a second-century schismatic movement claiming to possess later revelations from the Holy Spirit. Tertullian's reference would indicate that the basic structure of the service among the Montanists was the same as was found in the church

generally. The sister communicated her revelations after church and not during the assembly. The phrase translated "regular services" occurs in *On Flight in Persecution* 14.1 on the necessity to "assemble together" even in times of persecution.

[6] *On the Crown* 3.3. Tertullian's point seems to be that the example of the Lord's institution at the last supper was to partake of the communion as part of a meal (Chs. VIII and XI) and so in the evening and for all to partake directly. Church practice, however, was to separate the Lord's supper from a common meal so as to take it at dawn and to administer the elements by the hands of those presiding (but from the hands of deacons in VIII.4).

[7] As by Joseph Crehan, *Early Christian Baptism and the Creed* (London: Burns Oates & Washbourne, 1950), Appendix 6. Cf. R. M. Grant, *After the New Testament* (Philadelphia: Fortress, 1967), pp. 55f.

[8] R. P. Martin, "The Bithynian Christians' *Carmen Christo,*" *Studia Patristica,* Vol. 8 (*Texte und Untersuchungen* 93, 1966), pp. 259-65.

[9] See Chapter XIII, notes 28 and 29.

[10] C. W. Dugmore, *The Influence of the Synagogue upon the Divine Office* (Westminster: Faith Press, 1966), pp. 81ff.

[11] Pierre du Bourguet, *Early Christian Painting,* Compass History of Art (New York: Viking Press, 1965), pp. 14ff.; Michael Gough, *The Early Christians,* "Ancient Peoples and Places" (London: Thames and Hudson, 1961); André Grabar, *Christian Iconography* (Princeton, N. J.: Princeton University Press, 1968), pp. 87ff.

[12] Eusebius, *Church History* 4.23.11. Other references include Irenaeus, *Against Heresies* 4.33.8 for the reading of Scriptures in the church and exposition based on them and Tertullian, *Prescription of Heretics* 36, which refers to the churches where the authentic writings of the apostles are read. Clement of Alexandria, *Miscellanies* 7.7.49 refers to Scripture reading at home before dinner, cited p. 147.

[13] See also *Second Clement* 19 cited below; Irenaeus in note 12; *Apostolic Constitutions* 2.54.1; and cf. 1 Timothy 4:13.

[14] It has been suggested that *Second Clement* is a homily based on Isaiah 54:1, which is quoted in chapter 2.

[15] Greek text and English translation by Stuart Hall, *Melito of Sardis:*

On Pascha and Fragments, Oxford Early Christian Texts (Oxford: Clarendon, 1979).

[16] It is claimed as the oldest Latin sermon, from the end of the second century, and interpreted as a polemic against Jewish Christians rather than an invitation to conversion by its latest editor, Dirk van Damme, *Pseudo-Cyprian Adversus Iudaeos: Gegen die Judenchristen, Die älteste Lateinische Predigt*, "Paradosis" XXII (Freiburg, 1969), pp. 62f., 89-91. Cf. his "Pseudo-Cyprian, *Adversus Judaeos*: The Oldest Sermon in Latin?" *Studia Patristica*, Vol. VII (Berlin, 1966), pp. 299-307.

[17] Raniero Cantalamessa, *L'omelia "in S. Pascha" dello pseudo-Ippolito di Roma* (Milan, 1967). There is an edition of the Greek text with French translation in *Sources Chrétiennes*, Vol. 27 (Paris, 1950) by P. Nautin, who places the homily in the late fourth century.

[18] *Didache* 13; *Apostolic Tradition* 5, 6, and 20.9.

[19] Lukas Vischer, *Tithing in the Early Church*, Facet Books (Philadelphia: Fortress Press, 1966), pp. 13ff.

VIII

Early Accounts
of the Lord's Supper

"He ... took bread and when he had given thanks, he broke it"

Some New Testament Texts: 1 Corinthians 11:23-26; 10:16; Matthew 26:26-29; Mark 14:22-25; Luke 22:17-20; Acts 20:7-11.

SOURCES

IGNATIUS: Be careful, therefore, to employ one eucharist, for there VIII.1 is one flesh of our Lord Jesus Christ and one cup for unity with his blood, one altar, as there is one bishop together with the presbytery and deacons who are my fellow servants, in order that whatever you do may be done according to God. (*Philadelphians* 4)

No one should perform any of the things pertaining to the church apart 2 from the bishop. Let that be considered a dependable eucharist which is done by the bishop or by whomever he appoints. (*Smyrnaeans* 8)

DIDACHE: [9] Concerning the eucharist, give thanks in this way: First 3 concerning the cup, "We give thanks to you, our Father, for the holy vine of David, your Servant,[1] which you made known to us through Jesus your Servant. To you be the glory forever." Concerning the broken bread, "We give thanks to you, our Father, for the life and knowledge which you made known to us through Jesus your Servant. To you be the glory forever. As this broken bread was scattered upon the mountains and being gathered together became one loaf, so may your church be gathered together from the ends of the earth into your kingdom. Because the glory and the power are yours through Jesus Christ forever." No one is to eat or drink of your eucharist except those who have been baptized in the name of the Lord. For also concerning this the Lord has said, "Do not give that which is holy to the dogs."

[10] After you are filled, give thanks in this way: "We give thanks to

VIII.   you, Holy Father, for your holy name which you made to dwell in our hearts and for the knowledge, faith, and immortality which you made known to us through Jesus your Servant. To you be the glory forever. You, Lord Almighty, created all things on account of your name, and you gave food and drink to human beings for their refreshment, in order that they might give thanks to you, but you graciously bestowed on us spiritual food and drink and life eternal through your Servant. Above all we give thanks to you, because you are mighty. To you be the glory forever. Remember, Lord, your church to deliver her from every evil and to perfect her in your love, and gather her that you have sanctified from the four winds into your kingdom which you prepared for her. Because the power and the glory are yours forever. Let grace come and this world pass away. Hosanna to the God of David. If any is holy, let him come. If any one is not, let him repent. Maranatha. Amen." But allow the prophets to give thanks as they wish.

[14] Having earlier confessed your sins so that your sacrifice may be pure, come together each Lord's day of the Lord, break bread, and give thanks. No one who has a quarrel with his fellow is to meet with you until they are reconciled, in order that your sacrifice may not be defiled. For this is what was spoken by the Lord, "In every place and time offer to me a pure sacrifice, because I am a great king, says the Lord, and my name is marvelous among the nations." (9; 10; 14)

4   JUSTIN: After we thus wash him who has been persuaded and has given his consent, we take him to the place where those called the brethren have gathered together to make fervent prayers in common on behalf of themselves and of the one who has been illuminated in baptism and of all others everywhere. We pray that we who have learned the truth may be counted worthy also to be found good citizens through our works and keepers of his commandments so that we may receive the eternal salvation. When we cease from our prayers, we salute one another with a kiss. Next there is brought to the president of the brethren bread and a cup of water mixed with wine. Taking these he sends up praise and glory to the Father of all through the name of his Son and of the Holy Spirit and makes thanksgiving at length for the gifts we were counted worthy to receive from him. When he completes the prayers and thanksgiving, all the people present sing out their assent by saying "Amen." "Amen" in Hebrew means "May it be so." When the president has given thanks and all the people have made their acclamation, those called by us deacons give to each of those present to partake of the bread and wine mixed with water for which thanksgiving has been given, and they carry some away to those who are absent. (*Apology* I, 65)

5   HIPPOLYTUS: Let the deacons present the offering to the bishop. When he lays his hands on it, with all the presbyters, let him say the

thanksgiving. "The Lord be with you." And the people shall say: "And VIII. with your spirit." [And the bishop shall say:] "Lift up your hearts." [And the people shall say:] "We have them with the Lord." [And the bishop shall say:] "Let us give thanks to the Lord." [And the people shall say:] "It is meet and right." Let him continue thus:

We give thanks to you, O God, through your beloved Servant Jesus Christ, whom in the last times you sent to us as a Savior and Redeemer, and Messenger of your will; who is your inseparable Word, through whom you made all things and in whom you were well pleased; whom you sent from heaven into the virgin's womb and who was conceived within her and was made flesh and demonstrated to be your Son being born of Holy Spirit and a virgin; who fulfilling your will and preparing for you a holy people stretched forth his hands for suffering that he might release from sufferings them who have believed in you; who when he was betrayed to voluntary suffering that he might abolish death and rend the bonds of the devil and tread down hell and enlighten the righteous and establish the covenant and demonstrate the resurrection: Taking bread he offered thanks to you and said, "Take eat; this is my body which is broken for you." Likewise also the cup, saying, "This is my blood which is shed for you. When you do this, make my memorial." Remembering therefore his death and resurrection we offer to you the bread and the cup giving thanks to you because you made us worthy to stand before you and minister to you. And we pray that you would send your Holy Spirit upon the offering of your holy church, that you would grant to all who partake of your holy [mysteries] to be united that they may be filled with the Holy Spirit for the confirmation of faith in truth. That we may praise and glorify you through your Servant Jesus Christ through whom glory and honor be to you with Holy Spirit in your holy church now and for ever world without end. Amen. . . .

And the bishop shall give thanks according to the aforesaid. It is not altogether necessary for him to recite a prayer according to a brief form, no one shall prevent him. Only let his prayer be thanksgiving to God, but let each one pray according to his own ability. If indeed he is able to pray suitably with a grand and elevated prayer, this is a good thing. But if on the other hand he should pray and recite a prayer in a moderate manner, no one shall prevent him. Only let his prayer be correct and orthodox. (*Apostolic Tradition* 4; 10)[2]

DISCUSSION

In this chapter the main concern will be the ceremony of the Lord's supper and the general meaning of it. Succeeding chapters will deal with two special ideas associated with this central act of Christian worship. For the present, note that the common name in second-century authors is *eucharist*.[3] We have kept the English form of this Greek word (*eucharistia*, "thanksgiving") in the translations of many passages because it had become a technical designation for the Lord's supper. The Greek word means "thanksgiving" or "giving of thanks." The verb form of the word occurs in the New Testament accounts of the last supper for the thanks expressed by Jesus. The verb form still means "I thank you" in modern Greek. In some passages it is difficult to know whether the noun should be given a literal (general) or a technical sense. Wherever some form of the phrase "give thanks" occurs in the translations some form of the word *eucharistia* (verb *eucharisteō*) is in the original.

The designation eucharist was already applied in the second century not simply to the prayer but also to the act as a whole (VIII.1, 2) and to the elements over which the thanks were said (IX.3). Later Irenaeus will call the service a "thank offering" (Ch. X for the sacrificial idea of the Lord's supper). This terminology is an instance of a part coming to stand for the whole. But it is notable what part of the ceremony stood for the whole–the thanksgiving. The Lord's supper was the church's great moment of thanksgiving. The church's basic act of prayer and worship was to give thanks. That says something significant about the church life of the early Christians and the quality of their life in Christ. Hence, in the prayers at the Lord's table there was a remembrance of all of God's gifts. But preeminently the eucharist was centered on the spiritual blessings which came through Jesus Christ.

Ignatius (VIII.1, 2) was very concerned about church unity. The followers of false teachings were holding their own schismatic assemblies. Part of Ignatius' program to deal with false teachers and their divisive influence was to center all congregational activities under one head, the bishop (see XIV.9 and Ch. XIV for the development of church organization). He presided at worship, as Justin's "president" (cf. VII.2), and so had charge of the eucharist. The bishop was normally the one who preached as well as the one who presided over the liturgy in the second century. This arrangement was not a matter of validity but of good order. Ignatius places no limitations on whom the leader of the congregation might invite to conduct the service.

The Lord's supper was a constant feature of the Sunday service. There is no second-century evidence for the celebration of a daily eucharist.[4] The eucharist was the climax of the Christian worship service and that which distinguished it from the Jewish synagogue service. What preceded the Lord's supper was variable. The normal order was a synagogue type service of instruction from the Scriptures and prayer (VII.2), but the eucharist could be preceded by a baptismal service (VIII.4) or the ordination of church officers (VIII.5), both normally performed on a Sunday. Thus Justin, *Apology* I, 65 (VIII.4) is describing a baptismal eucharist, whereas chapter 67 (VII.2) is describing an ordinary Sunday eucharist. This accounts for the apparent repetitiousness so close together in his narrative. The manner of celebrating was the same, but the circumstances were different. Hippolytus's account (VIII.5) is in the context of instructions concerning the ordination of a bishop. After his ordination the new bishop proceeded with the celebration of the liturgy. Hippolytus gives the new bishop a model to guide him in what to say and do.

The central place of the Lord's supper in early Christianity is abundantly indicated by all types of sources. It was found symbolized in Gospel accounts prior to the last supper. Two favorite scenes in early Christian art were the turning of water to wine at Cana and the multiplication of the loaves and fish. (Under the influence of the latter, fish are shown even in representations of the Lord's supper.)[5] These two events were brought together by Irenaeus as signs of the (eucharistic?) food and drink God gives Christians.[6]

Our sources which give sample prayers (VIII.3, 5) are careful to state that one is not bound by what is recorded. This was still an age of free prayer, and set liturgies were some two hundred years away.[6a] Nevertheless, there was a need for guidance, and there was a concern that things be done properly. Certain expressions early became stereotyped, and a certain structure and pattern of procedure and praying soon became fixed by repetition. What Justin said the president prayed about (and see his fuller statement in X.2) agrees well with the recorded prayers from early times.

The Jewish affinities of the *Didache* are everywhere in evidence and nowhere more so than in the primitive atmosphere which surrounds the simple prayers of its eucharist. The Jewish meal began with a ceremony of breaking bread and saying a prayer; thus the author used a word for bread which literally means "fragment," the "broken bread." As a prayer was said over a piece of bread, so there was a prayer over the cup of wine. Hence, the author speaks of the "cup," standing for the contents (this too was Jewish), because the cup was held as the prayer was spoken.

The reverse order of cup and then bread, the context of a meal ("after you are filled") with the long thanksgiving prayer coming afterwards, and the separate mention of a eucharist in chapter 14 have raised the question whether chapters 9-10 are describing the eucharist proper, a love feast, or some combination of the two. The alternative interpretations are legion: (1) chapter 9 is a eucharist followed by an *agapē* (love feast); (2) chapters 9-10 are an *agapē* with the eucharist only mentioned at 14; (3) chapters 9-10 are an *agapē* leading up the eucharist proper which remains undescribed; (4) chapters 9, 10, and 14 are all talking about a eucharist which may or may not have been in the context of a common meal; (5) chapter 9 is a meal and chapter 10 is the eucharistic prayer proper. The last has the virtue that it can be fitted into the scheme of the Passover meal (which is given below). It would seem strange for a manual of church life which gives detailed instruction on baptism (III.5) and many other features of conduct to give so much attention to a fellowship meal and omit the Lord's supper. Chapter 14 is not a repetition, but is concerned with proper observance of the weekly rite. Therefore, we accept this as an account of the Lord's supper as observed in certain early Jewish Christian circles and seek an explanation for its apparent anomalies.

The early rabbinic directions for the Passover meal instruct that a benediction be said over a cup of wine before the meal begins, a benediction be pronounced on the unleavened bread, and at the close of the meal a benediction over another cup (the "cup of blessing") that was the thanksgiving for the meal. More was done, of course, but I have selected the pattern which holds for other formal meals too.[7] The same procedure would seem to be reflected in the long text of Luke 22:14-20 where a cup is partaken of, bread is distributed, the supper is eaten, and another cup is blessed. In the church's usage the bread which was blessed before the meal and cup over which thanks were given at the end of the meal were brought together. Thus Matthew and Mark relate only those parts of the last supper which were significant for the church's liturgical usage. If those manuscripts of Luke which give the long text preserve the original, then Luke alone has given a fuller account of the whole meal.[8] The Didachist may have preserved the pattern of a typical Jewish religious meal in his account of the eucharistic celebration by the church.

Since there was a prayer for the breaking of bread and a prayer said over a cup of wine (if this was served) in the ordinary Jewish table prayers, Jesus' procedure at the last supper was not distinctive. What was new was the significance he gave to the bread and wine in relation to his death and its meaning.

There was some dispute in rabbinic circles whether at an ordinary meal the order should be benediction over the food and then the wine or wine and then food.[9] The writer of the Didache could simply reflect the latter practice, while giving a eucharistic understanding to the elements. The order of the cup first and then the bread may have been known in some Christian circles: for evidence may be cited the manuscripts of Luke 22 which give a shorter text, omitting the end of verse 19 and all of verse 20 with its reference to the second cup, and Paul's order in 1 Corinthians 10:16.[10] If this was the case, we may conclude that the order in which the elements were observed was not of crucial importance. The evidence strongly supports the conclusion that in the order of events at the last supper it was the bread first and the cup later to which Jesus gave the special significance. The present text of the Didache here reflects an aberration from what survived as normal church practice. An emendation in the text offers an attractive resolution of the difficulty. The removal of the rubrics, "First concerning the cup" and "Concerning the broken bread," leaves us with only two prayers, one before the meal which would have been said over the bread (ch. 9) and one after the meal which would have been said over the cup (ch. 10). The two resultant prayers are remarkably parallel in structure. If the compiler, misled by the initial reference to the "vine of David," misunderstood the prayers, his insertions could have created the reversed order, which never existed anywhere in actual practice.[11] Such excisions, however, must remain speculative.

The eucharist in the *Didache* appears to be set in the context of a social meal. This may have been the usual setting in the early days of the church. Jesus instituted the memorial of himself during the celebration of a religious meal. The disorders at Corinth (1 Corinthians 11:17-34) were occasioned by the circumstances of a common meal. As gathered together, perhaps in a house church, to eat together would have been the time when the necessary elements were present for the communion. But very soon, perhaps under the influence of such instructions as Paul gave the Corinthians, the eucharistic celebration was separated from the common meal. The evidence of Pliny (VII.1) is usually taken as implying this separation in Bithynia at the beginning of the second century. Justin's accounts (VII.2; VIII.4) leave no room for a meal. In the second century the fellowship meal developed separately as the "love feast" (for which see Ch. XI).

The prayers in the *Didache* may have been punctuated, as in Jewish synagogue practice, by congregational responses. The recurring phrase, "To you be the glory forever," sounds like such a congregational acclamation to the thanksgiving expressed by the leader of the prayers. The phrases at the close of the post-supper thanksgiving also may constitute a dialogue between the leader and the people (see below).

Many things one might have expected in the eucharistic prayers are missing in the *Didache*. The prayers seem to be an adaptation of Jewish table prayers, and with little change might have been spoken by non-Christian Jews. Most notable is the absence of any specific mention of the death of Christ. Perhaps the prayers originated in a setting too close to the death of Christ; on Jewish soil the crucifixion was an embarrassment to Christian Christological claims. Other aspects of the faith found more natural expression and assumed greater importance. Thus there is the strong note of thanksgiving for the spiritual blessings wrought by God through Jesus Christ. And the notice of "knowledge," "life," and "immortality" may be taken as in a way compensating for the lack of attention to the passion.[12]

The main features of the *Didache's* account, in addition to thanksgiving, are fellowship and eschatology. The eating together demonstrates the sense of fellowship. The *Didache* is concerned with intra-community unity. The fellowship aspect is brought out by the requirement that the members confess their sins and be at peace before they partake. The instructions in chapter 14 stress repentance and reconciliation. As an expression of the unity of the church, the eucharist is not to be defiled by quarreling and division within the group. A communal confession of sin and not only private reconciliation may be indicated.

The eucharist, furthermore, as the fellowship meal of the redeemed, is for the baptized alone. The same requirement occurs in Justin (IX.3). Later liturgical sources uniformly call for dismissal of unbaptized persons and those under discipline before the Lord's supper. The application of "Give not that which is holy to the dogs" (Matthew 7:6) may be surprising, but is not so far-fetched as one might assume. The elements, because of the use to which they were consecrated, were counted as "holy things." "Dogs" in Jewish usage referred to non-Jews (see Mark 7:27f.) and would have been taken over by Jewish Christians in reference to those outside the redeemed community of spiritual Israel. The emphasis on the church, and Christianity as a community religion, is notable in this document.

The image of the bread (grain) "scattered upon the mountains" unites the themes of fellowship and eschatology. The grain has been brought together to form one loaf of which the one body partakes. Accordingly, the author prays for the gathering together of the dispersed church from all parts of the world into the heavenly kingdom of God. The expectation of the end-time dominates the atmosphere of the *Didache*, becoming quite explicit in chapter 16. The eucharist is related to this expectation and the restoration of personal fellowship with the departed Lord. There is a longing for the end of the world and the coming of Christ. Thus the community prayed *Marana tha*. This is an Aramaic phrase to be translated "Our Lord, come!" It was part of the liturgical language of the first Palestinian Christians and survived untranslated on Greek soil (1Corinthians 16:22). It expressed the fervent hope of the early Christians for the return of Christ. This eschatological aspect tended to be weakened or lost in later prayers. Thus Tertullian speaks of Christians praying for the delay of the end (VII.3).[13]

Justin (VIII.4) describes the "first communion" of a newly baptized ("illuminated" or "enlightened") convert. Partaking of the eucharist was the first act expressing one's participation in the fellowship of the church.[14] The theme of spiritual knowledge is maintained, as is the atmosphere of thanksgiving. The Lord's supper is still the meaningful communion of the redeemed people of God. The sense of fellowship, mutual love, and peace within the community is expressed by the exchange of a kiss. The kiss was a form of greeting and served as a sign of brotherhood.[15] This expression of being members of one spiritual family had been in use as a Christian greeting from apostolic times (Romans 16:16; 1 Corinthians 16:20; 1 Peter 5:14) and was a regular feature in early liturgies. The elements over which thanks were expressed were sent to those Christians who were absent from the assembly. Thus there was an effort made to incorporate even those who could not be present into the unity and fellowship of the gathered faithful.

The prayer of thanksgiving was the sacrifice offered by all Christians (Ch. X). The prayer was offered to God "in the name of his Son and of the Holy Spirit." The contents of the prayer included thanksgiving for creation and for deliverance from evil (X.2). The whole congregation joined in the thanksgiving by ratifying the prayer with an "Amen." This was another liturgical word from the original Palestinian heritage of the church that survived in later worship (Ch. XII, note 29). The word was a common acclamation in the Old Testament, and as Justin explained to his Greek readers, it means "Let it be so." The word was an endorsement of what was spoken. In the synagogue the "Amen" was the congregational response to the prayers of the leader. It appears everywhere in early Christian accounts of worship and in liturgies in the same way. Justin's word for the manner in which the people spoke the "Amen" we have alternatively rendered "sing out their assent" and "make their acclamation." The word was used in classical Greek with the meanings "assent with a shout of applause," "sing praises." The twin ideas of "sing out" and "assent" (or "acclaim") served Justin's purpose well to convey to his readers the manner in which the "Amen" was spoken (a chant, as in Jewish liturgical prayers) and its significance (a ratification of the prayer).

The elements used were ordinary food which Jesus had endowed with special significance. Justin uses the common word for "bread" or loaf, in contrast to the *Didache* (above). He further specifies that the wine was the ordinary table drink, not straight wine but wine mixed with water. Ordinarily one did not have to specify that wine meant diluted wine; quite to the contrary, one had to specify "unmixed" wine. Justin, as an apologist, had to defend Christians against charges of misconduct, so he wants the sober character of Christian gatherings to be clear. It might be supposed that Justin refers to separate cups of water and wine. His word for wine is literally "mixture," so the reference to water could seem redundant otherwise. Moreover, in the baptismal eucharist in Hippolytus' *Apostolic Tradition* (as distinct from the regular Sunday eucharist) the newly baptized was given the cup of mixed wine ("the antitype of the blood"), a cup of milk with honey as a sign of entering the promised land and becoming spiritual children, and a cup of water as a sign of the washing from sins.[16] In defense of the translation adopted it may be said that the parallels of Justin's statements suggest that he is using "mixture" to mean "wine," as was not uncommon, necessitating for his purposes the further specification that the diluting water was indeed present.

The prayer given by Hippolytus as a pattern continues to emphasize thanksgiving and to present a Christological focus. He elaborates on the benefits of the death of Christ. Some details of the ceremony are supplied from the description of the special baptismal eucharist. His account introduces features which were to be significant in the later development of the eucharistic liturgy. There are three main parts to the ceremony:

offerings, eucharistic prayer of sacrifice, and communion. The deacons bring in the bread and mixed wine, what was later known as the offertory. The prayer is prefaced by a dialogue between the bishop and the people, the *sursum corda* ("Lift up your hearts"). The whole people were called upon to offer the prayer of thanksgiving. Worship was a corporate act, not something done for the people. The laying of hands on the elements in accompaniment to prayer is shown in certain early catacomb paintings.[17] The gesture of laying on hands signified a blessing in early Christian practice.

Hippolytus' prayer incorporates two elements of great importance in the history of worship: the words of institution and the invocation of the Holy Spirit. The repetition of Jesus' words at the last supper (modified) is incorporated into the prayer itself. The invoking of the Holy Spirit is known as the *epiclesis*. The purpose in Hippolytus' prayer is the unifying of the church in the one Spirit. In later eucharistic theology the Latin church identified the repetition of the words of institution as the moment of the change of the elements into the real body and blood of Jesus (see Ch. IX). The Greek church identified the *epiclesis* as the moment of change. It is noteworthy to see both characteristic features in Hippolytus' prayer. They are both probably early elements in the service at the table. The respective halves of Christendom settled on different moments in the liturgy when a particular view of the change in the elements made it important to identify precisely the moment of the change. But in Hippolytus there is no conversion of the elements. The narrative of the institution justifies the church's practice, and the petition for the Holy Spirit does not function to change the elements but to change the people.

The prayer includes a specific remembrance of Jesus, the *anamnesis* ("memorial") and a statement of offering to God, the *oblation*. The presbyters, and deacons if there was need, then distributed the elements, and the recipients said "Amen" on reception.

With the abandonment of the meal and the move to Gentile contexts the expressions "breaking of bread" and "Lord's supper" disappeared, and the prayer of thanksgiving over the elements was united in the same consecration. The components of offertory, prayer of thanksgiving, breaking the bread, and communion remained constant for the future development.

BIBLIOGRAPHY

Kilmartin, E. J. and R. J. Daly. *The Eucharist in the West: History and Theology.* Collegeville: Liturgical Press, 1998.

Rordorf, Willy and others. *The Eucharist of the Early Christians* (New York: Pueblo, 1978).

Sheerin, Daniel J. *The Eucharist.* Collegeville: Liturgical Press, 1986.

NOTES

[1] The Greek word means both servant and child (son). We have adopted the translation "servant" because this same word is used in the Greek translation of the "Servant of the Lord" passages in Isaiah, which is probably the usage influencing Christian terminology. It was popular with the earliest Christians because of its double applicability to Christ, the Servant of the Lord and God's Son. It continued in liturgical language long after it ceased to be used otherwise in talking about Christ. See further p. 150.

[2] The translation is substantially that given by Gregory Dix, *The Treatise on the Apostolic Tradition of St. Hippolytus of Rome* (Reissued with Corrections; London: S.P.C.K., 1968), but modified according to the reconstruction by Bernard Botte, *La tradition apostolique de saint Hippolyte* (Münster, 1963).

[3] Other references include *Acts of John* 86; 110; *Acts of Peter* 2; Tertullian, *Prescription Against Heretics* 36.

[4] C. W. Dugmore, *The Influence of the Synagogue upon the Divine Office* (Westminster: Faith Press, 1966), pp. 55f.

[5] Klaus Wessel, *The Last Supper,* "Pictorial Library of Eastern Church Art" (Rechlinghausen: Aurel Bongers, 1967), pp. 5-12; Michael Gough, *The Early Christians* (London: Thames and Hudson, 1961), pp. 86-89. See Plates III and IV of this book.

[6] *Against Heresies* 3.11.5.

[6a] A. Bouley, *From Freedom to Formula: The Evolution of the Eucharistic Prayer from Oral Improvisation to Written Text* (Washington, D.C.: Catholic University of America Press, 1981).

[7] There were four separate cups passed around during the Passover meal–Mishna *Pesahim* 10. J. Jungmann, *The Early Liturgy* (London: Darton, Longman, and Todd, 1960), pp. 32-33, 40 considers prayer after the meal before taking the "cup of blessing" to be the origin of the Christian eucharistic prayer. For other studies, see T. J. Talley, "The Eucharistic Prayer of the Ancient Church According to Recent Research: Results and Reflections," *Studia Liturgica,* Vol. 11 (1976), pp. 138-158; repr. in Everett Ferguson, ed., *Worship in Early Christianity,* Studies in Early Christianity, Vol. XV (New York: Garland, 1993), pp. 88-108; E. Mazza, *The Origins of the Eucharistic Prayer* (Collegeville: Liturgical, 1995).

[8] For a defense of the long text of Luke on the basis of the usual Passover procedures, see Joachim Jeremias, *The Eucharistic Words of Jesus* (New York: Scribner's, 1966).

[9] Mishna, *Berakoth* 8.8.

[10] 1 Corinthians 11 shows that Paul knows the bread-cup order. He perhaps reversed the order in chapter 10 so that he can develop the concept of the body as he does in verse 17.

[11] Felix Cirlot, *The Early Eucharist* (London: S.P.C.K., 1939), Appendix I.

[12] The unusual features of *Didache's* communion prayers are thus different from another unique eucharistic prayer of the second century–*Acts of John* 109. There the Christ is addressed in the prayer and given a long list of titles; the prayer is more a vehicle of the author's peculiar spirituality than representative of actual practice in the church, except to the extent it testifies to the exercise of free prayer and shows why the orthodox moved more toward set forms.

[13] Also his *Apology* 33; *Scorpiace* 3. But he does pray for the end in *On Prayer* 5.

[14] For the order preaching, faith, baptism, eucharist see *Acts of Peter* 2.5; Pseudo-Clement, *Recognitions* 1.63; 6.15; *Homilies* 11.36.

[15] Tertullian, *On Prayer* 18 calls the kiss the "seal of prayer." Eleanor Kreider, "Let the Faithful Greet Each Other: The Kiss of Peace," *Conrad Grebel Review*, Vol. 5 (1987), pp. 29-49.

[16] *Apostolic Tradition* 23. For the ordinary table drink as wine much diluted with water, see Everett Ferguson, "Wine as a Table-Drink in the Ancient World," *Restoration Quarterly*, Vol. 13 (1970), pp. 141-153.

[17] Cf. Plate III. Cf. also the usage by the Jewish sectarians at Qumran –I Q Sa ii.20. On the *sursum corda* see Ch. XII, note 18.

IX

The Language of the Real Presence
About the Lord's Supper

"This is my body"

Some New Testament Texts: Mark 14:22-24 and parallels;
John 6:35-65; 1 Corinthians 10:16; 1 Timothy 4:4-5.

SOURCES

IGNATIUS: [The Docetists] avoid the eucharist and prayer because
they do not confess the eucharist to be the flesh of our Savior Jesus
Christ, which suffered for our sins and which the Father in his goodness
resurrected. (*Smyrnaeans* 7)

IX.1

I will make plain to you the dispensation in the new man Jesus Christ,
by his faith, his love, by his passion and resurrection. Especially will I do
so if the Lord should show me that all of you, to a person, come together
in the common assembly in grace from his name in one faith and in Jesus
Christ, "who was of the family of David according to the flesh," son of
man and son of God. The intention is that you obey the bishop and
presbytery with undisturbed mind, breaking the one bread, which is the
medicine of immortality, the antidote in order that we should not die but
live forever in Jesus Christ. (*Ephesians* 20)

2

JUSTIN: And this food is called by us eucharist. It is not lawful for any
other one to partake of it than the one who believes the things which
have been taught by us to be true, and was washed with the washing for
the remission of sins and for rebirth, and lives in the manner Christ
taught. We receive these elements not as common bread and common
drink. In the same manner as our Savior Jesus Christ was made flesh
through the word of God and had flesh and blood for our salvation, even
so we were taught that the food for which thanks have been given
through the prayer of the word that is from him and from which our

3

IX.   blood and flesh are nourished according to the bodily processes is the flesh and blood of that Jesus who was made flesh. For the apostles in their memoirs, which are called Gospels, delivered what was commanded them, that Jesus took bread, gave thanks and said: "Do this for my memorial; this is my body." Likewise taking the cup and giving thanks, he said: "This is my blood." And he gave it to them alone. (*Apology* I, 66)

4   IRENAEUS: How can they be consistent with themselves when they say the bread for which they give thanks is the body of their Lord and the cup his blood, if they do not say he is the Son of the Creator of the world? . . . How can they say that the flesh that is nourished from the body of the Lord and from his flesh comes to corruption and does not partake of life? Let them either change their views or avoid offering the bread and wine. But our view is in harmony with the eucharist, and the eucharist confirms our view. We offer to God his own things, proclaiming rightly the communion and unity of flesh and spirit. For as bread from the earth when it receives the invocation of God is no longer common bread but the eucharist, consisting of two things—one earthly and one heavenly—so also our bodies when they partake of the eucharist are no longer corruptible but have the hope of the resurrection to eternity. (*Against Heresies* 4.18.4,5)

5   But if the flesh is not saved, neither did the Lord redeem us with his blood nor is the cup of the eucharist a participation in his blood nor the bread which we break a participation in his body. . . . He acknowledged the created cup with which he moistens our blood as his own blood, and he confirmed the created bread from which our bodies grow as his own body. Since therefore the cup that has been mixed and the bread that has been made, from which things the substance of our flesh grows and is sustained, receive the word of God and the eucharist becomes the body of Christ, how do they say that the flesh that is nourished from the body and blood of the Lord and is a member of him is incapable of receiving the gift of God which is eternal life? (*Against Heresies* 5.2.2,3)

6   TERTULLIAN: Taking bread and distributing it to his disciples he made it his own body by saying, "This is my body," that is a "figure of my body." On the other hand, there would not have been a figure unless there was a true body. (*Against Marcion* 4.40)

7   CYPRIAN: The cup that is offered in commemoration of him is offered mixed with wine. When Christ says, "I am the true vine," the blood of Christ is certainly not water but wine. Neither is it possible to see that his blood by which we are redeemed and made alive is in the cup when there is absent from the cup the wine by which the blood of Christ is shown forth. (*Epistle* 63 [62].2)

CYRIL OF JERUSALEM: The bread and the wine of the eucharist IX.8
before the holy invocation of the worshipful Trinity was simple bread and
wine, but when the invocation is done, the bread becomes the body of
Christ and wine the blood of Christ. (*Lectures on the Mysteries* 1.7 [=
Catechetical Lectures 19.7])

For in the type of the bread there is given to you the body, and in the 9
type of the wine there is given to you the blood, in order that you may
become by partaking of the body and blood of Christ the same body and
blood with him. For even so we become bearers of Christ since his body
and blood are distributed in our members. (*Ibid.* 4.4 [= 22.3])

We beseech the loving God to send forth the Holy Spirit upon what is
offered in order that he may make the bread the body of Christ and the 10
wine the blood of Christ. For whatever the Holy Spirit touches he
sanctifies and changes. (*Ibid.* 5.7 [= 23.7])

GREGORY OF NYSSA: He disseminates himself through that flesh
whose substance comes from bread and wine in every one who believes 11
in the economy of grace, blending himself with the bodies of believers, as
if by this union with what is immortal, a human being too may become a
partaker in incorruption. He gives these things by the power of the
benediction through which he transelements the natural quality of these
visible things to that immortal thing. (*Catechetical Oration* 37)

AMBROSE: But this bread is bread before the words of the sacraments.
When consecration has been added, from bread it becomes the body of 12
Christ. Let us, therefore, prove this. How is it possible for that which is
bread to be the body of Christ? By consecration. In whose words then is
the consecration? Those of the Lord Jesus. [The next chapter quotes the
words of the last supper as repeated by the priest, and the explanation
concludes:] Before the words of Christ the cup is full of wine and water.
When the words of Christ have operated, then is made the blood which
redeems the people. (*On the Sacraments* 4.4.14–4.5.23)

DISCUSSION

The questions raised in later ages, especially in the Reformation and
post-Reformation controversies about the Lord's supper, were not raised
in the earliest period. The dominant conceptions in regard to the Lord's
supper were those noted in the last chapter–thanksgiving for God's gifts,
the memorial action related to this, fellowship, and eschatological hopes.
Other concepts, however, were also present which were to have a great
development in the future. These ideas introduce us to the origins of
Catholic sacramental theology. It is well to look at these in order to
determine more clearly what these ideas meant at the beginning. That

will be the task of this and the following chapter.

In discussing the language of the real presence in the early centuries, three aspects of the problem are to be kept in mind: the identification of Christ with the elements of the Lord's supper, the benefits conferred by communion, and the consecration which effects the change in the elements. These aspects are distinct but in time merged in their significance.

The basis for the identification of Christ with the elements was the words of institution by Jesus at the last supper, "This is my body," "This is my blood." A certain amount of the "realistic" language in the early church is simply the repetition of the New Testament language, with no reflection on its meaning. The main context, however, in which the close identity of the elements and the flesh and blood of Jesus is stressed is to be found in the opposition to heretical teaching. A major threat to early Christian beliefs came from Docetism. The word is derived from the Greek verb "to seem," "to appear." There were those who believed that Jesus did not have a real or true human body but that he only seemed or appeared to be a real man. He came in appearance, so there was not a true incarnation. This view was continued by the Gnostics of the second century, with whom it was linked with the belief that matter was associated with evil. Thus the divine Spirit, Christ, could not have been contaminated by an actual involvement in all that pertains to fleshly life. This is why Ignatius and Tertullian, for instance, use the word "flesh" and not "body" in talking about the elements of the Lord's supper. The "realism" of the early writers was an opposition to the Gnostic disparagement of the flesh. Orthodox writers affirmed that union of flesh with Spirit is possible. Of course, the use of actual material elements from the created world in the Lord's supper gave them a powerful argument against the heretical denial of the goodness of creation. It also gave them an argument for the real human nature of Jesus. He was true flesh and blood, since it was the material objects bread and wine which he had used to show forth the nature of his human body. This circumstance accounts for much of the literal language of early Christians about the Lord's supper.

The anti-heretical thrust of the language of the real presence makes it difficult to determine any metaphysical thought about the real presence. Indeed the case might be made that initially there was none. In Hebrew thought it is function that is important (word equals deed). In prophetic symbolism deeds and words stood for the reality they represented and had the power to effect that for which they stood.[1] If Jesus' actions at the last supper are interpreted in this frame of reference, then the elements had the power or function of the body and blood. On the other hand, in Greek philosophy substances are important. An important aspect of the development of Christian doctrine was the putting of Christian beliefs, which grew out of a primarily Hebraic-Jewish context, into the language of Greek philosophy.[2] This process may be illustrated in the development of the Christological controversies of the ancient period. A similar development may be postulated in regard to the Lord's supper. Hellenistic Christianity defined the value of the Lord's supper in terms of a change in the elements, not just a change in their use or function.

As to the second aspect of this study, the benefits conferred by partaking of the elements, John 6 appears to have been the source. Immortality was thought to be conferred through partaking of the elements endowed with the life-giving power of the Savior. The ideas of the Synoptic institution narrative ("This is my body") and John ("He who eats this bread will live forever") are united in Irenaeus. Participation in the elements brings about union with Christ and his resurrection. The blessings of life and immortality are spiritually received through the power of Christ.

That which gave the special character to the elements, whether as "body and blood" or as vehicles of spiritual life, was the consecration. Prayer consecrated something to a special use, according to Jewish and early Christian thought. Prayer over the meal dedicated it to the use of the participants for their nourishment, in accordance with God's creative design (1 Timothy 4:4-5). Similarly, prayer over the bread and wine dedicated the elements to their particular use as a memorial of Christ. They were no longer "common" bread and wine. They had become "holy" through the special association which now attached to them. No consideration of the nature of consecration or the precise moment when it was effected appears in the early sources. In the fourth century, however, the idea of a conversion of the elements finds expression. When that occurred, it became important to define the moment of the change. If one followed the "institution" narrative strand of thought, then it was natural to conclude that the repetition of the words of Jesus constituted the decisive moment. This was the emphasis in the West, as may be seen in Ambrose (IX.12). If one thought in terms of the coming of the divine life as the important aspect, then it was natural to make the invocation of the Holy Spirit or the personal Word as the decisive moment when the divine power entered the elements. This was the line followed in the eastern churches and may be seen in Cyril of Jerusalem (IX.10). Both developments are late, and the second-century texts can best be explained if the reader understands the prayer of thanksgiving as a whole rather than some particular part of it as constituting the "consecration" of the elements.

With this sketch of our understanding of the main ideas we may turn to look at some of the specific texts.

Ignatius clearly represents the anti-heretical thrust in his references to the Lord's supper . He indicates that some Docetists were so "spiritual" in their religion that they abstained from the church's services of prayer and eucharist so as to avoid the material elements (IX.1). Ignatius repeatedly emphasizes the humanity of Jesus Christ, at once both God and man.[3] The material elements indicate a real flesh, and their use is a defense against a Docetic view of Christ. The one assembly of the faithful was a safeguard against the divisive influences of the false teachers. Ignatius has a great deal to say about unity, the oneness of the Christian faith (VIII.1).[4] The "altar," or "place of sacrifice" for him is the church in assembly where the sacrifice of prayer is offered to God.[5] Selections VIII.1 and IX.1, 2 demonstrate that Ignatius' organizational concern had to do with the unity of the church; the "one bishop" with the presbytery and deacons, like the one eucharist, was a center of loyalty, and this oneness may be stressed more in theory and polemic than was practiced in reality (see Ch. XIV).

Ignatius also appears to give the first statement about the supernatural benefits to be found in the partaking of the eucharist in his phrase "the medicine of immortality" (IX.2). "Breaking one bread" is the "antidote that we should not die." Once more, the anti-heretical emphasis on unity is in the forefront. But Ignatius seems to give special powers to the bread itself. The material element was a means of spiritual blessing. Nevertheless, it has been argued that Ignatius is attributing the medicinal value not to the bread but to the "breaking of bread."[6] In other words, the gift of eternal life is found in the common assembly where one is united with Christ in the one faith. To partake of false teaching, in contrast, is to take deadly medicine.[7]

Justin's explanation of the eucharist (IX.3), which follows his account of the rite (VIII.4), has been a battleground, for everyone has read his opinion into Justin's words. This is possible, because, with some elaboration, Justin repeats the words of the Scriptures. The bread and wine are real material elements. Even after the prayer of consecration they are what nourish the body through the change which takes place in digestion. The interest in Justin's statement especially derives from the implication that some change takes place before this. The elements are not "common" food any more. This may not be significant, but Justin's further statement compares them to the incarnation. As Christ became flesh, so the bread and wine become flesh and blood. Does Justin mean a conversion has been effected? Or does he suggest, like Irenaeus after him (IX.4), that as the divine has become human, so the material now has a heavenly reality added to it? Or does he only stress the reality of the incarnation since we have to do with material reality? We prefer the last, because realist terminology in the second century is so often anti-Gnostic. The second alternative is possible, since on many points Irenaeus seems to be an elaboration of anticipations in Justin. The first we consider unlikely, at least as regards any extreme change in the nature of the elements. The true literalists in the second century were some fringe Gnostic groups who introduced ideas of magic.[8] Elsewhere Justin is explicit that the bread and wine are a "memorial" of the body and blood.[9]

Justin was struggling to interpret to his pagan readers the Jewish and early Christian idea of a change in function that carried realistic power, but his analogy to the incarnation (itself a difficult concept to pagans) together with his illustration of human digestion could be read as literal realism, which in spite of being ambiguous and problematic was soon to have a powerful doctrinal development. We would conclude that the only "change" is the change involved in the consecration of the elements as a memorial of the body and blood. That leads us to the next difficult feature of Justin's cryptic description: the prayer which effects the consecration.

The common term in the comparison between the incarnation and the consecration of bread and wine as the body and blood is the "word" (logos). Jesus Christ became flesh "through the word of God," and the "eucharistizing" takes place "through the prayer of the word that is from him." Almost every word in the Greek is ambiguous and even a literal English translation does not adequately suggest the options. The central issue is whether "word," if used with same meaning in both places, is the spoken word or the personal Word. The principal interpretations, based on later liturgical developments, have been that Justin refers either to the words spoken by Jesus at the institution or to an invocation of the heavenly Word. Either interpretation may be defended, but each is full of objections. If "word" in both places is the divine Logos, then there is support for the second interpretation of the preceding paragraph. But we look in vain for other examples of an invocation of the Logos in early literature, and the construction is strained. If the parallel use of "word" is not to be stressed, and if "word" in the second part is the narrative of institution, there is agreement with the following quotation of these words. But is that properly a "prayer"? Perhaps it would be better to think of the "word" as an unspecified formula of prayer which Justin thought derived from Christ[10] or the pattern of thanksgiving which Christ had set. Returning to the idea of a parallel usage of "word," we have the possibility that it is God's creative or declarative word, in which case the second clause is a prayer for God's word to be operative in making bread and wine equal the body and blood and so a "consecration by the word of God and prayer."

Irenaeus shows the change from the early Docetism combatted by Ignatius to the later Gnosticism (IX.4, 5; X.4), for the issues now were not just the nature of Christ but also the nature of the material creation, the relation of Christ to the Creator, and the resurrection of the body. Irenaeus argues that the heretics must acknowledge that the earth is the Lord's or cease to employ those elements which they deny are his. Christ could not have acknowledged the bread and the mixed cup as his body and blood if he belonged to another Father.[11] Since the material elements receive the divine potency of the body and blood, our flesh which is nourished with the eucharist does not go to corruption but partakes of life.

Irenaeus has the realist terminology but not the realist thought. There is no conversion of the elements. Indeed, if there were any change in the substance of the elements, his argument that our bodies–in reality, not in appearance–are raised would be subverted. The bread has the effect of the body; it is sanctified but is not changed materially. Although there is no change of the elements, they are made capable of something else. A heavenly reality is added to the earthly reality. The genuine writings of Irenaeus do not explain what this heavenly "thing" is, whether the Holy Spirit,[12] the literal body and blood (unlikely), or the heavenly Logos.

Irenaeus is the first to speak explicitly of a consecration "when it receives the invocation of God." Irenaeus has been seen as referring to an invocation (*epiclesis*) for the Holy Spirit. His other references to the body and blood would indicate the use in his services of the words of institution, but that they were thought of in as consecratory is not said. It is best to take his "invocation of God" as a general reference to the prayer of thanksgiving. Elsewhere he speaks of the "sanctifying" of the gifts through "giving thanks."[13] The early centuries were not exercised with a "moment" of consecration, for they had not become concerned with a conversion in the elements. The prayer of thanksgiving effected the hallowing of the material for a spiritual purpose.[14]

The Alexandrian writers Clement and Origen viewed the elements as a symbol, or an allegory. They preserved the distinction between the elements and that which they symbolized.[15] The presence of Christ is a spiritual one (more real because spiritual, in their view of things). Consecration gives to the elements the potency of the heavenly reality of which the material elements are a type. Here it is well to remember that in ancient thought a symbol partakes of the reality symbolized to a degree greater than is true in modern thought. Some symbols can be very meaningful to us–the wedding ring or the national flag. If we think of our emotional reaction to a desecration of such a symbol, we may get closer to the realm of ancient perceptions. At any rate, just the language of "symbolism" does not mean what we might think. Although there is a distinction between the symbol and the thing symbolized, the "reality" is in some sense "there." But neither does this agree with later Medieval views of a change into a real body and blood of Christ.

The same situation prevails in the writings of Tertullian and Cyprian. When they use the language of popular piety they call the elements the body and blood of Christ. Thus Tertullian can speak of the flesh that "feeds on the body and blood of Christ" that the soul might be nourished on its God.[16] He speaks of the pain felt when any bread or wine falls on the ground.[17] This is carried further by Cyprian who can pass on almost superstitious sounding stories about the results of profanation of the consecrated elements.[18] Yet both men when they speak with precision distinguish the symbol from what it represents. The bread was a "figure" of the body. But Tertullian turns the word *figura* against the Docetism of

Marcion (IX.6). The language of symbolism does not help those who deny a real body to Jesus. The bread would not be a figure unless there was first a true body of which it was a figure. There is no shadow without a substance to cast the shadow. Similarly, for Cyprian, literal language about drinking Christ's blood is balanced by language of remembrance ("commemoration"–X.5) and representation ("shown forth"–IX.7). Both symbolism and realism are present in the thought of Cyprian and Tertullian. The symbolism concerns bread and wine as signs. The realism concerns the spiritual gift that the sign carries with it.[19] For Hippolytus, too, the bread and wine are the antitypes, or likenesses of the reality portrayed.[20] His consecration prayer (VIII.5) contains both the words of institution and petition for the Holy Spirit, but there is no suggestion of a change in the elements.

Popular piety tended to make a straight identification of the elements with Christ. This simple, unreflective type of realism is seen in the inscription of Abercius, which speaks of receiving the fish, Christ, in the eucharist (XIII.11 and discussion there, especially note 33 and cf. Plate III).

In the fourth century the idea of a change in the elements themselves, and not just in their purpose (use) or power (effects), becomes explicit. There also appears the distinctive western and eastern explanations of what it is that accomplishes the change, whether the repetition of the words of institution or the invocation of the Holy Spirit.[21] In general the East was more "mystical" and the West more "literal."

Cyril of Jerusalem (IX.9, 10) tried to explain what happens. The Holy Spirit, sent down upon the elements by God in response to the celebrant's prayer, not only sanctifies but also changes. One becomes united with Christ through the participation. The moment of the change is identified with the invocation (*epiclesis*). This may still refer to the prayer as a whole in our first selection from Cyril but is a specific petition for the Holy Spirit in the third. Gregory of Nyssa (IX.11) had a more elaborate explanation: the food becomes the body of Christ (itself nourished with the same kind of food), and the physical body is absorbed in his Deity. So, by taking of his body, one shares in Christ's immortality. By "body" it seems clear that he and Cyril are thinking of the glorified body and not just the crucified body. The novelty of Gregory's thought is in a measure indicated by the new terminology he employs. The gifts are "transelemented" into something else.

As Cyril and Gregory have followed the invocation and communion strand of thought, Ambrose (IX.12) picks up the institution and "giving of thanks" strand. But he is no less explicit in his realism about the body and blood. If the treatise *On the Sacraments* is genuine, as is now generally accepted, Ambrose gave the first full and clear definitions to what became characteristic in the Latin church.[22] It was climaxed in the definition of the dogma of transubstantiation, which was achieved in the eleventh to thirteenth centuries. According to that dogma the substance of bread and wine is changed into the substance of the body and blood while the accidental properties of taste and appearance remain those of bread and wine. Transubstantiation was an explanation of how the change in the elements occurred; the belief in the fact of a change was much earlier.

It seems there was a twofold line of development that went something like this. On one hand, consideration of the benefits of partaking of the Lord's supper led to a consideration of the divine life received. The idea of the power in the elements led to a consideration of the invocation of the Holy Spirit as the means that brought about the spiritual blessings. On the other hand, the realist language in the anti-heretical polemic emphasized a literal identity of Christ with the elements. This centered attention on the words of institution and made them the central idea in effecting the presence of Christ. The introduction of the sacrificial idea produced the medieval doctrine concerning the Mass. But the idea of sacrifice had to expand from the prayers to the elements to the Christ present in the elements. To that development we turn in the next chapter.

BIBLIOGRAPHY

Crockett, W. R. *Eucharist: Symbol of Transformation.* New York: Pueblo, 1989.

Ferguson, Everett. "The Lord's Supper in Church History: The Early Church Through the Medieval Period." *The Lord's Supper: Believers Church Perspectives.* Ed. Dale R. Stoffer. Scottdale, PA: Herald Press, 1997. Pp. 21-45.

Lampe, G.W.H. "The Eucharist in the Thought of the Early Church," *Eucharistic Theology Then and Now.* "Theological Collections," 9. London: S.P.C.K., 1968. Pp. 34-58.

MacDonald, A. J., ed. *The Evangelical Doctrine of Holy Communion.* Cambridge: W. Heffer & Sons, 1930.

NOTES

[1] For the acceptance of prophetic symbolism in the interpretation of the Christian sacraments cf. A. D. Nock, "Hellenistic Mysteries and Christian Sacraments," in *Early Gentile Christianity and its Hellenistic Background* (New York: Harper Torchbook, 1964), p. 125; reprinted in *Essays on Religion and the Ancient World,* ed. Zeph Stewart (Oxford: Clarendon, 1972) Vol. 2, p. 804. Note H. Wheeler Robinson's phrase

"representative realism" in his article "Hebrew Sacrifice and Prophetic Symbolism," *Journal of Theological Studies*, Vol. 43 (1942), pp. 135, 137f.

2 A thesis of Adolf Harnack's *History of Dogma*, trans. Neil Buchanan (New York: Dover, 1961 reprint), Vol. 1, pp. 41ff.

3 For example II.3; XIII.2; *Smyrnaeans* 1; *Romans* 3; *Ephesians* 19.

4 Cf. also *Magnesians* 7; *Ephesians* 13.

5 VIII.1; *Ephesians* 5 and see our next chapter.

6 Graydon F. Snyder, "The Text and Syntax of Ignatius, *Pros Ephesious* 20:2c," *Vigiliae Christianae*, Vol. 22 (1968), pp. 8-13, argues the case on textual, syntactical, and interpretive grounds. It may be added that this view fits better the context and Ignatius' stress on the assembly of the church against schismatic assemblies.

7 *Trallians* 6.

8 The Gnostic Marcus managed to color the wine during his consecratory prayer to give the appearance of actual blood–Irenaeus, *Against Heresies* 1.13.2. Clement of Alexandria, *Excerpts from Theodotus* 82 speaks of "bread . . . sanctified by the power of the name and not the same in appearance as when received, but transformed by power into spiritual power." Did the kind of realism represented by these Gnostics have something to do with the orthodox emphasis on spiritual benefits?

9 In *Dialogue with Trypho* 70 Justin says that Isaiah 33:13-19 refers to "the bread which our Christ delivered to us to make into a memorial of his having been made flesh for the sake of those who believe in him and for whose sake he suffered, and to the cup which he delivered to us to make into a memorial of his blood by the giving of thanks." Cf. X.2. The different terminology from the *Apology* (addressing pagans) used in addressing a Jew is noteworthy.

10 E. G. C. F. Atchley, *On the Epiclesis of the Eucharistic Liturgy and in the Consecration of the Font* (Oxford, 1935), chapter 3.

11 *Against Heresies* 4.33.2, which brief statement brings out the point of the argument in the longer passages we have quoted.

12 This is found in the spurious Fragment 37, which appears to have been an ingenious combination of Irenaeus' eucharistic conceptions in terms of later Greek ideas.

13 *Against Heresies* 4.18.6.

[14] Origen, *Against Celsus* 8.33 refers to the prayer of thanksgiving that makes the bread a "sacred body," which sanctifies the participants. Note in Plates III and IV the hands extended in blessing at the giving of thanks.

[15] Charles Bigg, *The Christian Platonists of Alexandria* (Oxford: Clarendon Press, 1886), pp. 103-107, 219-222. Among the principal references are Clement, *Instructor* 1.6.43, where John 6 is interpreted as the partaking of faith, of the Holy Spirit, and of the Divine Word; 2.2.19f., where wine is the symbol of the sacred blood and the real presence is that of the Spirit; Origen, *Commentary on Matthew* 11.14, "the typical and symbolical body"; *Commentary Series in Matthew* 85; *Homily in Leviticus* 7.5.

[16] *On the Resurrection of the Flesh* 8.3.

[17] *On the Crown* 3.4.

[18] *On the Lapsed* 25.

[19] C. W. Dugmore, "Sacrament and Sacrifice in the Early Fathers," *Journal of Ecclesiastical History*, Vol. 2 (1951), pp. 24-37; reprinted in Everett Ferguson, ed., *Worship in Early Christianity*, Studies in Early Christianity, Vol. XV (New York: Garland, 1993), pp. 178-191.

[20] *Apostolic Tradition* 23.1.

[21] There was still variety with Greek writers attributing the change to the words of Christ and Latin writers speaking of the invocation. The language of symbolism persisted along with the newer conversion language. See the article by G. W. H. Lampe in the bibliography, pp. 51-52.

[22] Similar ideas in *On the Mysteries* 9.50-58; *On the Christian Faith* 4.10.125.

X

Sacrificial Ideas Associated with the Lord's Supper

"Offer ... the sacrifice of praise"

Some New Testament Texts: Hebrews 13:15; Romans 12:1; 15:27, 31; 2 Corinthians 9:12.

SOURCES

CLEMENT OF ROME: God commanded that offerings and services be   X.1
performed and that they not be done at random times and in a disorderly manner but at the appointed times and hours. He appointed by his supreme will both where and by whom he wishes to be served in order that all things may be done in a holy manner according to his good pleasure and may be acceptable to his will. Therefore those who make their offerings at the appointed times are acceptable and blessed, for they follow the laws of the Master and do no sin. To the high priest the proper ministries have been given, and the proper place has been assigned to the priests, and their own services are imposed on the Levites; the layman has been bound by the regulations for the laymen. (40)

JUSTIN: "The offering of fine flour, sirs," I said, "which was   2
commanded to be offered on behalf of those purified from leprosy was a type of the bread of the eucharist which our Lord Jesus Christ commanded to be made a memorial of the passion which he suffered on behalf of the people being purified in their souls from all evil. He commanded to do this in order that at the same time we might give thanks to God for having created the world with all things in it for the sake of human beings, for having freed us from the wickedness in which we were, and for having completely destroyed the principalities and powers by the one who accepted suffering according to his will. [There follows a quotation of Malachi 1:10-12.] He speaks beforehand then

X. concerning us Gentiles who in every place offer sacrifices to him, that is the bread of the eucharist and the cup similarly of the eucharist, since he said that we glorify his name but you profane it." (*Dialogue with Trypho* 41)

3 We [Christians] are the true high priestly race of God, as also God himself testifies when he said that "in every place among the Gentiles they offer pure and acceptable sacrifices to him." God does not receive sacrifices from anyone except through his priests. Therefore, God in anticipation testifies that all the sacrifices through the name of Christ are well pleasing to him which Jesus Christ delivered to be done, namely at the eucharist of the bread and of the cup, the sacrifices which are done in all the earth by Christians. But he rejects those sacrifices performed through those priests of yours [Jews]. . . . I also agree that prayers and thanksgivings performed by worthy men are the only sacrifices perfect and well pleasing to God. For these alone Christians undertake to make, even at the memorial of their solid and liquid food in which also is brought to mind the suffering that the Son of God endured because of them. (*Ibid.* 116, 117)

4 IRENAEUS: Giving directions to his disciples to offer to God the first fruits from his creation, not as if he were in need but so that they would not be unfruitful nor ungrateful, he took bread which is from created things and gave thanks, saying, "This is my body." And the cup likewise, which is out of the created things to which we belong, he confessed to be his blood, and he taught the new oblation of the new covenant. The church, receiving this from the apostles, offers in the whole world to God, who provides us with the means of sustenance, the first fruits of his own gifts in the new covenant. [Then follows Malachi 1:10f.] (*Against Heresies* 4.17.5)

5 CYPRIAN: That priest truly discharges the office of Christ who imitates what Christ did. He then offers a true and full sacrifice in the church to God the Father, if he proceeds so to offer according to what he sees Christ himself to have offered. . . . And because we make mention of his passion in all sacrifices (for the Lord's passion is the sacrifice which we offer), we ought to do nothing else than what he did. . . . As often as we offer the cup in commemoration of the Lord and his passion, let us do what it is known the Lord did. (*Epistle* 63 [62].14, 17)

6 CYRIL OF JERUSALEM: Then after the spiritual sacrifice, the bloodless worship, is completed, we entreat God over that sacrifice of propitiation for the common peace of the churches . . . . Then we commemorate also those who have fallen asleep . . . . We believe there will be a great benefit to the souls on behalf of whom the prayer is offered up while that holy and most awesome sacrifice is presented . . . .

We offer up the Christ who was sacrificed for our sins, propitiating . . . the X.
merciful God. (*Lectures on the Mysteries* 5.8-10 [=*Catechetical Lectures*
23.8-10])

APOSTOLIC CONSTITUTIONS: Remembering now his passion, his 7
death, his resurrection from the dead, his ascension into heaven, and his
approaching second appearance in which he is coming with glory and
power to judge the living and dead and to recompense each person
according to his works, we offer to you, our King and God, according to
his constitution this bread and this cup. We give thanks to you through
him because you have counted us worthy to stand before you and be
priests before you. We beseech you that you will look favorably upon
these gifts set forth before you, O All-sufficient God, and be pleased with
them to the honor of your Christ. Send down your Holy Spirit upon this
sacrifice, the testimony of the sufferings of the Lord Jesus, that he may
show this bread to be the body of your Christ and this cup the blood of
your Christ. May he do so in order that those who partake may be
strengthened for godliness, may attain remission of sins, may be delivered
from the devil and all his error, may be filled with the Holy Spirit, may
be worthy of your Christ, may attain eternal life when you are reconciled
with them, O Lord Almighty. (8.2.12 [59])

DISCUSSION

Clement of Rome (X.1) uses the regulations in the Old Testament
pertaining to sacrifice as an illustration of the good order which God
expects in the church. God, according to the Law of Moses, had
determined the times, place, and personnel of worship. Clement's entire
chapter forty, which we have quoted, is concerned with the Old
Testament sacrificial system. Christ is now the "High Priest of our
offerings" (36.1), which presumably are the "sacrifice of praise" (35.12).
In keeping with his illustration, Clement can speak of the activity of
Christian elders, especially it seems in the leadership of worship, as
"offering the gifts" (XIV.2). By analogy with the Old Testament,
Christian worship is described in the language of sacrifice. This was the
universal language of worship in the ancient world (Jewish and pagan),
and no other imagery was so readily understood or suitable.

The *Didache* is more explicit in the use of the Old Testament language
of sacrifice in reference to the Christian ministry and Christian worship.
The first fruits which formerly went to the priests are now to be given to
the Christian prophets, "for they are your high priests" (*Didache* 13, and
see our Ch. XIV). The prophets presided at the Lord's supper, hence
Christian worship (with special reference to the "breaking of bread") is
called a "sacrifice" (VIII.3). To be a pure sacrifice there must be
reconciliation in the community. The author cites Malachi 1:11 as

fulfilled in the Christian assemblies. This passage became the favorite Old Testament text in reference to the Lord's supper. Justin twice used it as a proof that God rejected the worship of the Jews and now accepted instead the worship of Gentile Christians, centered in the Lord's supper (X.2, 3).[1] Irenaeus, too, quotes Malachi 1:10f. in reference to the eucharist (X.4). Although the writer of the *Didache* is not explicit about what aspects of sacrifice are in his mind, we may relate his statements to what finds expression later in the second century and to the Jewish background. Thus one may see in the gifts brought for the support of the teachers and the poor (*Didache* 13) an offering (Deuteronomy 14:22-29; 26:1-15; Numbers 18:21-32), and in the prayers at the Lord's supper a thank-offering (the sacrifice of thanksgiving–note the way thanksgiving dominates the prayers, VIII.3), and perhaps in the Lord's supper itself the meal which the worshippers shared after bringing their offering (Leviticus 7:11-18).[2]

The church itself in early Christian thought was now God's temple where acceptable worship was offered to him. Ignatius can speak of the church as the "altar" outside of which one "is deprived of the bread of God."[3] Similarly the widows and other objects of Christian charity are called the "altar of God,"[4] because they devoted themselves to prayer and were supported out of the gifts brought to church at the assembly for worship (see Ch. XVII). The gifts brought by the faithful as a contribution to the church and especially for the poor continued to be referred to in the language of sacrifice–"gifts" and "offerings."[5] Thus Hippolytus used the same language about offering oil, cheese, and olives as he did about offering bread and wine to God.[6] For these things, too, "eucharist is made" (thanks are given). To bring them to God (in church) is "to offer" them.

The eucharist is explicitly called a sacrifice for the first time in our sources by Justin (X.2). The pure sacrifice of Malachi is the "bread and cup of the eucharist." The eucharist is a sacrifice of thanksgiving and so it fulfills Malachi's words. Justin, too, may be thinking of the bringing of the elements as the gift of the people.[7] His main emphasis, however, is on the sacrifice of praise and thanksgiving. The prayers are preeminently the sacrifice of Christians (X.3), for thanksgiving itself is a sacrifice. Thus Justin reverses his phrase and speaks of the "eucharist (thanksgiving) of the bread and cup" as the sacrifice of Christians. All Christians are priests, "the true high priestly race of God." The sacrifice is that of the whole community. All worship is a sacrifice, and the nature of Christian worship finds its climax in the great thanksgiving for God's gifts of creation and redemption pronounced in connection with the bread and wine. The Jews themselves had come to consider prayer the equivalent and then the substitute for animal sacrifices.[8] Justin agrees with the sentiment that "prayers and thanksgivings" are the perfect sacrifices, the only kind acceptable to God now. And, he affirms that these are the only sacrifices which Christians offer, and this preeminently at the Lord's supper.

For Justin the eucharist is a memorial of the passion of Christ.[9] Jesus' death was itself a sacrifice,[10] but there seems to be no equivalence made by Justin between Jesus' death and the sacrifice performed by thanksgiving. The remembrance is not a silent calling to mind; there is something "to do." It has been urged that Justin's language "do this memorial" should be translated "offer this memorial,"[11] that the memorial is itself a sacrifice. Within the thanksgiving context this may be correct. "To do" may mean "to offer" in a sacrificial setting. On the other hand, we think that Justin's use of "do" is influenced by the New Testament accounts more than by any Old Testament usage of "do" in a sacrificial context.[12] The "doing" is for the purpose of the giving thanks (Ch. VIII).

In the earliest writers it would seem, therefore, that the eucharist is called a sacrifice only in connection with Old Testament types and by way of contrasting the spiritual service of thanksgiving by Christians with the bloody sacrifices of Jews and pagans. Athenagoras speaks of the "bloodless sacrifice," the "rational service" of Christians, in contrast to the holocausts of the pagans.[13] So essential to divine service in the ancient world was sacrifice that pagans could only conclude that Christians were "atheists" because they had no temple and ceremonial cult. The principal phenomenon with which Christianity could be compared was a philosophical school, and the views of some of the philosophers provided the main pagan analogy to the Christians' idea of spiritual sacrifice. The Old Testament background and the surrounding religious world made the language of sacrifice inevitable in Christian usage, even when a different phenomenon was being expressed.

It was natural to move from the prayer as a sacrifice to the elements over which the prayer was said as a sacrifice. Particularly if, as seems likely, the bringing of the bread and wine as a contribution was described from the beginning as an offering, would it be easy to apply the language of sacrifice to the elements of the eucharist. The word eucharist itself also could have provided the bridge, as it was extended from the prayers to the whole action to the elements.

Irenaeus introduces a further development, for he speaks more explicitly of the bread and cup as an oblation (X.4). He identifies the sacrifice more closely with the elements by dwelling on the aspect of an offering of the first fruits of the earth (with which we may compare the *Didache*). That the bread and cup are themselves a sacrifice, "the new oblation of the new covenant," is perhaps more a verbal than a conceptual novelty. The Christian altar is in heaven, and "toward it our prayers and oblations are directed."[14] The Christian oblation is contrasted with the Jewish: "There were sacrifices by the people [Jews] and there are sacrifices in the church; but the species is changed inasmuch as they are offered by free men and not by slaves."[15] The thought is still moving in the framework of the fulfillment of Malachi 1, and the sacrifice is the thanksgiving for the first fruits of the earth.[16]

Irenaeus' attention to the elements themselves is due to his anti-heretical concern. Against Gnostics who considered the material creation evil, he brought forward the fruits of creation as intimately associated with the most sacred actions of the Christian religion (Ch. IX). He does connect the bread and cup with the body and blood (once more an anti-heretical insistence on the real, created humanity of Jesus), but with no suggestion that it is other than the first fruits which are being sacrificed to God. The ideas of sacrifice and real presence were to remain side by side for a long time before they were brought into closer relationship. Irenaeus has several passages on sacrifice, always the sacrifice of the church and not of a part of the church or by a special class.

Since worship as a whole was an act of spiritual sacrifice, it was natural to move from the prayers to the action of the eucharist as a whole as a sacrifice. This may be involved already in what the Didache and Justin say. On the other hand, the specific identification of the sacrificial act with what the celebrant did at the eucharist may not be in mind in even some of the later sources where it would be easy to assume this to be the case. Thus the eucharist in Hippolytus is dominated by the idea of sacrifice (VIII.5). The church offers bread and wine, gives thanks for this priestly privilege, and prays for the Holy Spirit to be sent into this food so that by partaking of the sacrificial food the church may partake of the Spirit. Hippolytus also uses this language freely in other contexts (see Ch. XI) that permit some precision in what he means by "offering" something: through prayer something becomes consecrated to God.[17] The accompanying action may be laying the gift on the table, raising it heavenward, or laying on the hand in blessing. The offering to God of gifts in kind is combined with the conception that prayer is the spiritual Christian sacrifice. Thus the emphasis is upon the act as a whole and the range of ideas is still that of the second century. There is no identification of the church's sacrifice with the sacrifice on the cross.

One may nonetheless see in Hippolytus connotations which point to the future. In the third century the language of sacrifice and priesthood was used more freely. Origen spoke often of the Christian ministers in terms of the Old Testament priesthood, especially in his allegorizing homilies, which drew spiritual lessons for the church from the Old Testament. Cyprian, the new convert become bishop, has both the language and concept of priesthood and sacrifice, He regularly uses "priest" for the Christian bishop, "altar" for the place of celebration of the eucharist, and "sacrifice" for the observance of it.[18] Cyprian carries further the transference (or narrowing down) of sacrificial ideas from the service of prayer to the consecrated elements, and he opened up a whole new era by a closer association of the eucharistic sacrifice with the sacrifice on the cross (X.5). He associated the elements, the idea of sacrifice, and the passion of Christ. The insistence in his passage on "doing what Christ did" pertains to an argument against some who used water alone in the eucharist. Cyprian says there must be wine mixed with the water (IX.7; cf. VIII.4) because that is what Christ used when he instituted the communion. Since our act is a commemoration, we must do what he did. This accounts for the attention to the elements. The Christian bishop offers a "true and full sacrifice," and this is the "sacrifice of his passion." Mention is made of the passion of Christ in the prayer, and this presumably controls what is meant by saying that "the Lord's passion is the sacrifice we offer." It is still the bread and not the body which is offered, so no independent value is given to the bread or to the eucharistic sacrifice. The setting is still the thank offering in commemoration of the Lord's passion. Nevertheless, such language may pass from the homiletical and polemical to the dogmatic.

Sacrificial ideas became more fully developed in the fourth century with Cyril of Jerusalem and the compiler of the *Apostolic Constitutions* (X.6, 7). The service had expanded from a sacrifice of thanksgiving to a sacrifice of propitiation and from the offering of the elements to an offering of Christ. The way to this propitiatory view of the eucharist had been opened by the actual combination in thought of those ideas which were at hand in the eucharistic developments of the preceding two centuries, namely the real presence of Christ in the elements and the association with the sacrifice on the cross. For Cyril "we offer up Christ." In the clear sacrificial language of the consecration prayer in the *Apostolic Constitutions*, one of the blessings to participants is the remission of sins. It is indicative of the direction of doctrinal thought that the blessings earlier assigned to baptism are here ascribed to the eucharist. The offering is also made "on behalf of" all who have pleased God from the beginning of the world; the parallels, however, may indicate that the meaning is "pray for," as in the remainder of the great intercession. Sacrificial language rivals the note of thanksgiving which prevailed earlier (Ch. VIII).

Fourth-century writers still spoke the language of commemoration: "It is evident to those educated in divine things that we do not offer another sacrifice, but we perform the memorial of that one saving sacrifice."[19] Or, they could speak of offering "the antitype" of the death on the cross.[20] But we have carried our survey enough beyond our normal chronological limits to see the course which was set for the future. Early Christian ideas had been brought together in a new combination and sacrificial notions had been refocused.

BIBLIOGRAPHY

Brilioth, Ynge. *Eucharistic Faith and Practice*. London: S.P.C.K., 1930.

Daly, R. J. *Christian Sacrifice: The Judaeo-Christian Background Before Origen*. Washington, DC: Catholic University of America Press, 1978.

Ferguson, Everett. "Spiritual Sacrifice in Early Christianity and Its Environment." *Aufstieg und Niedergang der römischen Welt*. Ed. H. Temporini and W. Haase. Berlin: Walter de Gruyter, 1980. Part II, Vol. 23.1, pp. 1151-1189.

Hanson, R.P.C. *Eucharistic Offering in the Early Church* (Bramcote, Notts.: Grove, 1979).

Stevenson, K. W. *Eucharist and Offering*. New York: Pueblo, 1986.

Young, Frances M. *The Use of Sacrificial Ideas in Greek Christian Writers from the New Testament to John Chrysostom*. Cambridge: Philadelphia Patristic Foundation, 1979.

NOTES

[1] He also cites the passage in *Dialogue* 28.

[2] Paul seems to compare the Lord's supper to the religious meal following the sacrifice–1 Corinthians 10:16-21.

[3] *Ephesians* 5 (quoted VI.22); cf. *Trallians* 7. In *Philadelphians* 4 (quoted VIII.1) Ignatius exhorts to "one eucharist," for there is "one altar," as part of his appeal for unity and thrust against those who held divisive assemblies apart from the main church.

[4] Polycarp, *Philippians* 4.3. Carolyn Osiek, "The Widow as Altar: The Rise and Fall of a Symbol," *The Second Century*, Vol. 3 (1983), pp. 160-169.

[5] J. A. Jungmann, *The Early Liturgy* (London: Darton, Longman, and Todd, 1958), pp. 41, 66f., 116-118, 171f.

[6] *Apostolic Tradition* 5, 6.

[7] Cf. VIII.4, "There is brought to the president," where the verb is the same as the "offer" of X.2.

[8] George Foot Moore, *Judaism* (Cambridge: Harvard University Press, 1927), Vol. II, pp. 14f., 218.

[9] Cf. *Dialogue* 70, quoted in Chapter IX, note 9.

[10] For example, *Dialogue* 40, but Justin seems to use sacrifice about the cross only in connection with Old Testament prophecy.

[11] Felix Cirlot, *The Early Eucharist* (London: S.P.C.K., 1939), Appendix IV.

[12] Luke 22:19 and 1 Corinthians 11.24-25 have the same phrases.

[13] *Plea for the Christians* 13; cf. *Odes of Solomon* 20; Justin, *Apology* I, 13 (quoted p. 83); Tertullian, *On Prayer* 28. Clement of Alexandria's small treatise on prayer beginning in *Miscellanies* 7.6.30ff. disparages pagan sacrifice and characterizes prayer as the "best and holiest sacrifice" and calls the altar "the congregation of those who devote themselves to prayers." The discussion has Hellenistic philosophical backgrounds but is set in a Christian context. In 7.7.49.4f. he lists giving teachings and money to the needy as sacrifices in addition to prayer.

[14] *Against Heresies* 4.18.6.

[15] *Ibid.* 4.18.2.

[16] Thanksgiving continued to dominate Irenaeus' sacrificial concept. Cf. "offering with giving of thanks" (*Against Heresies* 4.18.4), and at the beginning of that section he says that we make an offering, not because God needs it, but as a way of giving thanks for his gifts. Irenaeus does not define the act of sacrifice, but always connects it with thanksgiving.

[17] Hans Lictzmann, *Mass and Lord's Supper* (Leiden: E. J. Brill, n.d.), pp. 148-151.

[18] For instance, *On the Unity of the Church* 17.

[19] Theodoret, *Interpretation of Hebrews* 8.4, 5.

[20] Gregory Nazianzus, *Oration* 2.95.

XI
The Love Feast (Agapē)

"When you come together to eat"

Some New Testament Texts: Jude 12; 2 Peter 2:13 (in some manuscripts); 1 Corinthians 11:17-34.

SOURCES

IGNATIUS: It is not lawful either to baptize or to have a love feast apart from the bishop. (*Smyrnaeans* 8)   XI.1

CLEMENT OF ALEXANDRIA: If some using unchecked language   2
dare to call some sorry meal giving forth the odor of roast meat and sauces an *agapē*, they insult with pots and the flow of sauce the good and saving work of the Word, the sanctified *agapē*, and they blaspheme this name with drink and food and smoke. They are deceived by their thinking when they expect to buy the promise of God with dinners. For if we designate festive gatherings as either dinners, luncheons, or receptions, we would properly name this kind of meeting and would imitate the Lord who has not called such banquets *agapēs*,. . . .
Agapē is truly heavenly food, a rational banquet.
If "you shall love the Lord your God and your neighbor," this is the celestial feast in the heavens, but the earthly feast is called a meal, as has been shown from the Scripture. The meal occurs because of love, not love because of the meal, which is a proof of a generous and shared good will. . . . The person who eats of this meal shall obtain the best of the things which pertain to reality, the kingdom of God, since he has had a care here for the holy assembly of love, the heavenly church. Love then is a pure thing and worthy of God, and its work is generosity. . . . Love is not a meal, but let the banquet depend on love. . . .
It is admirable then to lift up our eyes to the true, to depend on the

XI.   divine food from above, and be filled with the contemplation of him who truly exists, so tasting of the only pure and sure delight. The food which comes from Christ shows this to be the *agapē*, which we must attain. (*Instructor* 2.1.4,3-4; 5,3; 6,1–7,1; 9,3)

3   TERTULLIAN: Our feast shows its motive by its name. It is called by the Greek word for love. Whatever is reckoned the cost, money spent in the name of piety is gain, since with that refreshment we benefit the needy. . . . As is so with God, there is a greater consideration for the lowly. If the reason for our common meal is honorable, appraise the subsequent order of procedure by its purpose. Since it is a religious duty, it permits nothing vile, nothing immodest. We do not recline at the table before prayer to God is first tasted. We eat the amount that satisfies the hungry; we drink as much as is beneficial to the modest. We satisfy ourselves as those who remember that even during the night we must worship God; we converse as those who know that the Lord listens. After the washing of hands and lighting of lamps, each one who is able is called into the center to chant praise to God either from the holy Scriptures or from his own talents. This is a proof of how much is drunk. Prayer in like manner concludes the meal. (*Apology* 39.16-18)

4   HIPPOLYTUS: Widows and virgins shall fast often and pray on behalf of the Church. The presbyters when they wish and the laity likewise shall fast.

The bishop cannot fast except when all the people also [fast].

For often some one wishes to bring an offering, and he cannot be denied and [the bishop] having broken [the bread] shall always taste of it, and eat with such of the faithful as are present.

And they shall take from the hand of the bishop one piece of a loaf before each takes his own bread, for this is "blessed [bread]"; but it is not the eucharist as is the Body of the Lord.

And before they drink let each of those of you who are present take a cup and give thanks and drink, and so take your meal being purified in this way.

But to the catechumens let exorcised bread be given; and they shall each offer a cup.

A catechumen shall not sit at table at the Lord's Supper.

And at every act of offering let him who offers remember him who invited him, for to this end he [i.e. the host] petitioned that they might come under his roof.

But when you eat and drink do it in good order and not unto drunkenness, and not so that any one may mock you, or that he who invites you may be grieved by your disorder, but [rather] so that he may pray [to be made worthy] that the Saints may come in unto him. For He said, Ye are the salt of the earth.

If you are all assembled [and] offered [what is called in Greek] an

apophoretum [i.e. something to be taken away] accept it from him [i.e. the XI.
giver] [and depart] and eat thy portion alone.

But if [you are invited] all to eat [together], eat sufficiently but so that there may remain something over that your host may send it to whomsoever he wills as the superfluity of the Saints, and he [to whom it is sent] may rejoice with what is left over.

And let the guests when they eat partake in silence without arguing. But [let them hearken] to any exhortation the bishop may make, and if any one ask any question, let an answer be given him. And when the bishop has given the explanation let every one quietly offering praise [to him] be silent until he [?the bishop] be asked again.

And if the faithful should be present at a supper without the bishop, but with a presbyter or deacon present, let them similarly partake in orderly fashion. But let every one be careful to receive the blessed bread from the hand of the presbyter or deacon. Similarly a catechumen shall receive the [same bread], [but] exorcised.

If laymen [only] are met together without the clergy let them act with understanding. For the layman cannot make a blessing [or, make the blessed bread].

And having given thanks let each one eat in the Name of the Lord. For this is pleasing to God that we should be jealous [?for his Name] even among the heathen, all of us sober alike. . . .

If at any time any one wishes to invite those widows who are advanced in years let him feed them and send them away before sunset.

But if he cannot entertain them at his house because of the circumstances, let him give them food and wine and send them away, and they shall partake of it at home as they please. (*Apostolic Tradition* 25-27)[1]

DISCUSSION

Jesus instituted the memorial of himself at the last supper in the context of a meal.[2] It seems that a meal provided the most convenient context in which the Lord's supper was observed by early Christians. At least this was the case at Corinth[3] and provided the occasion for the abuses which developed there. The *Didache* also sets the eucharist in the context of a common religious meal (VIII.3). The Roman governor Pliny places the Christian gathering for a common meal at a separate time from their "stated" religious assembly (VII.1). By this time in Bithynia, it would seem, the Lord's supper was separated from the meal. Even where an ordinary meal provided the setting for the Lord's supper, there is no reason to think the latter was not distinct in its observance and meaning.

The Greek word for love, *agapē*, was used by Christians in reference to certain of their religious meals together. Thus one specialized meaning for *agapē* was "love feast," the shared meal which was an expression of and proof of brotherly feeling and mutual concern. These meals were correctly named, for they were manifestations of brotherly love, as we shall see below. In addition to the passages cited, there are several other early occurrences of *agapē* in the sense of "love feast." Origen refers to Celsus' criticism of the Christians' love feasts as belonging in the same class with pagan secret associations.[4] The *Passion of Perpetua and Felicitas* relates how the martyrs in their last meal on the day before their martyrdom partook of an *agapē* "so far as they could."[5]

A close connection is indicated between the Lord's supper and the *agapē* by an apparent interchange of the terms. Ignatius (XI.1) mentions *agapē* immediately following a parallel reference to the eucharist (VIII.2). The importance he gives to the bishop's presence for an *agapē* as well as for a baptism suggests that he has an important religious gathering of the community in mind. It appears that the term *agapē* could be used for, or at least to include, the Lord's supper.[6] On the other hand, Hippolytus uses "Lord's supper" to refer to the *agapē* (XI.4). Apparently *agapē* was used for the meal, and eucharist for the memorial of the Lord. As they were separated in time, and perhaps in location, the love feast continued to be an important social and religious function of the Christian community.

Clement of Alexandria seems almost to protest against the designation *agapē* for the social meal (XI.2). He thereby attests the common word usage. Perhaps it is the almost exclusive use of *agapē* for the feast by some that concerns him. Clement typically emphasizes a spiritual interpretation of outward Christian observances. In view of this, he is very likely here not rejecting the *agapē*, either in name or in fact, but calling attention to its true motive and using it to direct attention to the true meaning of love. The meal itself is not love but exists because of love. It is one earthly expression of that higher spiritual reality which is "to love God and one's neighbor."

For many of the average Christians the central point of their Christian experience was the common meal. This importance, which seems indicated by our literary sources, may be confirmed by the early Christian catacomb paintings. These visual representations of what was most meaningful in their faith to the ordinary believers contain many depictions of a meal.[7] It is often difficult to know whether the last supper, a Lord's supper, a funeral meal, the heavenly banquet, a feeding miracle from the Gospels, or a love feast is indicated. Some would seem clearly to be the love feast, and the experience of these shared dinners has likely influenced the representation of other scenes.

The love feasts were clearly church activities, hence the importance placed on the presence of the bishop or another member of the clergy (XI.1, 4). It was a "church dinner," although held in a private home. As gatherings of small groups out of the community they were an important potential source of divisiveness and means for the spread of false teachings. It was important that these gatherings be tied to the whole church and integrated into its total life. A definite religious atmosphere and deportment characterizes the surviving accounts (XI.3, 4).

The love feast served functions of fellowship and charity for the early Christians. It was the social, convivial aspect which perhaps especially attracted many persons. The sharing of food by the wealthier with the poorer was an important means of charity. The host provided food for those chosen who sometimes did not eat at his house but received the food at home or accepted it to take home. The recipients were expected to pray for their benefactor, so sharing spiritual blessings in return for material ones (XI.4; cf. Ch. XVII). Clement (XI.2) appears to have the host in mind when he speaks of buying "the promise of God with dinners." Widows, the sick, or any of the poorer and needy members of the church might be invited. Any church-sponsored gathering would have been an occasion for sharing in which in the nature of the case the better off would have contributed more. This benevolent function of the *agapē* was what came to predominate, and it was with this purpose that vestiges of the *agapē* continued in the later centuries of the church.

The concerns in our sources about proper conduct are an indication that the social aspect was what counted for most of the participants in the second century. Moral disorders at the love feasts of some Gnostic groups were a source of slander against Christians.[8] Tertullian himself, after identifying with the Montanists, implies moral laxity at some love feasts in the great church.[9] The language of Clement suggests too much attention by some to the material side of the love feast at the expense of the spiritual side (XI.2). The prescriptions of Hippolytus would not have been necessary unless there was a need for tight regulation.

It is only at the end of the second century that we get detailed descriptions of what was done at a Christian love feast. It occurred in the late afternoon or early evening, the time of the principal meal in the day. Tertullian, rebutting pagan slanders, lays stress on the sober religious character of the gathering. It is an *agapē* because it benefits the needy; special consideration is shown for the lowly. There is prayer before all take their places at the table. The eating and drinking are moderate. After the meal hands are washed and the lights are lit, according to custom. Hymns provide the evening's entertainment.[10] The company is dismissed with prayer.

Hippolytus devotes the longest space of any of our sources to the *agapē*, but the variations in our textual authorities place much of the detail in his testimony in doubt. Nevertheless, the main lines of his evidence are sure and coincide with other information. Since the bishop is expected to be present and participate whenever some member of the church wants to hold a love feast, he can fast only when the whole church does so. A presbyter or deacon can preside, but laymen alone are not to have a love feast. This gives a definite "churchly" tone to the occasion. Perhaps, like Ignatius, Hippolytus was concerned to preserve the unity of the community; or his regulations may be designed to enhance the religious character of the *agapē* and especially to provide a safeguard against the disorders which had caused so much mischief. The bishop functioned in the way the head of the household or honored guest at Jewish religious meals did in pronouncing the blessing and distributing the bread with which the meal began. The similarity of Hippolytus' regulations to the religious character of Jewish meals indicates the primitive character of much that he says and points to the origins of these Christian practices in the Judaism from which the church had sprung.[11] The author distinguishes between the eucharistic bread and the "blessed bread." His use of the word "offer" throughout shows what connotation is to be given to this language in connection with the eucharist (Ch. X). "To offer" was to dedicate by prayer to a religious purpose. In the case of the *agapē*, that purpose was the relief of the poor. Since the love feast was a fellowship meal of Christians, those who were not baptized did not recline at table with the full members of the church, nor did they eat of the bread over which the blessing was said (an expression of brotherly unity) but were given bread over which an exorcism had been pronounced in order to deliver it from the sphere of demons. Each person apparently spoke his own blessing over the cup of wine and was expected to remember the host (benefactor) in his prayer. Hippolytus, like Tertullian, was concerned that the conversation and conduct not become rowdy.

These instructions for the beginning of the meal with prayer and conduct during the meal are well attested in the documents based on the original *Apostolic Tradition*. Some of the documents also give directions for distribution of the food to the poor, widows, and sick. The Ethiopic version, in a confused text, contains further information which may very well go back to Hippolytus or his time concerning the conclusion of the *agapē*.[12] It provides for the deacon to bring in a light and gives a prayer of thanksgiving for the close of the day and the gift of light to be pronounced by the bishop. When all rise from the meal, they sing psalms (cf. Tertullian in XI.3). Then a cup of mixed wine and water is held while a hallelujah psalm is recited. This coincides with Jewish meals, at which the formal conclusion is a blessing pronounced over a cup of wine.

The agreements of Tertullian and Hippolytus give us a good description of what the love feast was, or was intended to be, at the end of the second century. A clearer picture of its relation to the Lord's supper in earlier times is dependent on the discovery of new sources.

BIBLIOGRAPHY

Cole, R. Lee. *Love–Feasts: A History of the Christian Agapē*. London: Charles H. Kelly, 1916.

Ferguson, Everett. "Agapē Meal." *Anchor Bible Dictionary*. Ed. David Noel Freedman. New York: Doubleday, 1992. Vol. 1, pp. 90-91.

Keating, J. F. *The Agapē and the Eucharist in the Early Church*. London: Methuen and Co., 1901. Reprint New York: AMS Press, 1969.

Reicke, Bo. *Diakonie. Festfreude, und Zelos*. Uppsala, 1951.

NOTES

[1] Quoted from Gregory Dix, *The Treatise on the Apostolic Tradition of St. Hippolytus of Rome* (Reissued with Corrections; London: S.P.C.K., 1968). The witnesses to the text show the greatest variety in this section, and I have not attempted to copy Dix's textual signs. Brackets have been used both for editorial explanations and for some words having attestation in the sources but probably not part of the original. In the edition by Bernard Botte, *La tradition apostolique de saint Hippolyte* (Münster, 1963), the quoted materials are sections 23, 26-30, which is the numbering followed also in Geoffrey J. Cuming, *Hippolytus: A Text for Students* (Bramcote: Grove, 1976).

[2] Matthew 26:20-30 and parallels.

[3] 1 Corinthians 11:20-34.

[4] *Against Celsus* 1.1.

[5] 17 (5.4). The use of *agapē* in *Acts of Paul and Thecla* 25 is debatable and is not translated as love feast in the English edition of Schneemelcher, *New Testament Apocrypha*, Revised Edition (Louisville: Westminster/John Knox, 1992), Vol. II, p. 243; there is an unclear reference in a Coptic fragment of the *Acts of Paul* (Schneemelcher, *New Testament Apocrypha* II, p. 264). A clearer reference occurs in the *Acts of John* 84.).

[6] Cf. *Epistle of the Apostles* 15, where the *agapē* is closely associated with the remembrance of Jesus' death but may be regarded as distinct in significance, although occurring in the same setting.

[7] J. Wilpert, *Die Malereien der Katakomben Roms* (Freiburg, 1903),

plates 15, 27, 41, 62, 65, 133, 157, 167, 184, 265, 267; Pierre du Bourguet, *Early Christian Painting* (New York: Viking Press, 1965), plates 2, 75, 87, 89, 100; André Grabar, *The Beginnings of Christian Art* (London: Thames and Hudson, 1967), pp. 107, 112, 135. See our Plate IV.

[8] Jude 12; Justin, *Apology* I, 26; Clement of Alexandria, *Miscellanies* 3.2.10; 7.16.98; Minucius Felix 9; 30-31; Eusebius, *Church History* 4.7.11 says it was the conduct of certain Gnostics that gave rise to slander against Christians.

[9] *Fasting* 17.

[10] Tertullian's Montanist tract *Fasting* 13 makes derisive reference to singing a psalm at what is presumably an *agapē*.

[11] Felix L. Cirlot, *The Early Eucharist* (London: S.P.C.K., 1939), Chapter I and Appendix I.2. See our Chapter VIII for the main outlines of Jewish fellowship meals: each person giving thanks for his own cup, the blessing and breaking of bread by the one presiding, the meal, a final "food blessing" over a cup of wine at the end of the meal.

[12] Botte, *op. cit.*, places the Ethiopic addition at the first. Its location depends on whether the meal began before or after dark. It appears that the versions have misunderstood Hippolytus, and confusion is the result. Specifically, has the Ethiopic duplicated instructions for the beginning or the end of the meal?

PLATE I
"Baptism of Jesus." Chapel of the Sacraments, Catacomb of Callistus.

PLATE II
"Baptism." Chapel of the Sacraments, Catacomb of Callistus.

PLATE III
"Eucharistic Fish." Catacomb of Callistus.

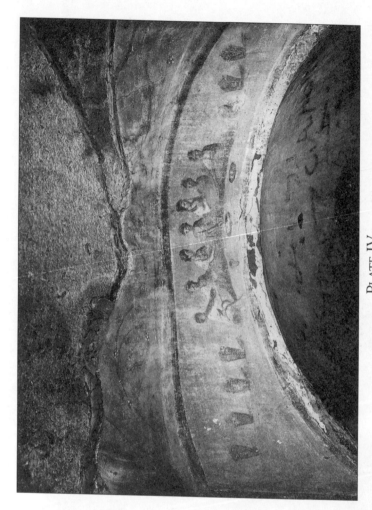

PLATE IV
"Fractio Panis." Greek Chapel, Catacomb of Priscilla.

PLATE V
"Good Shepherd." Chamber of Velatio, Catacomb of Priscilla.

PLATE VI
"Good Shepherd." Crypt of Lucina, Catacomb of Callistus.

PLATE VII
"Orans." Chamber of the Velatio, Catacomb of Priscilla.

PLATE VIII
"Orans." Catacomb of the Jordani.

XII
Some Early Prayers

"Many were gathered together and were praying"

Some New Testament Texts: Matthew 6:9-13; Acts 2:42; 4:24-30;
1 Timothy 2:1f., 8; 4:3-5; Ephesians 3:14-21; 1 Thessalonians 3:11-13.

SOURCES

PAPYRUS "MORNING PRAYER": XII.1
Helper of those who turn to you,
Light of those in the dark,
Creator of all that grows from seed,
Promoter of all spiritual growth,
have mercy, Lord, on me
and make me a temple fit for yourself.
Do not scan my transgressions too closely,
for if you are quick to notice my offences,
I shall not dare to appear before you.
In your great mercy,
in your boundless compassion,
wash away my sins, through Jesus Christ,
your only Child, the truly holy,
the chief of our souls' healers.
Through him may all glory be given you,
all power and honor and praise,
throughout the unending succession
of ages. Amen.[1]

PAPYRUS PRAYER FOR SALVATION: O God Almighty, who 2
created the heaven, earth, and sea, and everything in them, help me,
have mercy on me, wipe away my sins, and save me in the present and in

XII. the coming age through our Lord and Savior Jesus Christ through whom be the glory and might forever. Amen.[2]

3   PRAYER AT MEAL: Blessed be you, O Lord, who has nourished me from my youth and who gives food to all flesh. Fill our hearts with joy and gladness, that always having all we need, we may abound in every good work, in Christ Jesus our Lord, through whom glory, honor, and power be to you for ever. Amen. (*Apostolic Constitutions* 7.5.49.68)[3]

4   DOXOLOGY IN *SECOND CLEMENT*: To the only invisible God, Father of truth, who sent forth to us the Savior and Author of immortality, through whom was manifested to us the truth and the heavenly life, to him be the glory for ever and ever. Amen. (20.5)

5   GENERAL PRAYER FROM CLEMENT OF ROME: We shall pray that the Creator of the universe may keep unbroken the number of his elect in the whole world, making earnest entreaty and supplication through his beloved Servant Jesus Christ, through whom he called us from darkness into light, from ignorance into the full knowledge of his glorious name. Grant to us to hope on your name, the source of all creation. You opened the eyes of our heart in order to know that you alone remain the highest among the highest, the holy among the holy ones. You humble the pride of the haughty, you destroy the reasonings of the nations, you exalt the humble and humble the exalted, you make rich and you make poor, you cause to die and you cause to live, you alone are the benefactor of spirits and God of all flesh. You look into the depths, you behold the works of human beings, you are the helper of those in danger, the savior of those who despair, the creator and overseer of every spirit. You multiply nations upon the earth and you choose out of them those who love you through Jesus Christ your beloved Servant, through whom you trained, sanctified, and honored us.

We pray you, Master, be our helper and protector. Save those of us in affliction, have mercy on the humble, raise up the fallen, manifest yourself to those in need, heal the sick, bring back those of your people who are straying. Feed the hungry, ransom our prisoners, raise up the weak, comfort the faint-hearted. Let all the nations know you that you are God alone and Jesus Christ is your Servant and we are your people and the sheep of your pasture.

You made manifest the eternal constitution of the world through the things you performed. You, Lord, created the inhabited earth, you who are faithful in all generations, righteous in judgments, marvellous in strength and majesty, wise in creating and understanding in establishing the things made, good in the things seen, and kind to those who trust you, merciful and compassionate. Forgive us our lawlessness and unrighteousness, our transgressions and faults. Do not reckon every sin of

your servants and handmaidens, but purify us with the cleansing of your XII.
truth and direct our steps to walk in holiness of heart and to do the things
which are good and pleasing before you and our rulers. Yes, Lord, make
your face to shine upon us for good in peace in order that we may be
sheltered by your mighty hand and may be delivered from every sin by
your uplifted arm, and deliver us from those who hate us unjustly. Give
concord and peace to us and to all who dwell on the earth, even as you
gave to our ancestors when they called upon you devoutly in faith and
truth. May we be obedient to your almighty and glorious name and to our
rulers and governors on the earth.

You, O Master, by your majestic and ineffable might gave to them
imperial authority in order that we who know the glory and honor you
gave to them might be submissive to them, not opposing your will in
anything. Give to them, Lord, health, peace, concord, and stability in
order that they may administer blamelessly the dominion which you have
given them. For you, Master, heavenly King of the ages, do give to human
beings glory and honor and authority over what dwells on the earth. May
you, Lord, direct their counsel according to what is good and pleasing to
you so that by piously administering the authority you gave them with
peace and gentleness they may find mercy from you. You alone are able
to do these things and better things with us. To you we offer our praise
through the high priest and guardian of our souls, Jesus Christ, through
whom be to you the glory and the majesty both now and for all
generations for ever and ever. Amen. (59-61)

POLYCARP: Now may the God and Father of our Lord Jesus Christ 6
and Jesus Christ himself, the eternal high priest and Son of God, build
you up in faith, truth, gentleness, absence of wrath, patience, longsuffer-
ing, endurance, and purity. May he give you lot and share among his
saints, and us with you and with all under heaven who shall believe in
our Lord Jesus Christ and in his Father who raised him from the dead.
Pray for all the saints. Pray also for emperors, powers, and rulers, and for
those who persecute and hate you, and for enemies of the cross, so that
your fruit may be manifest among all, so that you may be perfect in him.
(Philippians 12)

POLYCARP'S PRAYER AT THE STAKE: O Lord God Almighty, 7
Father of your beloved and blessed Servant Jesus Christ, through whom
we have received full knowledge of you, the God of angels, powers, all
creation, and of all the race of the righteous who live before you. I bless
you that you have counted me worthy of this day and hour in order that
I might participate in the number of the martyrs, in the cup of your
Christ, for the resurrection of eternal life of both soul and body in the
immortality of the Holy Spirit. May I be received among them before you
today by a rich and acceptable sacrifice, even as you the unlying and true

XII.   God prepared, showed forth, and fulfilled. On account of this and for all things I praise you, I bless you, I glorify you through the eternal and heavenly high priest Jesus Christ, your beloved Servant, through whom to you with him and the Holy Spirit be the glory both now and in the coming ages. Amen. (*Martyrdom of Polycarp* 14)

8   AN AUTHOR'S PRAYER: Therefore, I invoke you, Lord God of Abraham, God of Isaac, God of Jacob and Israel, you who are Father of our Lord Jesus Christ, the God who through the abundance of your mercy has been well disposed toward us so that we might know you, you who made the heaven and the earth and rule over all, who are the only and true God, above whom there is no other God; through our Lord Jesus Christ, by whom is the dominion and gifts of the Holy Spirit, give to everyone who reads this book to know you, to be strengthened in you, and avoid every opinion which is heretical, Godless, and impious. (Irenaeus, *Against Heresies* 3.6.4)

9   IRENAEUS' PRAYER FOR THE CONVERSION OF HERETICS: We indeed pray that they may not remain in that pit which they themselves have dug . . . and that being converted to the church of God they may be lawfully begotten, that Christ may be formed in them, and that they may know the Framer and Maker of this universe, the only true God and Lord of all. We pray these things for them, loving them to a better purpose than they imagine they love themselves. For our love, since it is true, is for their salvation, if they will accept it. . . . Wherefore it does not weary us to extend our hand to them with all our strength. . . . May we be able to persuade them to cease from their error and to stop their blasphemies against their Maker, who is both the only God and the Father of our Lord Jesus Christ. Amen. (*Against Heresies* 4.25.7)

DISCUSSION

Prayer occupied an important place in the daily life of Christians. The *Didache* provided that one pray three times a day "in the manner the Lord commanded in his Gospel." There follows the text of the Lord's prayer as given in Matthew 6:9-13, with the addition of the doxology "Yours is the power and the glory forever."[4] Early Jewish writings provided for prayer three times a day. In place of the Jewish *Amidah* (the Eighteen Benedictions) and *Shema* (confession of faith) the *Didache* substituted the Lord's prayer. According to Jewish models and early Christian instructions, the Lord's prayer was not recited verbatim as a fixed form but was an outline or sketch of prayer that was either filled in or supplemented with one's own petitions.[5] Later the third, sixth, and ninth hours were fixed as Christian hours of prayer.[6]

In addition, provision was made at certain places for daily meetings at

the beginning of the day for communal prayer and instruction (VI.26).
The use of the first person singular in the papyrus "Morning Prayer"
(XII.1) indicates that it was for private prayer. Evening prayer before
retiring was private. Clement of Alexandria states, "Before partaking of
sleep it is a sacred duty to give thanks to God, since you have enjoyed his
grace and love, and so to go straight to sleep."[7] He adds, "Wherefore we
ought often by night to rise from the bed and bless God."[8] Christians
prayed before and after their meals. Although it is later before the
contents of table prayers were preserved (XII.3), there are abundant
references from early times that Christians did not partake of food
without thanksgiving (XVI.3).[9]

The Christian life was a life of prayer. Thus for Clement of Alexandria
the true Christian "prays throughout his whole life" and not just at the
third, sixth, and ninth hours.[10]

> His whole life is a holy festival. His sacrifices are
> prayers and praises, and reading from the Scriptures
> before meals, and psalms and hymns during meals and
> before bed, and prayers again by night.[11]

> And often communicate your thoughts to others,
> but especially to God at night even as in the day. For
> much sleep is not to keep you from your prayers and
> hymns to God.[12]

The pervasiveness of prayer in the lives of Christians may be seen in the
number of prayers written on potsherds and scraps of papyrus or inscribed
on tombstones, houses, and churches.[13]

Morning prayers were made facing the east: "Prayers are made looking
toward the sunrise in the east."[14] The posture for prayers at times might
be kneeling or prostrate.[15] Nevertheless, the characteristic Christian
posture for prayer was standing with arms outstretched and slightly raised
and the palms turned up to heaven.[16] The frequent literary texts are
confirmed by the numerous portrayals in catacomb paintings and on
sarcophagi.[17] This posture was common to Jews and pagans in antiquity.
The standard representation in art of a Christian, particularly of a
deceased person (since most of the surviving early Christian art is
funerary), is as an *orans*, a praying figure. The paintings may be a symbol
of piety, a portrait of the deceased in the perpetual adoration of God or
in intercession before him, or may represent the sanctity of the person.
The outstretched arms were a standard stylization for prayer, representing
for early Christians what Dürer's "Praying Hands" do for modern
Christians. Elevated hands formed the posture of prayer in the
congregational assembly and in private prayer. The "lift up your hearts"
of the preface to the eucharistic prayer (VIII.5) may have been the signal

for the people to rise and lift their arms. The lifting up of the hearts corresponded to the physical elevation of the hands.[18]

Incense, common in Hebrew and pagan worship, was rejected by Christians.[19] It was a material sacrifice, and, as an accompaniment to the spiritual sacrifice of prayer, was rejected in the same way as was instrumental accompaniment to singing (next chapter).

No congregational prayers were recorded, but we do have some good indications of the style and contents of the prayers in the worship assemblies. Clement of Rome (XII.5) gives the kind of prayer that he must have been accustomed to leading in church. It bears definite similarities to phrases in contemporary Jewish prayers and to prayers in later Christian liturgies. Clement moves into an actual prayer from a statement of what the Roman church would pray for. God's bestowal of saving knowledge through Jesus Christ occasions the transition from third to second person. The power of God is celebrated in his control over human affairs in a series of statements that is a composite of Scriptural phrases, rounded out by reference to God's election of the church and work of salvation by Christ. Praise is followed by petition as God is asked to be the helper of the needy, the prayer returning once more to the mention of Christ and the church. Clement next praises God as creator, but creation and redemption belong together, and this section leads into petitions for forgiveness and protection. This leads in turn to notice of earthly rulers, and it is clear that good relations with the government is a prime concern for the Roman church (the beginning of the letter mentions two persecutions). The prayer concludes with a renewed affirmation of faith and a doxology.

The letter of Clement was meant to be read in the assembly at Corinth (see Ch. VII, p.87 for the fact that it continued to be read there). Thus, as with Paul's letters, it is punctuated by doxologies.[20] This great prayer at the close may be compared to the brief prayers with which Origen closed his homilies.[21]

Nearly every phrase in Polycarp's prayer at his martyrdom (XII.7) has biblical or liturgical parallels. One need not be skeptical of the exact words. Some of the faithful may have overheard his prayer. Even if it is not reported verbatim, the church at Smyrna had heard Polycarp pray enough that they knew his characteristic phraseology. Indeed, if the prayer is wholly the composition of the author, we may have all the more reason to see its wording as a typical prayer from Polycarp adapted to the particular circumstances of his martyrdom. Only the particular Trinitarian form of the doxology may be doubted as belonging to the period of Polycarp. In the mentality of the early church, even martyrdom, or rather especially martyrdom, was approached with praise and thanksgiving. Not all were called to be martyrs; to be so called was a special gift from God to those whose faith was strong. At the hour of his arrest Polycarp's prayers were not for himself but for others and especially the church.[22]

Prayers for rulers come in for frequent reference in early Christian literature (in VII.3 it is the one item from the congregational prayers singled out for mention by the apologist Tertullian; XII.5, 6). Tertullian declares:

> Christians look up with hands outstretched . . . with head uncovered ... and pray without ceasing for all our emperors. We pray for long life for them, for security to the empire, for protection to the imperial house, for brave armies, a faithful senate, a virtuous people, the world at rest, whatever is desired by a person or Caesar.[23]

Such prayers were an existential concern in the age of persecution. These statements occur often in apologetic writings because Christians had to justify not offering sacrifice to the emperor. Their claim was that their prayers to the God who created the world and upheld the government were more effectual and a better proof of loyalty.

Other references to the objects of Christian petitions are more incidental. The prayers are especially for fellow Christians and their needs (XII.5, 6; VIII.4)[24] and are related to the hope for final salvation. But there was also concern for those who needed to be converted to the truth (XII.9).[25]

The dominant note of the early Christian prayers is praise, and this finds explicit expression in the doxologies. Such words of praise were in use in Judaism. They became a characteristic of Christian prayers as the uniform conclusion to a prayer (VIII.3 and 5 as well as those in this chapter). They also appear at the conclusion of books, letters, and sermons (XII.4 as an example) and as independent pieces (XIII.9). The doxologies are sometimes addressed to God alone (XII.4), sometimes to God and Christ (typically through Christ to the Father–XII.1, 2, 3, 5), sometimes to Father, Son, and Holy Spirit (XII.7). More characteristic would seem to be praise to God, through Christ, in the Holy Spirit (VIII.5; cf. VIII.4).[26] Thus there was summed up the doctrine of prayer: God was the goal, Christ the Mediator, and the Holy Spirit the sphere in which the church prays.

Christian prayer was addressed commonly to God the Father. God is presented as the Creator, the God who continues to act, and the God who cares for human beings. He is the Master and Almighty, but also Helper and Father of Jesus Christ. His past acts are the basis of praise and petition. Recitation of his benefits, or praise and thanksgiving, precede specific requests. The ascriptions to God are phrased in keeping with what entreaties will be made. The central concerns are with the spiritual blessings of salvation, but all human needs come within the scope of prayer. The centrality of redemption in Christ stands out. This was the great blessing that was the basis of prayer itself and of further petitions. The salvation is often presented in intellectual terms (knowledge) in the prayers. The principal novelty, the central distinguishing characteristic of Christian prayer, was the mediation of Christ. The prayer is always addressed through Christ, the Lord and Savior. He was at the heart of prayer as of all acts of worship. He was the "high priest" of Christian intercession. He was also frequently referred to as Servant (or Child).[27] The term originated in the Servant Christology of the earliest church (Acts 3:13, with reference to Isaiah 52:13 and other texts; 4:27). It disappeared from the language of the church of the second and later centuries except in prayers. The language of religion is always conservative, and the language of worship is the most conservative aspect of religion. Here was preserved a term from the earliest Jewish Christian belief, testifying to the conviction that Jesus was the chosen agent in the fulfillment of God's purposes for his people. That faith had a richer content in later ages, but the continued use of the term Servant preserved a continuity in prayer life with the earliest days of the church.

The general structure of the prayers is, following the address to God, to move from praise (often taking the form of recitation of God's mighty acts) and thanksgiving to petition, then to close with a doxology, ending as beginning with praise. Then the prayer was confirmed or ratified with an "Amen."[28]

Besides the "Amen" various other acclamations and ejaculations may also be considered as part of the prayer life of Christians. We find them in connection with the congregational prayers and hymns, as part of the Lord's supper celebration, in greetings, on inscriptions, at martyrdom, and in other contexts. Such expressions are "Amen" (Ch. VIII), "Hallelujah" (Ch. XIII), "The Lord be with you" (VIII.5), "Peace to you" (common in variations on epitaphs), "Lord have mercy", "Thanks to God" (the expression of the martyrs). Such short exclamations show how a sense of the presence of God permeated all of life. The people actively participated in the congregational prayers by their responses and acclamations.

The prayers preserved a strong sense of the community, of life in the church, in which the welfare of all was bound together. Thus Christians prayed together, and prayed "*our* Father." Prayer was the property of the whole people of God. All actively participated in the prayers of the church. Tertullian, *On Shows* 25, implies that "to raise your hands to God," to utter the "Amen," and to shout the doxology "forever" were alike the expressions of the whole congregation.[29]

There is a rich doctrinal content in the early prayers. They are a living confession of faith. They are deeply rooted in the great events of salvation, and they are closely related to the daily life activities and needs of the believers. There is a freshness, vitality, and reality about early Christian prayers. They are not mechanical or saying words. The closeness of God and the power of faith are real.

BIBLIOGRAPHY

Church, F. Forrester and Terrence J. Mulry. *The Macmillan Book of Earliest Christian Prayers.* New York: Macmillan, 1988.

Cunningham, Agnes. *Prayer: Personal and Liturgical.* Collegeville: Liturgical Press, 1985.

Hamman, A. *Early Christian Prayers.* Trans. Walter Mitchell. Chicago: Henry Regnery Co., 1961. A rich collection of the prayers from the early centuries of the church in translation.

_____. *La Prière.* II. *Les trois premiers siècles.* Tournai: Desclée, 1963. A thorough study of early Christian prayer based on the preceding collection of texts, but not translated into English.

Kiley, M., ed. *Prayer from Alexander to Constantine: An Anthology.* New York: Routledge, 1997.

NOTES

[1] Quoted from A. Hamman, *Early Christian Prayers,* (Chicago: Henry Regnery Co., 1961), pp. 62f. The prayer has been ascribed to the second century, but that is uncertain.

[2] Translated from A. S. Hunt and B. P. Grenfell, eds., *The Oxyrhynchus Papyri* (London, 1903), Vol. III, # 407, p. 12.

[3] The *Apostolic Constitutions,* although compiled in the late fourth century, incorporates earlier material. This prayer is from a collection of prayers included at the end of Book 7. It is of undetermined date, and from its contents might have originated at any age.

[4] *Didache* 8.2-3. The simpler form of the doxology indicates that this addition was quite early. Since all prayer ended with a doxology (see below), the liturgical use of the "Our Father" naturally led to the expansion of it to conclude with a doxology. On the practice of daily prayer, see Paul F. Bradshaw, *Daily Prayer in the Early Church* (New York: Oxford University Press, 1981).

[5] Gordon J. Bahr, "The Use of the Lord's Prayer in the Primitive Church," *Journal of Biblical Literature,* Vol. 84 (June, 1965), pp. 153-159. See especially Tertullian, *On Prayer* 10 and Origen, *On Prayer* 18 and 33. Also, F. H. Chase, *The Lord's Prayer in the Early Church,* "Texts and Studies," Vol. I:3 (1891). For the patristic commentaries on the Lord's

prayer see R. L. Simpson, *The Interpretation of Prayer in the Early Church* (Philadelphia: Westminster, 1965).

[6] Clement of Alexandria, *Miscellanies* 7.7.40.3; Tertullian, *On Prayer* 25; Hippolytus, *Apostolic Tradition* 31. C. W. Dugmore, *The Influence of the Synagogue upon the Divine Office* (Westminster: Faith Press, 1966), chapter IV, argues that these three hours were not taken from Jewish practice. Cf. D. Y. Hadidian, "The Background and Origin of the Christian Hours of Prayer," *Theological Studies*, Vol. 25 (1965), pp. 59-69; repr. in Everett Ferguson, ed., *Worship in Early Christianity*, Studies in Early Christianity, Vol. XV (New York: Garland, 1993), pp. 243-253.

[7] *Instructor* 2.4.44.2. Cf. his *Miscellanies* 2.23.145.1 and *Instructor* 2.9.77.1; Hippolytus, *Apostolic Tradition* 35.7; Tertullian, *On Prayer* 25 refers to prayer at the beginning and end of the day in addition to the third, sixth, and ninth hours.

[8] *Instructor* 2.9.79.2. For rising in the middle of the night for prayer see Hippolytus, *Apostolic Tradition* 36.8; Tertullian, *To His Wife* 2.5.

[9] "It is fitting for believers not to take food . . . before interposing prayer"–Tertullian, *On Prayer* 25; see Clement of Alexandria, *Instructor* 2.4.44.1 and note 11. For prayers at home, including at meals, see Balthasar Fischer, "The Common Prayer of Congregation and Family in the Ancient Church," *Studia Liturgica*, Vol. 10 (1974), pp. 106-124; repr. in Everett Ferguson, ed., *Worship in Early Christianity*, Studies in Early Christianity, Vol. XV (New York: Garland, 1993), pp. 224-242 (esp., pp. 235-242).

[10] *Miscellanies* 7.7.40.3. That all times and places are sacred and that silent or mental prayer may be prayed at any time are themes of this entire chapter. Cf. Tertullian, *On Prayer* 23 that one can pray at all times and places; Origen, *On Prayer* 12 and 31.4-7.

[11] *Miscellanies* 7.7.49.4.

[12] From a fragment assigned to Clement of Alexandria's "Exhortation to Endurance or To the Newly Baptized," translated by G. W. Butterworth in the Loeb Classical Library.

[13] See the collection of some of these in Hamman, *op. cit.*, pp. 62ff., 78ff.

[14] Clement of Alexandria, *Miscellanies* 7.7.43.6; cf. Tertullian, *To the*

Nations 1.13; *Apology* 16; Origen, *On Prayer* 32. Facing east in prayer was common in the Mediterranean world.

[15] Justin, *Dialogue* 90; *Acts of Paul and Thecla* 24; Origen, *On Prayer* 31.3.

[16] Clement of Rome 2 and 29; Athenagoras, *Plea* 13; Clement of Alexandria, *Miscellanies* 7.7.40.1; Tertullian, *Apology* 30; *On Idolatry* 7; *On Prayer* 17; *Acts of Paul and Thecla* 34. Tertullian, *On the Crown* 3 and *On Prayer* 23 discusses the times for kneeling (a sign of humility) and for standing (a sign of joy and boldness). Standing was the practice on the Lord's day in honor of the resurrection. Note Justin (VII.2) for the congregation rising for prayer. Stretching out the arms became a symbol of the cross for Christians–*Odes of Solomon* 42.

[17] See the different styles reproduced in illustrations 188 to 194 in André Grabar, *Christian Iconography* (Princeton, N. J.: Princeton University Press, 1968) and illustrations 25, 26, 58, 96-98, 102, 104, 113-115, 119, 120, 135, 140, 146 in the same author's *The Beginnings of Christian Art* (London: Thames and Hudson, 1967). See our Plates III, VII, VIII.

[18] Some confirmation for this suggestion may be found in Hippolytus' instructions for the love feast (*Apostolic Tradition* 36). The dialogue between the bishop and people that introduced the eucharistic prayer (VIII.5) preceded the thanksgiving at the love feast, but with one exception. The "Lift up your hearts" was not to be said, likely because the prayer at the dinner was said reclining and not standing, as was the eucharistic prayer. Everett Ferguson, "The Liturgical Function of the `Sursum corda'," *Studia Patristica*, Vol. XII (1975), pp. 360-363.

[19] Justin, *Apology* I, 13; Athenagoras, *Plea* 13; Irenaeus, *Against Heresies* 4.17.6; Clement of Alexandria, *Instructor* 2.8.67; Tertullian, *Apology* 30.

[20] 20.12; 32.4; 43.6; 45.7; 50.7; 58.2; 64.1; 65.2.

[21] Some of these are quoted by Hamman, *op cit.*, pp. 40ff. Clement of Alexandria's *Who Is the Rich Man?* and *Second Clement* (XII.4) and Melito, *On the Passover* close with doxologies.

[22] *Martyrdom of Polycarp* 7-8.

[23] *Apology* 30.4; see also Theophilus, *To Autolycus* 1.11; Athenagoras, *Plea* 32.

[24] See Justin's summary statement in *Apology* I, 13, quoted on p. 83.

[25] Cf. Clement of Alexandria, *Miscellanies* 7.7.41.6-7 for prayer "for the conversion of our neighbors."

[26] Basil in the fourth century discussed the presence of the two forms "in the Holy Spirit" and "with the Holy Spirit" (the latter making the Spirit a joint recipient of the praise with the Father and the Son) and cited examples of their respective use (*On the Holy Spirit* 25.58ff.).

[27] See also VIII.3, 5 and note 1 to Chapter VIII.

[28] See Origen, *On Prayer* 33 for the components of prayer: address to God, praise, thanksgiving, confession of sins, petitions and intercessions, concluding doxology.

[29] For the "Amen" as a congregational response see VII.2 and VIII.4 and discussion in Chapter VIII, p. 99. Later Jerome tells us that the Roman basilicas sounded like a clap of thunder when the "Amen" was voiced (*Commentary on Galatians* 1.2).

XIII
Some Early Christian Hymns and Poetry

"Sing psalms, hymns, and spiritual songs"

Some New Testament Texts: 1 Corinthians 14:15, 26; Ephesians 5:19; Colossians 3:16; Mark 14:26; Luke 1:14-17; 1:46-55; 1:68-79; 2:14; Philippians 2:6-11; 1 Timothy 3:16.

SOURCES

IGNATIUS: For your deservedly famous presbytery, worthy of God, is XIII.1 attuned to the bishop as strings to a harp. Therefore by your concord and harmonious love Jesus Christ is being sung. Now all of you together become a choir so that being harmoniously in concord and receiving the key note from God in unison you may sing with one voice through Jesus Christ to the Father. (*Ephesians* 4)

2

There is one Physician,
  both fleshly and spiritual,
    begotten and unbegotten,
God who came in the flesh,
    true life in death,
both of Mary and of God,
    first passible and then impassible,
Jesus Christ our Lord. (*Ibid.* 7.2)

3

ODES OF SOLOMON 11:
My heart was circumcised
  and its flower appeared;
Grace bloomed in it
  and it bore fruit to God.
The Most High circumcised me with his Holy Spirit
  and exposed my secret parts before him.
He filled me with his love;

XIII.   his circumcision became for me salvation.

> I have run in the way of truth in his peace;
>> from the beginning to the end I have received his understanding.
> I was established on a solid rock
>> where he placed me.
> The murmuring water approached my lips;
>> I drank from the fountain of the Lord's life in his abundance.
> I became intoxicated with the immortal water,
>> but my intoxication did not deprive me of reason.

> I turned away from vanities to the Most High, my God,
>> and I was enriched by his gifts.
> I forsook the foolishness which lies on the earth;
>> I stripped it off.
> I cast it from me;
>> the Lord restored me with his own garment.
> He reinstated me in his light;
>> he brought me to life again with his incorruption.

> I became as the land
>> which flourishes and rejoices in its fruits.
> The Lord became to me as the sun
>> upon the face of the earth.
> My eyes became bright;
>> and my face was sprinkled with dew.
> My nostrils were gladdened
>> by the sweet odor of the goodness of the Lord.

> He led me into his paradise,
>> where is the luxurious wealth of the Lord.
> [I beheld fruitful trees in season;
>> their natural growth was their crown.
> Their branches flourish and their fruits were rejoicing.
>> Their roots grow from a deathless land.
> A river of joy was watering them;
>> and I encircle the land of their eternal life.]

> I worshipped the Lord
>> on account of his glory.
> And I said, "Lord, blessed are those who have been planted in
>> your land,
>> who have a place in your paradise,
> Who grow in the growth of your trees,
>> who turned from darkness to light."

Behold, your good laborers make good conversions   XIII.
　from wickedness to what is excellent.

The bitterness of the plants in your earth will be changed;
　all things are becoming according to your will.
Blessed are those who perform sacred rites with your waters,
　eternal reminders from your faithful servants.
There is much room in your paradise;
　and nothing is useless, but all bears fruit.
Glory be to you, O God,
　in your paradise of eternal delight.
Hallelujah.[1]

ODES OF SOLOMON 16:   4
As the work of the husbandman is the ploughshare;
　And the work of the steersman is the guidance of the ship:
So also my work is the Psalm of the Lord;
　My craft and my occupation are in his praises;
Because his love hath nourished my heart,
　And even to my lips his fruits he poured out.
For my love is the Lord
　And therefore I will sing unto him.
For I am made strong in his praise,
　And I have faith in him.
I will open my mouth
　And his spirit will utter in me
The glory of the Lord and his beauty;
　The work of his hands and the fabric of his fingers;
The multitude of his mercies,
　And the strength of his Word.
For the word of the Lord searches out the unseen thing
　And scrutinizes his thought.
For the eye sees his works,
　And the ear hears his thought.
It is he who spread out the earth,
　And settled the waters in the sea:
He expanded the heavens,
　And fixed the stars;
And he fixed the creation and set it up. . . . [11 lines omitted]
And there is nothing that is without the Lord;
　For he was before any thing came into being.
And the worlds were made by his Word,
　And by the thought of his heart.
Glory and honor to his name.
Hallelujah.[2]

XIII.5   *ODES OF SOLOMON* 41:
> Let all the Lord's children praise him,
>> And let us appropriate the truth of his faith.
> And his children shall be acknowledged by him;
>> Therefore let us sing in his love:
> We live in the Lord by his grace;
>> And life we receive in his Messiah.
> For a great day has shined upon us;
>> And marvellous is he who has given us of his glory.
> Let us, therefore, all of us unite together in the name of the Lord;
>> And let us honor him in his goodness:
> And let our faces shine in his light;
>> And let our hearts meditate in his love,
>> By night and by day.
> Let us exult with the joy of the Lord.
>> [Christ speaks:]
> All those that see me will be astonished,
>> For from another race am I.
> For the Father of truth remembered me;
>> He who possessed me from the beginning.
> For his riches begat me, and the thought of his heart:
>> [Odist:]
>> And his Word is with us in all our way,
> The Saviour who makes alive and does not reject our souls:
>> The man who was humbled, and was exalted by his own righteousness
> The Son of the Most High appeared in the perfection of his Father;
>> And light dawned from the Word
> That was before time in Him;
>> The Messiah is truly one;
> And he was known before the foundations of the world,
>> That he might save souls for ever by the truth of his name:
> Let a new song arise from them that love him.
> Hallelujah.

6   GREEK MORNING HYMN (*GLORIA*):
> Glory in the heavens to God,
> and on earth peace,
> to men, favor.
> We praise you,
> we bless you,
> we worship you,
> we give thanks to you,
> on account of your great glory,
> Lord, heavenly King,
> God the Father Almighty;

Lord, only Son,   XIII.
Jesus Christ;
and Holy Spirit.
O Lord God,
the Lamb of God,
the Son of the Father,
you who take away the sins of the world,
have mercy upon us;
you who take away the sins of the world,
receive our petition;
you who sit on the right hand of the Father,
have mercy on us.
Because you only are holy,
you only are Lord,
Jesus Christ,
unto the glory of God the Father. Amen.[3]

Each day I will bless you,
and I will praise your name forever, and forever.
Count us worthy, O Lord, that this day
we may be kept guiltless.
Blessed are you, O Lord the God of our Fathers.
Your name is worthy of praise and is glorified forever. Amen.

Blessed are you, Lord, teach me your judgments. [3 times]
Lord, you have been a place of refuge for us from generation
    to generation.
I said, Lord, have mercy on me,
heal my soul, because I have sinned against you.
Lord, I have fled to you for protection;
teach me to do your will, because you are my God;
because beside you is a spring of life,
in your light we shall see light;
extend your mercy to those who know you.

GREEK EVENING HYMN: 7
Gracious light of the holy glory
    of the holy, blessed,
    immortal, and heavenly Father,
    Jesus Christ!
Having come to the setting of the sun,
    seeing the evening light,
    we hymn the Father and the Son
    and the Holy Spirit of God.
Worthy are you at all times

XIII.   to be praised with holy voices,
           Son of God, the giver of life.
           Therefore the world glorifies you.[4]

8   FRAGMENT OF CHRISTIAN HYMN, with musical notations:
Let none of God's notable [creatures]
. . . . be silent, nor the light bringing stars
cease [from praise] . . . . . .
. . . . Let all the fountains of rushing rivers praise our
Father, Son, and Holy Spirit. Let all the angels respond, Amen,
Amen. Power, praise,
. . . . . . to the only Giver of all good things. Amen. Amen.[5]

9   A DOXOLOGY:
Praise is your due,
hymns are your due,
glory is due to you,
Father, Son, and Holy Spirit,
due to you always.
Amen.[6]

10   AN ACROSTIC HYMN:
      . . . .
      . . . .
      In order that you may receive eternal life.
You have escaped the heavy ordinance of lawless .
      . . . .
      . . . . to love.
You have come to the marriage of the King,
      Marriage . . . .
      . . . . in order that you may not be destroyed.
Speak no more in double words
      . . . .
      . . . .
Some come as sheep
      in their manner, but inwardly they are wolves;
      recognize them from afar.
Seek to live with the saints,
      seek that you may receive life,
      seek that you may escape from the fire.
Hold the hope which you have learned;
      the day which the Lord set for you
      is known to no one.
God, after arranging many things, came;
      having won a triple victory over death

. . . .
Jesus suffered for these;
  having said that I offer my back,
  in order that you might not fall in death.
The ordinances of God are good;
  they remain for examples in all things
  in order that you may receive the good life.
[Jesus] washed in the Jordan,
  washed for an example;
  he has the pure bath.
Having remained on the mountain he was tempted.
. . . .

. . . .
Now work out the inheritance,
  now is the time for you to give,
  even now to those in great hunger.
God said to care for strangers,
  the strangers and the helpless;
  show hospitality in order that you may escape the fire.
God sent him in order to suffer.
  He received eternal life;
  he preached the power of immortality.
He preached the gospel to his servants, saying:
  The poor receive the kingdom
  to be children, of the inheritance.
He was scourged as an example
  in order that he might provide an influence for all;
  he has broken death in order that it might be destroyed.
In order that after dying you may see the resurrection,
  in order that you may see the eternal light,
  in order that you may receive the God of lights.
O the refreshments of those who sorrow,
  but, O, the leapings of the unfaithful,
  O the fearful fire for the wicked.
You have come under grace freely;
  listen to the petitions of the poor;
  speak no more arrogantly.
The fire is fearful;
  it is always fearful;
  the fire is fearful to the wicked.
Christ . . . .
  Christ is the support of the saints,
  Christ is the fire to the wicked.
. . . .
  Sing psalms with the saints;

XIII.   speak always to feed the soul.
. . . .
Never forget the things you have learned,
the things that he spoke to you that you might receive.[7]

11   INSCRIPTION OF ABERCIUS:
The citizen of an elect city, I made this tomb
while I was alive so that I might have here a place for my
    body during time.
Abercius is my name, a disciple of the pure shepherd
who feeds his flock of sheep on hills and plains,
who has large eyes looking around everywhere.
He taught me the faithful writings of life.
He sent me to Rome to behold a kingdom
and to see a queen with golden robe and golden sandals.
I saw a people there who bore a shining seal.
And I saw the plain of Syria and all the cities, even Nisibis,
when I crossed the Euphrates. Everywhere I had companions
and I had Paul as a guide. Everywhere faith led the way
and set before me food, everywhere the fish from the spring,
mighty and pure, whom the pure virgin caught
and gave this to the friends to eat always,
having sweet wine, giving mixed wine with bread.
While standing by, I Abercius said for these things to be
    inscribed here.
Truly I am seventy-two years old.
May every one who understands and agrees with these things
    pray for Abercius.[8]

DISCUSSION

The Psalms of the Old Testament continued to be used by Christians in their worship (VII.4). In addition, the new religious energy released by Christianity found expression in the creation of many new hymns. New Testament scholarship has now identified several such hymns, or portions of hymns, embedded in the text of the New Testament.[9]

The same kind of critical analysis has revealed hymnic material in Ignatius (XIII.2 as an example). Ignatius refers to a harp by way of comparison (XIII.1), and that is the only way musical instruments are referred to in the earliest Christian writers. He draws his picture of congregational unity from what he had often experienced–the participation of the whole congregation in singing to God through Christ.[10]

Quite notable is the Christ-centered and almost confessional character of the earliest Christian hymns. Eusebius quotes an anonymous writer from the late second century who wrote against the heresy that the Savior was only a man and who adduced the hymns of the church as an evidence of its faith: "All the psalms and odes which have been written by faithful brethren from the beginning praise Christ as the Word of God and speak of him as a God."[11] One of the notable things about Christian worship to the Roman governor Pliny was the reciting of hymns to "Christ as to a God" (VII.1). Although prayer was normally addressed to God, hymns were often addressed to Christ (and even the Old Testament Psalms were understood in the church as about Christ). The praise of Christ continued to be a central element in songs produced in the centuries after the New Testament and Ignatius.

Some poetry is included in this chapter, for we do not know what was actually sung in worship. The inscription of Abercius, obviously, was not. Some of the materials that have been called hymnic may not have been sung in worship either. Again, we cannot always make a distinction between prayers and hymns when these are found on papyrus.[12] Jews and Christians practiced a cantillation of the Scripture lections as well as the prayers, which makes them approximate hymns.[13] Hymns are poetic prayers, and prayers in elevated prose often approximate poetry. Indeed, early Christian poetry and hymns, following their Semitic models, generally do not follow the metric patterns of Greek and Latin poetry, and so may be called "prose hymns." Some of the formal devices which do appear in developed (Byzantine) Christian usage and which seem to be related to Semitic rather than Greek models are the following: use of acrostics, use of parallelism of clauses, rhyme and similar endings of words giving an effect like rhyme, the same number of syllables in verses of a strophe, and similar placing of strong accent in verses to aid in cantillation. The flourishing of blank verse and other less rigid poetic forms in modern literature may prepare us to appreciate the freer forms of ancient Hebrew and Christian psalmody.

Hymn writing especially flourished in Syriac speaking Christianity.[14] Syriac is the language in which the earliest Christian "song book" survives, the collection of forty-two songs known as the *Odes of Solomon*. The *Odes* are commonly ascribed to the early second century.[15] It can be sustained that they are Christian, not only in present form, but in composition. How the name of Solomon came to be attached to them is something of a mystery. There is no obvious effort in the contents to project back to the historical Solomon. The connection may be nothing more than the fact that Solomon was ascribed a large number of songs (1 Kings 4:32). Or the association of Solomon with Wisdom, and the appearance of Christ as the speaker in some of the *Odes*, may indicate that the connection comes through an association of Solomon with Christ, the heavenly Wisdom.

Although some of the *Odes* use the language of the first person singular in reference to religious experience (sometimes this would seem to be

Christ who is speaking), they seem to have been designed for corporate worship. In a further effort to give the *Odes* a context, J. H. Bernard argued that they were used for baptismal services.[16] This would seem to go a bit far, but baptismal language and allusions are prominent and many of the songs can be thought of as initiation hymns. It is probably a mistake, however, to think of the collection as having a single setting. In terms of structure, many of the *Odes* begin with a comparison and end with a Hallelujah (as XIII.4).

The *Odes* have been suspect of Gnosticism, but this seems an unnecessary inference. They express such pure religious sentiments that almost anyone could have used them, and Christian history exhibits many examples of one group using another's songs. But there is nothing here that an orthodox writer may not have said. On an early dating the *Odes* would belong to the spiritual atmosphere in Syria before orthodox and fully Gnostic positions were sharply distinguished, but other scholars see indications of polemic against Marcionites and Manichaeans (third-century dualists). Their spirituality is not unlike that of Ignatius, and there is much the same atmosphere of thought as is found in him.

A good many of the certainly second-century hymns which survive are Gnostic or suspect of Gnosticism. Heretics made good use of the power of popular verse in spreading their ideas.[17] And on the purely religious side of its expression, much in Gnosticism made an appeal to a rational spirituality which found a natural expression in elevated poetry. Among these products of Gnostic religious poetry may be mentioned the hymn of Christ with his apostles in the *Acts of John*,[18] the Naassene hymn quoted by Hippolytus,[19] and the "Hymn of the Soul" (also known as "Song of the Pearl") preserved in the later *Acts of Thomas*.[20] Because matters of interpretation would divert us from our main purposes, these have been omitted from our discussion. Bardesanes, at the end of the second century, was known as a prolific writer of hymns in Syriac,[21] but later doubts about his orthodoxy meant that his works were not preserved and were replaced by the works of later authors, such as Ephraim the Syrian.

If a conjecture is correct, an addition to second-century hymnic material is to be found in the Bodmer Papyri. On the back of the last page of Melito of Sardis' sermon *On the Passover* there is a liturgical fragment:

> Praise the Father, you saints!
> Sing to the mother [the church?], you virgins!
> Let us praise, let us exalt exceedingly, O saints!
> You have been exalted, brides and bridegrooms,
> Because you have found your bridegroom, Christ.
> Drink into the wine, brides and bridegroom,
> . . . . [22]

If this fragment is from Melito, as is what precedes it, then it belongs to the second century. It has been suggested that it was part of a hymn chanted after baptism and after the homily on Exodus 12 but before the eucharist, and that it is referring to the newly baptized who have taken their vows to Christ and become a part of his spouse, the church. The fragmentary nature, of course, leaves all of this speculative. Melito's sermon itself contains many hymn-like passages, and it is an indication of the indefinite line distinguishing certain types of prose from poetry in the language milieu of early Christianity that Melito's sermon has been studied in relation to later Byzantine hymnography.[23] It is part of a tradition of poetic homilies.

Some present-day hymn books include Clement of Alexandria's hymn to Christ that concludes his treatise *Instructor*. "Shepherd of Tender Youth" is sometimes called the "earliest known Christian hymn," which was not inaccurate for the state of knowledge a century ago. It is evident from the foregoing that this statement is no longer correct. Moreover, it seems unlikely that Clement's composition was intended for the liturgy of the church. If it was not purely a poetic piece, then it may have been chanted by Clement's students in his school. Such exercises are known among followers of Hellenistic philosophers, and Clement's composition would have been a fitting piece for his students.

Turning to compositions which did have a definite liturgical history in the church, we have two ancient hymns from the Greek church which have continued in modern usage, the *Gloria* and "Hail Gladdening Light" (as it is rendered in some modern hymn books). The *Gloria* in Latin translation has held a place in the usage of the Western church. The Greek original, with the title "Morning Hymn," is contained in the biblical codex *Alexandrinus*, dated early fifth century (XIII.6).[24] At the end of the book of Psalms in this codex and in succeeding manuscripts of the Greek Old Testament there are collected the biblical odes (the songs from other parts of the Bible). They were used in addition to the Psalms in worship. *Alexandrinus* has ten songs from the Greek Old Testament, three from Luke, and then the *Gloria*, which is the song of the angels in Luke 2:14 expanded for liturgical use. It is possible that the Old Testament songs had been brought together in the pre-Christian period for use in the Hellenistic synagogue, so the collection could be quite early. The position of the *Gloria* in this collection and in a biblical manuscript would argue that its composition was quite early, at the latest we might think the third century. The exact wording, of course, could be any time up to the date of the manuscript.

There were various expansions of the brief Lukan text as the song was used in worship: *Apostolic Constitutions* 7.5.47 (63-66), which contains a slightly later form than that preserved in codex *Alexandrinus* and entitled a "Morning Prayer"; the Latin liturgy; and indeed even to the present it is a favorite text for musical scores. The structure is as follows:

(1) the biblical text,[25] (2) praise to the Trinity individually, (3) petition to Christ, and (4) glory to the Father. It looks as if the biblical text was first expanded in words of worship to God; then it was given a Trinitarian form with brief words about Christ and the Holy Spirit; finally, in the manner of confessional statements (Ch. II), a Christological addition was made.

The "Evening Hymn" (XIII.7) has been universally acclaimed as one of the most beautiful pieces from Christian antiquity. It belongs probably to the second century. Basil of Caesarea, who makes the first literary reference to it, refers to the song's antiquity and is not able to say who its author was. He explains that the words were a thanksgiving spoken at the time of the lighting of the lamps in the evening.[26] The hymn is addressed to Christ, the "gracious light" and the "giver of life."

The acrostic hymn (XIII.10) is found in a papyrus from the early fourth century, and the editors think the date of composition is not likely to be much earlier than the actual manuscript. The hymn is an alphabetic acrostic (from alpha to omega), such as was employed in Old Testament Psalms (e.g. 119). There are twenty-four lines of three members each. Each letter of the Greek alphabet in sequence provides the initial letter of the first word of each of the three members of a line. We have tried to show this feature in the translation by using indentation where the acrostic letter is repeated. The three members of a line each have the same metric quantity. Use of the hymn in a liturgical setting is uncertain. It addresses in the second person singular another believer (perhaps newly baptized ?). The theme is the salvation accomplished through the works of Christ.

The fragmentary third-century papyrus from Oxyrhynchus containing a portion of a Christian hymn with musical notation (XIII.8) is the only thing of its kind from the early centuries of the church. As for contents, it is somewhat exceptional among our surviving remains in its call for all of creation to join in the praise of Father, Son, and Holy Spirit.[27]

The musical notations, however, are what make the fragment unique. We really know very little about how Christians actually rendered their hymns in the earliest centuries. Conclusions are deduced from Jewish singing (most of the sources for which are later than the beginning of the Christian era), Greek music, and the medieval church music (both Latin and Byzantine). From these sources some idea may be obtained of how the singing was probably done.

This technical subject is beyond our intentions here, and we have kept our attention mainly on contents. Some features of the usual musical rendition by Christians, however, should be noted. The performance was more in the nature of what is called a chant than it was melodic. The more melodic compositions are attested only for the fourth century. Even then, the singing was homophonic, and not polyphonic as in modern harmonies. Furthermore, until the latter part of the fourth century the psalms were performed responsorially.[28] That is, the main content was sung as a solo by the cantor (*psaltēs* he was called in the church) with the congregation repeating the last words or responding with a refrain or acclamation. Antiphonal singing in which the congregation was divided into two choirs and chanted alternately came in alongside the responsorial chant in the late fourth century.[29]

In Christian hymnography the words were the important thing and melodies were adapted to the words. This was possible where the words were chanted and so were not bound to a rigid form of meter. The priority of the words and the form of rendition ensured that the singing was done without instrumental accompaniment. Indeed, an instrument had no function in these simple chants with their emphasis on the content of praise. There is no certain evidence of the use of instruments in the Christian liturgy until the later Middle Ages.[30] Because of the associations of musical instruments with immorality and idolatry in the pagan world, the church fathers took a very dim view of them in any setting and interpreted the Old Testament references to instruments in worship either as allegories or as part of the Mosaic dispensation replaced in the Christian dispensation.[31]

The inscription of Abercius is included as a sample of clearly non-liturgical poetry. It is an epitaph prepared by Abercius for his own tombstone. Abercius was bishop of Hieropolis in Phrygia and died around A.D. 200. The complete text of the inscription is contained in a fourth-century "Life of Abercius," but the major part of the inscription itself has been discovered and placed in the Vatican Museum. Since this inscription was copied, in part, in an inscription dated A.D. 216 and since the general period of Abercius' life is known, the inscription can be confidently dated at the end of the second century. It is one of our earliest certain Christian inscriptions. Its significant references to Christian faith and practice bear on many of the aspects of church life considered in other chapters: the world-wide Christian fellowship, the seal of baptism (e.g., III.4), the eucharist of bread and mixed wine, Christ born of a virgin, and Christ the good shepherd[32] and the fish.[33]

In these early hymns and poems one can sense the vibrancy and joy in the Christian faith with which "Christ is sung."

BIBLIOGRAPHY

Church, F. Forrester and Terrence J. Mulry. *The Macmillan Book of Earliest Christian Hymns*. New York: Macmillan, 1988.

Foley, Edward. *Foundations of Christian Music: The Music of Pre-Constantinian Christianity*. Collegeville: Liturgical Press, 1996.

McGuckin, J. A. *At the Lighting of Lamps: Hymns of the Ancient Church*. Harrisburg: Morehouse, 1995.

McKinnon, J. W., ed. *Music in Early Christian Literature*. New York: Cambridge University Press, 1987.

Quasten, Johannes. *Music and Worship in Pagan and Christian Antiquity*. Washington, DC: National Association of Pastoral Musicians, 1983.

NOTES

[1] Translated from the Greek text edited by Michel Testuz, *Papyrus Bodmer X-XII* (Geneva, 1959). The manuscript is third century. This is the only one of the *Odes* for which there is a Greek text. It is entitled simply "Ode of Solomon," but it agrees substantially with Ode 11 of the Syriac text, except that the lines within the brackets are not represented in the Syriac. I have departed from the markings of the manuscript in my division into lines, for the sake of sense units in English.

[2] This selection and the next are quoted from the translation of the Syriac in Rendel Harris and Alphonse Mingana, *The Odes and Psalms of Solomon* (Manchester, 1920). A more recent edition of the Syriac and English translation is provided by James H. Charlesworth, *The Odes of Solomon* (Missoula [Atlanta]: Scholars Press, 1977) and English translation in James H. Charlesworth, ed., *The Old Testament Pseudepigrapha*, Vol. 2 (Garden City: Doubleday, 1985).

[3] The *Apostolic Constitutions* and manuscript T of the Psalms omit the remainder. It is likely that this remainder represents two separate pieces, marked by the spacing between lines in our translation. So H. Leclercq, "Hymnes," *Dictionnaire d'archéologie chrétienne et de liturgie*, Vol. VI (Paris, 1924), col. 2849.

[4] Translated from the Greek text in W. Christ and M. Paranikas, *Anthologia graeca carminum christianorum* (Leipzig, 1871), p. 40. See Antonia Tripolitis, "*Phos Hilaron*: Ancient Hymn and Modern Enigma," *Vigiliae Christianae* Vol. 24 (1970), pp. 189-196.

[5] Edited in *Oxyrhynchus Papyri* Part XV (London, 1922), pp. 21-25, No. 1786 by B. P. Grenfell and A. S. Hunt. In our translation the words in brackets have been supplied to indicate the line of thought probably taken in the omissions but with no pretensions of making a restoration. For an improved edition and discussion of the musical aspects, see E. Wellesz, "The Earliest Example of Christian Hymnody," *Classical Quarterly* 39 (1945), pp. 34-45, and A. W. J. Holleman, "The

Oxyrhynchus Papyrus 1786 and the Relationship Between Ancient Greek and Early Christian Music," *Vigiliae Christianae*, Vol. 26 (1972), pp. 1-17.

[6] Quoted from A. Hamman, *Early Christian Prayers* (Chicago: Henry Regnery Co., 1961), p. 145.

[7] Our translation is made from Charles Wessely, *Les plus anciens monuments du Christianisme écrits sur papyrus* in *Patrologia Orientalis*, Vol. 4 (1907), No. 28, pp. 205ff. The hymn has also been edited and translated by B. P. Grenfell and A. S. Hunt in *Amherst Papyri* I (London: Oxford U. Press, 1900), pp. 23-28, and E. Preuschen, "Ein altchristlicher Hymnus," *Zeitschrift für die neutestamentliche Wissenschaft*, Vol. 2 (1901), pp. 73-80.

[8] Translated from the text given by H. Leclercq, "Abercius," *Dictionnaire d'archéologle chrétienne et de liturgie*, Vol. I (Paris, 1924), col. 74.

[9] On Christian use of the Psalms see J. A. Lamb, *The Psalms in Christian Worship* (London: Faith, 1962), and Everett Ferguson, "Athanasius' 'Epistola ad Marcellinum in interpretationem Psalmorum'," *Studia Patristica*, Vol. 16.2 (1985), pp. 295-308. Reinhard Deichgräber, *Gotteshymnus und Christushymnus in der frühen Christenheit* (Göttingen, 1967), and Gottfried Schille, *Frühchristliche Hymnen* (Berlin, 1965), include a great deal more as hymnic than most New Testament scholars do.

[10] Socrates, *Church History* 6.8.95 attributes to Ignatius the introduction of responsive chants (*antiphōnōn hymnōn*) by the congregation, but his evidence is so late as to be dubious. In any case, the congregation participated; it was only later that choirs gave the responses instead of the congregation. On musical imagery see Robert Skeris, *Chroma Theou: On the Origins and Theological Interpretation of the Musical Imagery Used by the Ecclesiastical Writers of the First Three Centuries with Special Reference to the Image of Orpheus* (Altötting: Coppenrath, 1976); Everett Ferguson, "The Active and Contemplative Lives: The Patristic Interpretation of Some Musical Terms," *Studia Patristica*, Vol. XVI (1985), pp. 15-23; idem, "Toward a Patristic Theology of Music," *Studia Patristica*, Vol. XXIV (1993), pp. 263-283.

[11] *Church History* 5.28.6. For prayer and hymns to Christ cf. Origen, *On Prayer* 14.6–15.1 and *Against Celsus* 8.67. *Sibylline Oracles* Book VI (Schneemelcher, *New Testament Apocrypha*, Vol. II, pp. 663-664) is a "Hymn to Christ." Daniel Liderbach, *Christ in Early Christian Hymns* (Mahwah: Paulist Press, 1999).

[12] A. Hamman, *Early Christian Prayers* (Chicago: Henry Regnery Co., 1961), contains hymns as well in his collection. "Hymning" was used of non-melodic praise, for example Origen, *On Prayer* 33.

[13] Eric Werner, *The Sacred Bridge* (New York: Columbia U. Press, 1959), p. 26 and chapter 4.

[14] Origen, *Against Celsus* 8.37, says that in the early church each person prayed and sang in his own language.

[15] Michel Testuz, the editor of *Ode* 11 in the Bodmer papyri (XIII.3 and note 1), is among those who favor Greek as the original language of the *Odes*, but James H. Charlesworth in numerous publications has articulated the current majority view of a Syriac original (in Charlesworth's wording an "early form of Syriac" "when Aramaic was shaping it"). He also speaks for the larger majority that dates the collection before 125, or at the latest 135. See now his *Critical Reflections on the Odes of Solomon*, Vol. 1: *Literary Setting, Textual Studies, Gnosticism, the Dead Sea Scrolls and the Gospel of John* (Sheffield: Sheffield Academic Press, 1998), pp. 18, 78-136 (on the language), and 283. A third-century date is argued by H. J. W. Drijvers, "Odes of Solomon and Psalms of Mani: Christians and Manicaeans in Third-Century Syria," *Studies in Gnosticism and Hellenistic Religions Presented to Gilles Quispel*, ed. R. van den Broek and M. J. Vermaseren (Leiden: E. J. Brill, 1981), pp. 117-130; cf. his "Facts and Problems in Early Syriac-Speaking Christianity," *The Second Century*, Vol. 2 (1982), pp. 157-175 (esp. 166-169); repr. in Everett Ferguson, *Missions and Regional Characteristics of the Early Church*, Studies in Early Christianity, Vol. XII (New York: Garland, 1993), pp. 251-269.

[16] *Odes of Solomon* in *Texts and Studies*, Vol. 8.3 (Cambridge, 1919).

[17] A fourth-century synod at Laodicea, canon 59, sought to forbid any psalms composed by private individuals and not in the canon of Scripture from the services of the church, but this was not effective.

[18] Chapters 94-96.

[19] *Refutation of All Heresies* 5.5.

[20] Chapters 108-113.

[21] The number given is 150, after the number in the Psalter.

[22] Othmar Perler, *Méliton de Sardes, Sur la Pâque* in "Sources

Chrétiennes," No. 123 (Paris, 1966), p. 128. Perler thinks this fragment represents a liturgical dialogue for a Quartodeciman Easter celebration in which the vigil of Saturday night ended with an *agapē* and eucharist on Sunday morning (cf. *Epistle of the Apostles* 15). This piece was used before the *agapē*–Othmar Perler, *Ein Hymnus zur Ostervigil von Méliton?* "Paradosis" XV (Freiburg, 1960), pp. 88f.

[23] See especially Melito's *On the Passover* 68-71; 82-83; and 103-105. It is notable that each of these passages has Christ as its theme and might as easily be included in our selection of confessional passages. E. J. Wellesz, "Melito's Homily on the Passion: An Investigation into the Sources of Byzantine Hymnography," *Journal of Theological Studies*, Vol. 44 (1943), pp. 41-52.

[24] The treatise *On Virginity* attributed to Athanasius directs that in the morning one is to say the Gloria and quotes the opening lines with the indication that the rest is so familiar, like the Psalms, it need not be quoted in full (ch. 20). B. Capelle, "Le texte du 'Gloria in Excelsis,'" *Revue d'histoire ecclésiastique*, Vol. 44 (1949), pp. 439-457 argues that an ante-Nicene hymn to Christ was transformed into a hymn addressed to the Father.

[25] That the meaning of the original in Luke 2:14 was "Peace among men of God's good pleasure" (i.e. his elect) see Ernst Vogt, "'Peace Among Men of God's Good Pleasure' Lk. 2:14" in *The Scrolls and the New Testament*, ed. Krister Stendahl (New York: Harper, 1957), pp. 114-117.

[26] *On the Holy Spirit* 29.73.

[27] For a close parallel see Origen, *Against Celsus* 8.67.

[28] In Acts of John 94 referred to in note 18 Jesus instructs that after he sings a verse the apostles are to respond with "Amen," and so the apocryphal hymn is constructed. Tertullian, *On Prayer* 27 refers to psalms at the close of which the company responds. Most interesting is Eusebius' use of Philo's description of the Therapeutae, a first-century Jewish sect, in *On the Contemplative Life* (esp. 80). Eusebius (*Church History* 2.17) thought Philo was really referring to Christians. He mentions their composing "songs and hymns to God in all kinds of meters and melodies" (section 13) and then (22) refers to their customs "which exactly agree with the manner observed by us," including, "the hymns which we are accustomed to recite, how while one sings in a decorous manner, keeping time, the rest listen in silence and join in singing the endings of the hymns."

[29] Egon Wellesz, *A History of Byzantine Music and Hymnography* (Oxford: Clarendon Press, 1961), p. 35. Basil of Caesarea (d. 379), *Letter* 207.3 describes antiphonal, responsorial, and unison singing as all employed by his church.

[30] James McKinnon, "The Meaning of the Patristic Polemic against Musical Instruments," *Current Musicology*, Spring, 1965, pp. 73f., 78f., 80f., based on his unpublished dissertation "The Church Fathers and Musical Instruments," Columbia University, 1965. The patristic evidence is collected and studied in my *A Cappella Music in the Public Worship of the Church*, third edition (Ft. Worth: Star Bible Publications, 1999).

[31] William Green, "Ancient Comment on Instrumental Music in the Psalms," *Restoration Quarterly*, Vol. 1 (1957), pp. 3-8. One notable exception to the uniform patristic condemnation of musical instruments is Clement of Alexandria, *Instructor* 2.4, but his approval of the lyre is for a private banquet, and early church writers never contemplate instruments in public worship. See also my work referred to in note 30 and the correction of the interpretation of a passage from Gregory of Nyssa sometimes cited as favorable to instruments in my "Words from the PSAL-Root in Gregory of Nyssa," *Studien zu Gregor von Nyssa und der Christlichen Spätantike*, ed. Hubertus R. Drobner and Christoph Klock (Leiden: E. J. Brill, 1990), pp. 57-68.

[32] The most common portrayal of Christ in early Christian art is as the Good Shepherd—see, for example, Michael Gough, *The Early Christians*, "Ancient Peoples and Places" (London: Thames and Hudson, 1961), pp. 90ff. See our Plates VII, VIII.

[33] There is a striking visual illustration of Abercius' words in the Catacomb of Callistus where a painting shows a large fish on a small table with one person laying hands on it in blessing and another person standing by with hands uplifted in prayer. The scene evidently represents Christ as the fish present in the church's eucharist. See our Plate III. For the fish symbolism see page 38, note 5.

XIV

The Organization
of the Early Church

"They appointed elders for them in every church"

Some New Testament Texts: Acts 14:23; 20:17, 28; Ephesians 4:11;
Philippians 1:1; 1 Timothy 3:1-13; 4:14; 2 Timothy 4:5; Titus 1:5-9.

SOURCES

DIDACHE: Elect therefore for yourselves bishops and deacons who are   XIV.1
worthy of the Lord, men who are meek, not lovers of money, true, and
tested. For they minister to you the service of the prophets and teachers.
Do not look down on them, for they are your honored men along with
the prophets and teachers. (15)

CLEMENT OF ROME: The apostles were delivered the gospel for us   2
from the Lord Jesus Christ; Jesus Christ was sent from God. Christ
therefore is from God and the apostles are from Christ. They both then
came in good order by the will of God. When they received his comands
and were fully convinced by the resurrection of our Lord Jesus Christ and
had full faith in the word of God, they went forth in the confidence that
the Holy Spirit gives preaching the gospel that the kingdom of God is
about to come. They preached district by district and city by city and
appointed their first converts, after testing them by the Spirit, as bishops
and deacons of those who were going to believe. . . . For thus the
Scripture says somewhere, "I will appoint their bishops in righteousness
and their deacons in faith." . . .

Our apostles knew through our Lord Jesus Christ that there would be
strife concerning the name of the episcopate. For this cause and having
received perfect foreknowledge, they appointed those we mentioned
above and afterward gave the rule that if they died other tested men
should succeed to their ministry. The men therefore who have been

XIV.   appointed by the apostles and afterward by other eminent men with the consent of the whole church and who have ministered unblameably to the flock of Christ humbly, quietly, and unselfishly, men who have been well testified to for many years by all, these men we do not consider it just to expel from their ministry. For it will be no small sin to us if we cast out from the episcopate those who have offered the gifts unblameably and holily. Blessed are those elders who have died previously and had a fruitful and perfect departure. They have no fear that someone remove them from their established place. For we see that you have removed some who have conducted themselves well from the ministry which has been unblameably honored by them. (42, 44)

3   HERMAS, SHEPHERD: The old woman came and asked me if I had already given the book to the elders. I replied that I had not given it. "That is all right," she said, "for I have words to add. When I have finished all the words, they shall be made known by you to all the elect. You shall write therefore two books and you shall send one to Clement and one to Grapte. Clement then shall send it to the cities abroad, for that is his duty. Grapte shall admonish the widows and orphans. But you shall read it for this city with the elders who preside over the church." (Visions 2.4.2-3=8.2-3)

4   The stones which are square, white, and fit into their joints are the apostles, bishops, teachers, and deacons who walked according to the holiness of God and did the work of overseeing, teaching, and serving the elect of God purely and piously. Some have fallen asleep, but some are still alive. They always agreed among themselves, had peace among themselves, and listened to one another. (Ibid. 3.5.1=13.1)

5   He showed me men sitting on a bench and another man sitting on a chair, and he said, "Do you see those seated on the bench?" "Yes, sir," I said. "These," he said, "are faithful, and the one sitting on the chair is a false prophet." (Mandate 11.1=43.1)

6   POLYCARP: Likewise the deacons are to be unblameable before his righteousness as servants of God and Christ and not of people. They are not to be slanderers, double tongued, nor lovers of money, but self controlled in all things, compassionate, attentive, walking according to the truth of the Lord, who became the servant of all. . . . Wherefore it is necessary that . . . you be subject to the elders and deacons as to God and Christ. . . .

And the elders are to be compassionate, showing mercy to all, turning back those who have strayed, looking after all the weak, not neglecting widows or orphan or poor. But "providing always for that which is good before God and others," they are to abstain from all wrath, partiality, and unjust judgment, and are to be far from all love of money, not quickly believing bad reports, not relentless in judgment, knowing that "all are debtors of sin." (*Philippians* 5.2,3; 6.1)   XIV.

IGNATIUS: Give heed to the bishop in order that God may also to   7
you. I am devoted to those who are submissive to the bishop, presbyters,
and deacons, and may I have a part with them in God. (*Polycarp* 6)

Likewise all are to respect the deacons as Jesus Christ, even as the   8
bishop is a type of the Father, and the presbyters are as the council of God
and as the college of apostles. Apart from these it is not called a church.
(*Trallians* 3)

All of you follow the bishop, as Jesus Christ does the Father, and the   9
presbytery as the apostles, and respect the deacons as the commandment
of God. No one should do anything which pertains to the church without
the bishop. (*Smyrnaeans* 8)

IRENAEUS: When we make appeal to the tradition that is from the   10
apostles, which is preserved in the churches by the successions of elders,
they oppose tradition and say that they are wiser not only than the elders
but also than the apostles and have discovered the genuine truth.
(*Against Heresies* 3.2.2)

We are in a position to make an accounting of those who were   11
appointed as bishops in the churches by the apostles and of their succes-
sors. (*Ibid.* 3.1)

Wherefore it is necessary to obey those who are the elders in the   12
church, who possess the succession from the apostles, as we have shown,
and who with the succession to the episcopate received the trustworthy
gift of the truth according to the pleasure of the Father. (*Ibid.* 4.26.2)

For all those heretics are very much later than the bishops to whom the   13
apostles committed the churches. (*Ibid.* 5.20.1)

CLEMENT OF ALEXANDRIA: Innumerable such commands have   14
been written in the holy books with reference to chosen persons, some to
presbyters, some to bishops and deacons, others to widows. (*Instructor*
3.12.97.2)

It is possible even now for those who have exercised themselves in the   15
Lord's commandments and have lived perfectly and knowingly according
to the Gospel to be enrolled in the elect body of the apostles. Such a
person is truly a presbyter of the church and a true deacon of the will of
God, if he do and teach the things of the Lord. He has not been ordained
by men, nor regarded righteous because a presbyter, but enrolled in the
presbyterate because righteous. . . . The grades here in the church, of
bishops, presbyters, deacons, are in my opinion imitations of the angelic
glory. (*Miscellanies* 6.13.106.1-2 and 107.2)

Indeed Paul altogether accepts the man who is husband of one wife,   16
whether he be presbyter, deacon, or layman, if he conducts his marriage
unblameably. (*Ibid.* 3.12.90.1)

XIV.17   Similarly also in the church the elders preserve the most excellent part and the deacons the ministerial. (*Ibid.* 7.1.3.3)

18   When after the death of the tyrant John removed from the island of Patmos to Ephesus, he used to journey by request to the neighboring districts of the Gentiles, in some places to appoint bishops, in others to regulate whole churches, in others to set among the clergy some one man, it may be, of those indicated by the Spirit. . . . When this bishop accepted the trust and made every promise, the apostle once again solemnly charged and adjured him in the same words. After that he departed to Ephesus; but the presbyter took home the youth who had been handed over to him, and brought him up. (*Who Is the Rich Man that Is Saved?* 42)

19   TERTULLIAN: Their [heretics'] ordinations are thoughtless, capricious, changeable. At one time they put novices in office, at another time men who are bound to some secular employment, at another time men who have apostatized from us. . . . Nowhere is advancement easier than in the camp of rebels. . . . And so today one man is their bishop, tomorrow another; today he is a deacon who tomorrow is a reader; today he is a presbyter who tomorrow is a layman. For even on laymen do they impose the duties of priesthood. (*Prescription of Heretics* 41.6-8)

20   Are not even we laics priests? It is written, "He has made us a kingdom also, and priests to his God and Father." The authority of the church and the honor for those dedicated to God through the seating of them in the order has established the difference between the order and the people. Accordingly, where there is no session of the ecclesiastical order, you offer, you baptize, and you are priest alone for yourself. Where indeed there are three, there is a church, although they are laics. (*Exhortation to Chastity* 7.3)

21   APOSTOLIC CHURCH ORDER: The deacons, doers of good works, searching about everywhere day and night, neither despising the poor nor regarding the person of the rich, shall acknowledge the oppressed, and not exclude him from a share in the collections of the congregation, but compel those having possessions to lay up for good works, in consideration of the words of our teacher. 'Ye saw me hungry, and did not feed me;' for those who have been deacons of good report and blameless purchase to themselves the pastorate. (22)[1]

22   ORIGEN: Consider . . . cities where Christians are not yet found, some one arrives and begins to teach, labors, instructs, leads to the faith, and finally becomes himself the ruler and bishop for those whom he taught. (*Homily on Numbers* 11.4)

23   Some Christians, therefore, have made it their work to travel around not only to cities but also to villages and country houses in order to make others pious toward God. And one would not say that they did this on

account of money, when they would not even accept their sustenance. XIV.
(*Against Celsus* 3.9)

EUSEBIUS: And many more besides these were well known in those 24
days who take the first place in the succession of the apostles. They being
pious disciples of such great men built upon the foundations of the
churches which had been laid in every place by the apostles. They spread
the Gospel more and more widely and scattered the saving seeds of the
kingdom of heaven far and near throughout the whole world. . . . Then
setting out on their journey they performed the work of evangelists, being
zealous to preach to those who had not yet heard the word of faith and to
deliver to them the written form of the divine Gospels. When they only
laid the foundations of the faith in foreign places, they appointed others
as pastors and entrusted to them the care of those recently brought in and
they themselves went on again to other countries and peoples with the
grace and cooperation of God. . . . It is impossible for us to record by name
all those in the first succession after the apostles who became pastors or
evangelists in the churches throughout the world. (*Church History* 3.37)

For there were yet many evangelists of the word at that time [after the 25
mid-second century]. . . one of whom was Pantaenus. (*Ibid.* 5.10.2)

DISCUSSION

The *Didache* describes the time of transition from an itinerant, inspired
ministry of apostles (missionaries ?), prophets, and teachers to a local
ministry, chosen by the community, of bishops and deacons. The
traveling prophets and teachers spoke the word of the Lord and
conducted the public worship. Provision is made in the *Didache* for a
prophet or teacher to settle in the community and be supported for his
ministry by offerings of first fruits as the priests of the Old Testament had
been (chs. 11-13; see quotation on p. 220). The local uninspired men
(XIV.1) now succeed to the honor (including support) of these men and
to their public ministry of teaching and conduct of worship.

The combination "bishops and deacons" was a more common one than
"elders and deacons." Overseer and servant made a more natural pair; the
natural contrast to elder was "younger." Nevertheless, the terms bishop
and elder appear to have been used interchangeably in early
post-apostolic Christianity, even as they appear in the New Testament.
Several sources indicate the existence of a plurality in a local church,
which was also true of the elders in Jewish communities in New
Testament times (XIV.1, 2, 3, 6).[2]

The *Letter* of Clement of Rome was written to deal with a certain
disturbance in the church at Corinth. The Corinthian church had
deposed some of its elders, unjustly in the view of the Roman church.
After discussing the virtues of faithfulness, repentance, hospitality,

obedience, and humility and the sins of strife, jealously, and rebellion, all with appropriate Old Testament texts and examples, the author comes in chapter forty to treat specifically of the Corinthian situation. In chapters forty to forty-four he lays down the principle that church order is divine. Then follows a section warning against opposition to the righteous (45-48) and exhorting to love (49-50) and concluded with a practical application—submit to the elders or depart (51-58).

The passages of present interest (XIV.2) are introduced with reference to Old Testament regulations about the times, places, and personnel of worship (X.1). It is characteristic of Clement to take examples from the past and move to a present application. His point is summarized in the statement: The high priest, the priests, the Levites, and the laymen each have their proper functions. Clement is talking about the Old Testament. If he has a direct analogy to the church in mind, Christ is the high priest for him (36.1; 61.3; 64), so the bishops would be the priests and deacons would be the Levites. But this may be overdrawing his analogy. The main point is obeying God's order. Clement does use priestly language in reference to the Christian ministry at worship. The word we have translated "ministry" (XIV.1, 2) is a word used in the Old Testament for priestly services. The sacrifices of the Christian ministry are praise and thanksgiving, worship as a whole (see Ch. X). People, however, not only use words, but words use them, and by the time of Cyprian in the third century the language of priesthood was no longer an Old Testament analogy but an established designation for officers in the church. Clement affords the first use in Christian literature of the language of "laity" in contrast to ministers. In the Bible "the people" (*laos*, from which laity is derived) is a noble concept, "the people of God," and refers to the whole of God's elect. As God's elect, all participated in the "priesthood" (1 Peter 2:5, 9). Someone has observed that the organizational history of the second and third centuries, therefore, is not the story of the emergence of the priesthood but the emergence of a distinct laity not exercising a priestly ministry (cf. XIV.20).

Clement, in his argument, next established the principle of order in reference to the Christian ministry: Christ–apostles–bishops and deacons (XIV.2a). This has been cited as the first passage presenting the idea of apostolic succession. If so, it is not such according to any recognizable later form of the doctrine. There is a succession here, but it is a succession of order and of time. There is no succession of functions from Christ to the apostles or from the apostles to the bishops. If there is, it includes the deacons as well. There is in this passage apostolic institution of particular positions in the church, apostolic appointment of the first occupants of those positions, and apostolic provision for a continuation of the same form of ministry. Clement's appeal to prophetic support for this church order is misguided. His quotation from Isaiah 60:7 was inaccurately made from memory or was taken from a text now unknown to us.

Clement next argues that it is sin to rebel against God's order by inserting other ministers in the place of those duly chosen. Once more he begins, in chapter 43, with the Old Testament, referring to the rebellion against the priesthood of Aaron and the method of Moses in Numbers 17 to confirm the divine choice. The parallel with the Christian age, if any is intended beyond the principle of obedience to constituted authority, makes the apostles = Moses and the bishops = the prophets "testifying together to the laws laid down by Moses." The contemporary application (XIV.2b) is that the apostles had taken advance action to establish the proper men in the ministry of the church. Besides the apostles, "other approved men" had made appointments; we may think of Timothy and Titus in the New Testament. The appointments were made with the approval of the whole congregation.[3] Clement uses "bishop" and "elder" for the same men, and indicates the presence of a plurality in each church.

Hermas identifies Clement as the corresponding secretary of the Roman church (XIV.3). His evidence agrees with Clement's about a plurality of elders or bishops in the church. The "elders preside over the church." Although Hermas never uses bishops and elders in the same context, in the way Clement does, permitting us to decide whether they refer to the same functionaries or to different ones for him, there does not seem to be a place for the singular bishop in what he writes. The presence of such a presiding elder could be indicated by XIV.5 if it could be established that the bench was for the elders and the chair for the bishop, but Hermas calls the presiding teacher a "prophet." Elsewhere he speaks of those with a desire for the "first places" and of "the leaders of the church who occupy the chief seats,"[4] but in another passage he refers to a desire for the "chief seat."[5] When Hermas lists the functionaries of the church (XIV.4), he inserts "teachers" between bishops and deacons. Probably this is a general reference which would include evangelists and all charged with a teaching function in the church.

Second Clement (see VI.25) likewise mentions none higher than the elders in the church. They teach and exhort the assembled brethren. The author himself seems to be an official teacher.[6]

Polycarp (XIV.6) gives instructions concerning righteousness to various groups in the church. He moves from a general exhortation to specific groups: wives, widows, deacons, younger men, and then elders. This combination of social and age groups with specific offices is not unlike 1 Peter and the Pastorals in the New Testament. The association with age groups may account for his somewhat unusual order and somewhat unusual pairing of the term elder with deacon. There seems no doubt that an office is being considered in what he says about deacons (servants) and elders (older men). Elders are in the plural and Polycarp says nothing about a separate bishop.

Polycarp's own writing, therefore, gives a different picture of church order from that provided by his correspondent Ignatius (XIV.7). Ignatius gives the first complete picture for a threefold ministry of bishop, elders, deacons, and he attests this order for his home church of Antioch and for the churches he addresses in Asia Minor. Indeed he can speak of "bishops who are appointed throughout the world."[7] This may be rhetorical; if not, it is no guarantee that they were the kind of bishops he describes. Only in addressing the church at Rome does Ignatius not mention a bishop; indeed in his letter to the Romans he does not discuss church order at all. This may be accidental, but it concurs with the evidence of Clement and Hermas that the Roman church still had a plurality of presbyter-bishops at the beginning of the second century. Ignatius had a great concern for unity, and he sees this unity symbolized in the single bishop in each church and preserved by obedience to him and his ministerial associates (VIII.1; IX.2; XIV.9). The declaration that apart from the threefold ministry the name of church is not given (XIV.8) is not so much a matter of the necessity of having all three kinds of officers in order to have a church as it is a declaration that a schism from the already established ministry in a given locality does not constitute a church. It is notable that Ignatius almost invariably treats the officers of a church as a whole.

Ignatius appears to make exalted claims for the episcopal office. The bishop is in the place of God, but this seems to be a matter of symbolism and should not be pressed too far. There is no word about apostolic institution or apostolic succession for the position of the one bishop. Ignatius' bishop is a congregational bishop or pastor. He functions as president of the presbytery. What is new is Ignatius' restriction of the word bishop to a single member of the presbytery. This person has an identifiable distinctness which sets him apart from the presbyters with whom he works cooperatively. Ignatius does speak of himself as "bishop of Syria."[8] This is typical of his hyperbolic language, for Antioch was the chief church of Syria. It may be an indication that Antioch was the only church in Syria to have monepiscopacy, for a large city church would have advanced in its organization beyond that of the smaller rural churches.

Ignatius addresses Polycarp as "bishop of the church of the Smyrnaeans," and Polycarp must have occupied such a position in relation to the church at Smyrna that Ignatius could identify him within his pattern of church government. When Polycarp addresses the church at Philippi, however, he identifies himself as "Polycarp and those who with him are presbyters."[8a] Hence, Polycarp may not have thought of himself in the same way Ignatius did, nor have made the sharp distinction between the "chief elder" and the "college of elders" that can be read into Ignatius. At least, the absence of a singular bishop at Philippi is notable. It has been suggested that Polycarp does not refer to a bishop there because the office was temporarily vacant. For that reason the church at

Philippi turned to the nearby Polycarp with a request for instruction in righteousness. Further, it is theorized that the Valens mentioned as a deposed presbyter, perhaps for the mishandling of church funds (ch. 11 of Polycarp's letter to Philippi), had held the office of bishop.[9] All of this may very well be so, but as far as the strict evidence goes we do not learn about monepiscopacy from Polycarp or about its existence at this time at Philippi.

The Ignatian pattern of one bishop and a plurality of elders and deacons spread over the churches and became the normal church order by the later second century. Irenaeus and Clement of Alexandria (XIV.11, 13, 14, 15) recognize the sole bishop in a church; nevertheless they continue to call the bishop an elder. Evidently the bishop was still a "chief elder" or "president of the presbytery" and not in a wholly distinct order. This usage occurs in crucial passages. Thus, when Irenaeus is tracing the "apostolic succession" in the churches as an argument against the new doctrines of the Gnostics, he speaks of the "successions of the elders" (XIV.10). Irenaeus certainly knew the bishop as holding a distinct office from that of the presbyters. He interprets Acts 20:17, 28 as meaning that bishops from other churches in Asia besides Ephesus were present inasmuch as Paul addressed "bishops" in the plural.[10] Apparently bishops could still be called elders in his time, but elders could not be called bishops. Hence, it is probably the "episcopal" member of the presbytery which Irenaeus has in mind and not all presbyters when he speaks of a succession from the apostles. With the "succession to the episcopate" a person received "the gift of the truth" (XIV.12). Some have thought of this as a gift conferred at ordination; on the other hand, the general argument of Irenaeus requires that truth itself be the gift.[11] Apostolic succession for Irenaeus was from one holder of the teaching chair to the next, and with the position came the heritage or tradition of Christian doctrine from apostolic days which it was the new incumbent's duty to proclaim and pass on.

Clement of Alexandria can speak of "presbyters [elders], deacons, and laymen" (XIV.16) in listing the composition of the church. This accords with later traditions that at first the church at Alexandria was governed by elders, who chose a presiding member out of their number. Only under Demetrius at the beginning of the third century did the bishop attain a greater measure of control and independence in accord with the pattern elsewhere.[12] Clement uses the text of 1 Timothy 3:2, 12, which has spoken about a bishop and a deacon, and refers it to a presbyter and a deacon. He apparently knows the bishop as a distinct individual, but when he gives an inclusive description of official ministries in the church (XIV.17), elders and deacons comprehend the whole. Clement has been appealed to as evidence that monepiscopacy took its rise in Asia under the auspices of the apostle John. But the form of the tradition handed down by Clement which includes the report of John appointing bishops in Asia uses the terms bishop and elder interchangeably for the same man (XIV.18). For Clement the interior spiritual life is the most important thing. He represents piety's protest against the increasing institutionalization of the church (XIV.15).

Tertullian's protest against the developing hierarchy and externalizing of Christianity perhaps led him into schism. The two selections from Tertullian contrast his viewpoint after he identified with the Montanists (XIV.20) with that he held while championing the viewpoint of the great church (XIV.19). He shows the emphasis on good order in the episcopally organized church at the beginning of the third century in opposition to the looseness and freedom of the Gnostic groups. His language as a Montanist shows the extent to which the clerical (referring to those in the *order* of the church as distinguished from the rest of the people, the "laity") and priestly concepts of the ministry were accepted. He notes that it was the custom of the church which had made the sharp distinction between layman and clergy.[13]

By the time of Origen in the third century the threefold ministry of bishop, presbyters, and deacons was everywhere accepted. One statement from him (XIV.22) suggests how monepiscopacy may have arisen: the locating of an evangelist in a given community.[14] The evidence of terminology discussed above on the interchange of the terms elders and bishops and the continued use of the word elder in reference to the singular bishop would argue that the single bishop arose out of the presbytery. Perhaps both views have an element of truth. A likely hypothesis is that the settling of a prophet, teacher, or evangelist in a given community (as the *Didache* had provided for) gave a single leading figure in a church. On the death of such figures, local presbyteries tended to produce out of their own number a "successor" to the unique leadership role played by the apostolic or inspired leader (Hermas' references to a "prophet" and the "chair" [XIV.5] and ambition for the chief seat(s) [notes 4 and 5] may reflect a similar situation.). This development would have occurred in the late first or early second century when the last representatives of the apostolic generation and of the inspired ministry were dying out, which is the time the evidence points to for the transition to monepiscopacy in the churches.

The second-century literature is notably silent about the word "evangelist." That the function continued is indicated by later sources (as for example XIV.23, 24, 25). The activities of evangelists on the frontiers of the Christian mission is part of the reason for their absence in the literature. Very little has survived of the story of the Christian missionary enterprise in the second century. For another thing, the men who might be recognized as evangelists or preachers are often present under another title, especially that of "teacher," by which name such notable Christian leaders as Pantaenus (XIV.25), Justin, Clement of Alexandria, and others are known. There were "evangelists . . . and teachers"; the teachers wrote books, so we know of them, but we do not know about the evangelists. Others, for the most part, if they did not become elders or bishops themselves, saw their functions absorbed in the threefold ministry.[15]

All aspects of leadership which belonged to the college of elders soon were exercised by the bishop. Second-century bishops (VII.2) presided at worship (especially the Lord's supper), gave the public teaching, administered the church's funds (especially in benevolence and hospitality), and represented the church in correspondence. One function which the college of presbyters kept to themselves in the second century appears to have been church discipline (VII.3 and next chapter).

Less is known, in general, about the functions of deacons. A previously cited passage indicates their role as assistants at worship (VIII.4). They continued to be closely associated with the bishop as his chief assistants, especially in material affairs (XIV.21).[16] The documents which lie behind the *Apostolic Church Order* (about 300) have been placed in the second century.[17] If this is so, we have excellent evidence for the way early deacons functioned as the "eyes and ears" of the bishop in learning the needs of the congregation and then in ministering to those needs. In its present form the *Apostolic Church Order* shows how the office of a deacon was coming to be viewed as a stepping stone to higher "ranks" and no longer as a lifelong calling.

BIBLIOGRAPHY

Campenhausen, Hans von. *Ecclesiastical Authority and Spiritual Power in the Church of the First Three Centuries*. London: Adam and Charles Black, 1969.

Ferguson, Everett, ed. *Church, Ministry, and Organization in the Early Church Era*. Studies in Early Christianity, Vol. XIII. New York: Garland, 1993.

Gore, Charles. *The Church and the Ministry*. New edition revised by C. H. Turner. London: Longmans, Green, and Co., 1919.

Harnack, Adolph von. *The Constitution and Law of the Church in the First Two Centuries*. London: Norgate and Williams, 1910.

Lienhard, Joseph T. *Ministry*. Wilmington: Michael Glazier, 1984.

Lightfoot, J. B. "The Christian Ministry," *Saint Paul's Epistle to the Philippians*. Grand Rapids, Michigan: Zondervan, 1953 reprint.

Telfer, W. *The Office of a Bishop*. London: Darton, Longman & Todd, 1962.

NOTES

[1] Quoted from A. Harnack, *Sources of the Apostolic Canons*, translated by L. A. Wheatley (London: Adam and Charles Black, 1895), pp. 21f.

[2] For the plurality of elders, add the Christianized version of the *Ascension of Isaiah* 3.23f. (about A.D. 100). The *Sibylline Oracles* 2.264 has the combination "elders and reverend deacons." It is difficult to decide whether the emperor Hadrian's letter to Servianus (Vopiscus, "Life of Saturninus" 8, in *Scriptores Historiae Augustae*) that mentions "bishops of Christ" and "Christian presbyter" intends the same or different functionaries, but its evidence is of questionable value. The original identity of bishops and elders was known by fourth-century Christian writers–see the references in J. B. Lightfoot, *St. Paul's Epistle to the Philippians* (Grand Rapids: Zondervan, 1953 reprint), pp. 98f.

[3] Selection by the congregation is provided for in Hippolytus, *Apostolic Tradition* 2, and was the common mode of choice in the early church. For other methods of selection, see Everett Ferguson, "Origen and the Election of Bishops," *Church History*, Vol. 43 (1974), pp. 26-33.

[4] *Similitudes* 8.7.4=73.4 and *Visions* 3.9.7=17.7.

[5] *Mandate* 11.12=43.12.

[6] Note also *Second Clement* 17.5, "Woe unto us because we were not obedient to the elders when they taught us concerning our salvation."

[7] *Ephesians* 3.2. The development of monepiscopacy is surveyed by E. G. Jay, "From Presbyter-Bishops to Bishops and Presbyters," *The Second Century*, Vol. 1 (1981), pp. 125-162.

[8] *Romans* 2.2.

[8a] Cf. the "Letter of the Corinthians to Paul" in the *Acts of Paul* 8.1: "Stephanus and the presbyters who are with him."

[9] Robert M. Grant, *After the New Testament* (Philadelphia: Fortress Press, 1967), pp. 53f.

[10] *Against Heresies* 3.14.2.

[11] Einar Molland, "Irenaeus of Lugdunum and the Apostolic Succession," *Journal of Ecclesiastical History*, Vol. 1 (1950), pp. 12-28; repr. in Everett Ferguson, ed., *Church, Ministry, and Organization in the*

Early Church Era, Studies in Early Christianity, Vol. XIII (New York: Garland, 1993), pp. 194-210. See Chapter II, note 11.

[12] W. Telfer, "Episcopal Succession in Egypt," *Journal of Ecclesiastical History*, Vol. 3 (1952), pp. 1-13.

[13] Tertullian's Montanist tract *On Monogamy* 12 is one of the first clearly defined uses of the word *clergy*.

[14] The same theory is expressed later by Theodoret. See my survey of the major interpretations of the rise of monepiscopacy, "Church Order in the Sub-Apostolic Period: A Survey of Interpretations," *Restoration Quarterly*, Vol. 11 (1968), pp. 225-248.

[15] On the evangelistic office in the second century and the general organizational developments in the early church see my article "The Ministry of the Word in the First Two Centuries," *Restoration Quarterly*, Vol. 1 (1957), pp. 21-31.

[16] Hippolytus, *Apostolic Tradition* 9. On the evidence in general see J. G. Davies, "Deacons, Deaconesses and the Minor Orders in the Patristic Period," *Journal of Ecclesiastical History*, Vol. 14 (1963), pp. 1-15; repr. in Everett Ferguson, ed., *Church, Ministry, and Organization in the Early Church*, Studies in Early Christianity, Vol. 13 (New York: Garland, 1993), pp. 237-251; G. W. H. Lampe, "Diakonia in the Early Church," in James I. McCord and T. H. L. Parker, eds., *Service in Christ* (Grand Rapids: Eerdmans, 1966), pp. 49-64; J. M. Barnett, *The Diaconate: A Full and Equal Order*, rev. ed. (New York: Seabury, 1994).

[17] Adolph Harnack, *Sources of the Apostolic Canons* (London: Adam and Charles Black, 1895), pp. 1-27, 46-53.

XV
Church Discipline

"Repent of this wickedness of yours and pray to the Lord"

Some New Testament Texts: Matthew 16:19; 18:15-20; Acts 8:12, 13, 18-24; Hebrews 6:4-8; 10:26; James 5:16; 1 John 1:9; 5:16f.

SOURCES

DIDACHE: In the assembly confess your transgression, and do not come to your prayer with an evil conscience. (4.14) XV.1

HERMAS, SHEPHERD: All the sins which they formerly committed 2
shall be forgiven to all the saints who have sinned up to this day, if they repent with their whole heart and remove double-mindedness from their hearts. For the Master swore by his glory to his elect: when this day has been fixed, if there is still sin, they shall not have salvation. For repentance for the righteous has an end. The days of repentance have been fulfilled for all the saints, but there is repentance for the Gentiles until the last day. (*Visions* 2.2.4-5=6.4-5)

After that great and holy calling [baptism], if any one who has been 3
tempted by the devil should sin, he has one repentance. But if he sins and repents continually, it is unprofitable to such a man. Scarcely shall he live. (*Mandates* 4.3.6=31.6)

Do you think that the sins of those who repent are forgiven 4
immediately? Not at all. But it is necessary for the one who repents to torture his soul, to be very humble in all his deeds, and to be afflicted with various tribulations. (*Similitudes* 7.4=66.4)

CLEMENT OF ALEXANDRIA: The one who has received forgiveness 5
of sins ought to sin no more. For in addition to the first and only repentance of sins (this would be of those practised before in the first and

XV.   heathen life–I mean sin done in ignorance) there is proposed for the
       moment for those who have been called a repentance that cleanses the
       soul from trespasses in order that faith may be established. Since the Lord
       knows the heart and foreknows what will happen, he foresaw from the
       beginning the fickleness of humanity and the craft and cunning of the
       devil. . . . Therefore, being full of mercy, he gave a second repentance to
       those who, although believers, fall into any trespass in order that if any
       one after his calling should be tempted by force or deceit he might still
       receive one repentance which is not to be repented of. . . . The person
       who has turned from the heathens and the former manner of life to the
       faith has attained the forgiveness of sins once. But the person who has
       afterward sinned and then repents, although having attained pardon,
       ought to be afraid since this one is no longer washed to the remission of
       sins. (*Miscellanies* 2.13.56.1-58.1)

6   It ought to be known then that those who fall into sin after baptism are
       those who are subjected to discipline; for the deeds done before baptism
       are remitted, and those done after are purged. (*Ibid.* 4.24.154.3)

7   If it should happen that on account of ignorance, weakness, or
       involuntary circumstances one should be ensnared in sins or
       transgressions after receiving the [baptismal] seal and redemption . . ., this
       one has not been absolutely condemned by God. For to every one who in
       truth turns to God wholeheartedly the doors are opened, and the thrice
       pleased father receives the son who truly repents. True repentance is to
       be no longer guilty of the same things but wholly to root out of the soul
       the sins for which one condemned oneself to death. . . .
          Thief, do you wish to receive forgiveness? Steal no more. Adulterer, be
       inflamed no more. Fornicator, be pure in the future. Extortioner, repay
       with interest. False witness, practice truth, . . .
          In order that you may take heart, having truly repented, that there
       remains for you a trustworthy hope of salvation, hear a story, not a story
       but an account concerning the apostle John which has been handed
       down and kept in memory. [There follows the record of a young man left
       by John with an elder of the church to raise, who was baptized but then
       became the leader of an outlaw band, and of John's going out to meet him
       and reclaiming him for the church.] When John approached, the robber
       embraced the old man. As he was able he spoke in his defense with
       lamentations and baptized himself a second time with tears. . . . The
       apostle prayed, kneeled down, and kissed his right hand as having been
       purified by repentance. He brought him back to the church and made
       intercession for him with profuse prayers. He struggled with him in
       continual fastings. With many soothing words he subdued his mind, and
       he did not depart before he restored him to the church. (*Who is the Rich
       Man that is Saved* 39-42)

8   IRENAEUS: When after much difficulty the brethren had converted

her [a deacon's wife who had been led astray by the magician Marcus], she   XV.
spent her whole time in confession, mourning and weeping. (*Against
Heresies* 1.13.5)

Some make public confession, but those who are ashamed to do this   9
and to some extent lose hope of the life of God either fall away entirely
or halt between the two opinions. (*Ibid.* 1.13.7)

EUSEBIUS: Natalius was persuaded by them to be called a bishop of   10
this heresy [Adoptionism] with a salary, so that he received from them
one hundred and fifty denarii a month. While he was with them, he was
admonished by the Lord many times through visions, for the compassionate God and our Lord Jesus Christ did not wish a witness of his own
sufferings [i.e. one who had confessed the faith before pagan rulers] to
depart from the church and perish. . . . When at last he was scourged by
the holy angels the whole night through and was tormented not a little,
he arose early in the morning and put on sackcloth and sprinkled himself
with ashes and with much haste and tears he fell down at the feet of
Zephyrinus the bishop [of Rome]. Rolling at the feet of the clergy and the
laity, he moved with his tears the compassionate church of the merciful
Christ. Although he made many petitions and showed the wounds from
the blows he had received, he was scarcely admitted to fellowship.
(*Church History* 5.28.10-12)

TERTULLIAN: This act [second repentance], which is most often   11
expressed by the Greek term, is *exomologēsis*, by which we confess our
transgressions to the Lord. Not that he is ignorant of them, but inasmuch
as by confession satisfaction is arranged, from confession repentance is
born, by repentance God is appeased. Thus *exomologesis* is a discipline for
human abasement and humiliation, enjoining that behavior which brings
mercy. It commands with regard to the very clothes and dress to lie in
sackcloth and ashes, to cover the body with soiled clothing, to lay the
soul low with lamentations, to exchange severe treatment for those sins
which were committed; for the rest to allow only plain food and drink,
not (to be sure) for the stomach's sake but the soul's. And for the most
part it commands indeed to strengthen prayers with fastings, to heave
sighs, to weep, to groan day and night to your Lord God, to fall prostrate
before the elders, to kneel before God's dear ones, to enjoin on all the
brothers to be ambassadors on behalf of your supplications.

All these things *exomologesis* performs so that it may make repentance
acceptable, so that it may honor God by the fear of danger, so that by
itself pronouncing judgment on the sinner may act in place of God's
wrath and by temporal afflictions may (I do not say frustrate but) expunge
eternal punishments....

With one or two is the church, and the church is Christ. Therefore
when you prostrate yourself at the brethren's knees, you are handling

XV.   Christ, you are entreating Christ. Likewise when they shed tears over you, Christ is suffering, Christ is supplicating the Father. (*On Repentance* 9, 10)

DISCUSSION

The early Christian community took seriously the problem of sin within its ranks. The ideal was that Christians should live above sin, once having been cleansed from their former manner of life. It soon became evident that all did not live up to the standard. Yet there was a strong feeling in the ancient church against forgiveness for post-baptismal sins.

The *Didache* required reconciliation of the members of the community with one another before participation in the breaking of bread (VIII.3). It is not clear whether the confession of sins enjoined in that passage is public or private, corporate or individual. Elsewhere the writer does call for a confession of sins "in church," or "in the assembly" (XV.1).[1] Again, it is not clear whether this was a corporate, liturgical prayer for forgiveness or a special confession by an individual who had fallen from the Christian standard of life.

The ultimate power of discipline in the church for wrongdoers was exclusion from communion.[2] The rule which excluded the unbaptized from the eucharist (VIII.3) kept from the table those who had fallen away from the Christian fellowship (IX.3 implies not only the necessity of baptism but also continued living according to the teachings of Christ). The second-century sources occasionally speak of those excluded from fellowship, and so from communion,[3] but do not give us details about how the ban was imposed. More is said about the procedure for readmission to the fellowship of the church, hence more attention will be given to this aspect of church discipline.

The *Didache* uses for "confess" the Greek word *exomologeō* (noun, *exomologēsis*). It is this word which is translated "confess" in the other selections. This word is from *homologeō*, the general word used for agreeing, confessing faults, professing faith or acknowledging a fact, and praising God. *Exomologeō* could have most of these meanings too, but it was the regular word for the confession of one's sins. In fact, it became the technical word for the public act whereby one sought restoration to the fellowship of the church from which that one had departed or had been excluded. Hence, Tertullian, writing in Latin, refers to the public confession by the Greek word (XV.11). *Exomologesis* had become a technical word just as *baptisma* and several other Greek words from the earliest Christian vocabulary did. They were not translated into other languages but were simply taken over with the corresponding spelling. It cannot be determined how early this technical usage of *exomologesis* came about; its occurrence in such documents as the *Didache* shows the general custom that made this terminology technical. The word itself indicates the verbal acknowledgment of transgression and the public nature of this acknowledgment.

Confession calls attention to the personal appeal for reconciliation and so to the public act performed for the sake of restoration. The word repentance calls attention to the inward state of penitence and thus to the state of forgiveness. Several authors refer to the means of forgiveness for post-baptismal sin and of readmission to the Christian community as repentance (XV.2-5, 11). In Greek the word is *metanoia*; in Latin, *poenitentia*, from whence comes the word penance. Penance is now used to refer to the sacramental or ecclesiastical discipline for the forgiveness of post-baptismal sins, as distinguished from the evangelical "penitence" associated with conversion. The idea of penance came from the usage of the word in reference to the acts of repentance which the quotations in this chapter show were required as a demonstration of the change of heart. In Latin the phrase was "to do repentance." The ancient significance of *poenitentia* was penitence, not penance. But the outward acts were expected to accompany it. The Biblical idea of repentance was a fundamental reorientation of one's life. This gave to the concept such a decisive once-for-all connotation that the early church was much exercised over the problem whether it was possible for there to be more than one repentance. The same word was used with reference to post-baptismal sins as to the pre-baptismal sins. To make a distinction from conversion or baptismal repentance, the phrase "second repentance" was adopted for the discipline of restoration to church fellowship.

The concern for sin by Christians is evident in the post-apostolic writings. There are frequent appeals to repentance in the apostolic fathers.[4] *Second Clement* may be regarded as a sermon on the theme of repentance. The entire *Shepherd* of Hermas may be regarded as concerned with the problem of forgiveness for post-baptismal sin. In this document the usage of *repentance* is at least approaching a technical sense.

The varied, and sometimes confused, statements in Hermas' diffuse work have led to a variety of interpretations of his message. Part of the difficulty comes from uncertainty over the background against which he is writing. The work may be seen as the opening wedge of a "laxist" tendency in the Roman church by its proclamation of the possibility of a post-baptismal repentance against a "rigorist" view that there could be no forgiveness offered by the church to backsliders (III.3). Or, the work may be seen as upholding a basically rigorist attitude while proclaiming a special repentance available to some for a limited time. Perhaps it is best not to try to schematize the teaching of the *Shepherd* on the subject of repentance and to see the author as involved in the dialectic between the demand for sinlessness and the actuality of involvement in the world. For instance, Hermas appears one time to offer repentance to apostates and at another time to deny it.[5] There is repentance for those who have denied the Lord in the past, but there is none for those who did so of set purpose or for those who are going to do so. In other words, repentance is always a present possibility but never a future promise.[6]

The Epistle to the Hebrews in the New Testament was apparently understood as teaching that there was no repentance for apostasy (6:4-8; 10:26-31). This seems to be the basis for the view expressed by "some teachers" (III.3) that there is no second repentance. The steady move by the Roman church away from this position perhaps accounts for its reservations about the canonical authority of Hebrews that persisted in the early centuries.

Hermas' proclamation of one repentance after baptism (XV.3) was retained by the church and remained the prevailing sentiment for a long time (XV.5). A disciplinary penance seems indicated by Hermas (XV.4), but this is a self-imposed affliction of the soul rather than an ecclesiastically-imposed regimen. Yet we know the church leaders exercised discipline from what is said about exclusion of apostates. These acts of self-discipline, elaborated in the documents from the end of the century, formed the basis for designating the restoration to the church a *repentance* and for directing attention to outward acts as a proof of the inward disposition.

Clement of Alexandria knew the *Shepherd* and accorded it considerable authority. He substantially reproduces the *Shepherd's* teaching on sin and repentance as concerns Christians (XV.5,6). He repeats the ideal of sinlessness for those who have once received forgiveness. There is a "second repentance" which is available once for those trapped by their own weakness or overcome by the devil's wiles. The post-baptismal sins are not simply forgiven; they must be "purged" by the disciplinary exercise of public repentance.

This public exercise finds its most circumstantial description in Tertullian (XV.11), but the notices in Irenaeus (XV.8,9) and Eusebius' account of the repentance of Natalius (XV.10) so closely accord with it that we may assume that we have here the normal practice of the church at large at the end of the second century.[7] These three examples are all from the West (North Africa, Gaul, and Rome), but the use of a Greek word to name the practice plus the allusions in Clement of Alexandria (XV.7) argue that the same was done in the eastern Mediterranean region too.

The process through which the Christian who had fallen into sin went in order to secure forgiveness and readmission to the Christian fellowship included the following activities: (1) Confession of one's sinfulness. It is not stated that the specific sin was confessed publicly. Later Origen and Cyprian say that this specific confession was made to the bishop or a confessor.[8] It would have been at his discretion whether the exact nature of the trespass was made known. In the case of known transgressions or open identification with a rival religious body (as in the case of Natalius) the nature of what was confessed would be known without a specific statement. (2) Acts of confession and repentance. One dressed in mourning attire, wept, fasted, and humiliated oneself before the assembly of the faithful. (3) Request for the prayers of the church. The elders appear as taking the leading role in the discipline of offenders. But the suppliant appears before the whole church in assembly and humbly beseeches their intercessions. The penitent kneels or makes prostration before the church. (4) Prayer. The suppliant prays for God's and the congregation's forgiveness. The church was acting in its role as the body of Christ and in keeping with Gospel passages in determining whether to grant its mercy. (5) Restoration to fellowship. The laying on of hands by the clergy was the sign of the reconciliation and return to the peace of the church; then the person was readmitted to communion.[9]

What is stated in Biblical passages about confession, repentance, and prayer has been ritualized or formalized. The penitential discipline was public because it was the act of the whole community to exclude and to readmit. There would have been private confessions to the clergy and spiritual counsel given. It is very much debated how early the evidence permits us to conclude that there was privately imposed penance by the bishop. Our sources from the end of the second and beginning of the third century are clear only for a public discipline.

The procedure was not superficial; this was no easy forgiveness. Such an ordeal was not likely to be desired more than the once that most writers allowed. The reluctance of some to submit even once (XV.9) is matched by Tertullian's own reluctance even to mention this "second plank" of salvation. In his treatise *On Repentance* he spends the first half of his writing on conversion repentance. His approach shows the parallel with baptism of this second forgiveness. He introduces the discussion of second repentance with hesitation for fear that its availability will encourage those who were not taking their Christian commitment as seriously as was desired.

Tertullian and Origen reflect a kind of classification of sins, although the boundaries are not precisely defined. Many of a rigorist mind thought the capital sins of idolatry, murder, and fornication (based on a particular interpretation of Acts 15:29) did not admit of forgiveness by the church in this life.[10] Exomologesis or second repentance functioned in regard to public acts by which one's faith was compromised such as attending gladiatorial contests and theatrical productions, participating in government offices, speaking ambiguously in regard to idolatry, or some fault in speech and conduct. Those persons who were less rigorous included all grave sins as subject to public discipline and forgiveness. The everyday sins of human nature, according to the classification, were forgiven by one's prayers and acts of piety. Origen specified almsgiving, forgiving others, converting a sinner, and love as bringing a forgiveness of daily faults.[11] The early church from their time on agreed that martyrdom ("baptism of blood") erased all sins, even that of apostasy. In fact, a believer who had not yet received baptism but was martyred was assured entrance into heaven. It was better to confess and be killed than to deny Christ in order to secure time to complete one's regular admission to the church.[12]

Tertullian was particularly attracted by a rigorist attitude toward morals and conduct. Hence, when the Montanist movement inaugurated a rigorist revival against the increasing accommodations with the world discernible in the great church, Tertullian identified with this movement. Tracts written during his Montanist days reject the possibility offered in *On Repentance*. The major sins, he argues, cannot be forgiven in this life; indeed the rigorous exclusion of those undergoing penitence helps them attain God's forgiveness at the judgment. This legalizing of the high standards of primitive Christianity continued to have its appeal.

The church at Rome was much exercised over the attitude which should be taken toward Christians who lapsed from the faith. Two schisms occurred in the third century over the matter—one made by Hippolytus and another more serious and lasting one by Novatian. Both men represented the rigorist tendency that would deny reconciliation to those guilty of major sins. They did not deny the possibility of salvation to such sinners but placed them in the condition of penitents whose final destiny was in the hands of God. The church could not declare forgiveness to those guilty of serious sins by granting reconciliation; God alone could forgive sins. In both cases the majority followed the path marked out by Hermas and without lowering the Christian moral demands took a more forgiving attitude. The church was to be a hospital for sick souls, not a society of the pure. Or, as Callistus, the rival of Hippolytus, put it, the church is like Noah's ark with both clean and unclean animals in it.[13] Callistus, in taking a lenient attitude toward those guilty of sexual sins, was not the complete innovator Hippolytus tried to make him out to be.

In spite of the rigorist tendency to be hesitant about granting reconciliation to those guilty of at least some sins, there were voices for allowing the church to extend her forgiveness to any of her children. So Dionysius of Corinth counselled.[14] And Clement of Alexandria's story of "John and the Robber" (XV.7; beginning cited XIV.18) was circulated to show the apostle's forgiveness to one of his converts who had become a leader of a robber band and so guilty of major crimes.

In the third century the penitential discipline was further systematized and organized, with varying periods of exclusion imposed for different sins and various stages imposed through which one must pass in returning to the full communion of the church.[15] The bishops in the third century successfully asserted their authority as the organs of the church for granting forgiveness. Cyprian struggled to maintain episcopal control of discipline and restoration.

Unfortunately, it has proved difficult in Christian history to maintain the tension between the ethical ideals of the Sermon on the Mount and the forgiving spirit of the one who spoke the words.

BIBLIOGRAPHY

Ferguson, Everett. "Early Church Penance." *Restoration Quarterly*, Vol. 36 (1994), pp. 81-100.

Karpp, Heinrich. *Die Busse: Quellen zur Entstehung des altkirchlichen Busswesens*. Traditio Christiana I. Bern: Lang, 1969. [Original Greek and Latin texts with German translations; French translations published Neuchâtel: Delachaux et Niestle, 1970.]

Poschmann, Bernhard. *Penance and the Anointing of the Sick*. London: Burns and Oates, 1964.

Rahner, Karl. *Theological Investigations*, Vol. 15: *Penance in the Early Church*. New York: Crossroad, 1982.

Telfer, W. *The Forgiveness of Sins*. London: SCM, 1959.

Watkins, O. D. *A History of Penance*. Vol. 1. *The Whole Church to A.D. 450*. London: Longmans, Green, and Co., 1920.

NOTES

[1] That phrase is missing from the parallel in *Barnabas* 19.12 and so is likely an addition to the original Two Ways source that is being employed by the compiler of the *Didache*.

[2] Werner Elert, *Eucharist and Church Fellowship in the First Four Centuries* (St. Louis: Concordia, 1966) develops the evidence that Christian fellowship was the basis for sharing in the eucharist, and those excluded from fellowship were excluded from communion.

[3] Cerdon (Irenaeus, *Against Heresies* 3.4.3); and Marcion (Pseudo-Tertullian, *Against All Heresies* 6.2; cf. Epiphanius, *Against Heresies* 42.1, 4). Tertullian, *Apology* 44 and 46 refer to disfellowship for immorality.

[4] Clement of Rome, *Epistle to Corinthians* 2; 7; 8; 57; *Second Clement* 8; 13; 16; 17.

[5] *Similitudes* 9.26=103.1-8 and *Visions* 2.2=6.1-8 versus *Similitudes* 6.2=62.1-7 and 8.6=72.1-6.

[6] Graydon F. Snyder, *The Shepherd* of *Hermas*, Vol. VI of *The Apostolic Fathers*, ed. R. M. Grant (New York: Nelson, 1968), pp. 36, 69-71. See Carolyn Osiek,*The Shepherd of Hermas: A Commentary*, Hermeneia (Minneapolis: Fortress, 1998).

[7] Celsus appears to allude to second-century Christian penitential practice in his words, "The lowly man humiliates himself shamelessly and improperly, prostrating himself face downward and grovelling upon his knees, clothing himself with wretched garments, and heaping dust on himself," quoted by Origen, *Against Celsus* 6.15. Cf. Tertullian, *On Modesty* 13.

[8] Origen, *Homily 2 on Psalm* 37; Cyprian, *On the Lapsed* 28. Tertullian, *On Prayer* 7 calls the general petition "Forgive us" in the Lord's Prayer an *exomologesis*.

[9] Cyprian *Epistles* 15 [10]; 16 [9]; 17 [11]; idem, *On the Lapsed*; *Didascalia* 7. All are third-century sources.

[10] Tertullian as a Montanist enlarged this list–*On Modesty* 19–but the items listed are reduceable to the three mentioned.

[11] *Homily on Leviticus* 2.

[12] Tertullian, *On Baptism* 16.2; Hippolytus, *Apostolic Tradition* 2.19; Origen, *Exhortation to Martyrdom* 30.

[13] Hippolytus, *Refutation of All Heresies* 9.7.

[14] Cited by Eusebius, *Church History* 4.23.6. Note the mercy extended by the martyrs of Lyons and Vienne to those who initially denied the faith–*Ibid*. 5.1.45f. Forgiveness for post-baptismal sin is prominent in the *Acts of Peter*; cf. especially chap. 10-11 for repentance, confession, and prayer.

[15] Gregory Thaumaturgus, *Canonical Epistle* 11 (a late third-century addition) lists the classes of penitents as follows: "Weeping takes place outside the gate of the place of prayer. The sinner who stands there must implore the faithful as they enter to pray for him. Hearing the word is within the gate in the fore-court. Here the one who has sinned ought to stand until the catechumens go out and then go out too. For after hearing the Scriptures and the teaching, it is said, let that one be put out and not be considered worthy to participate in prayer. Kneeling is within the entrance of the sanctuary in order that the one who was placed there may

leave with the catechumens. Standing is so that one may be associated with the faithful and not leave with the catechumens. Completion of the restoration is the participation in the holy things."

XVI

Christian Living
in the Second Century

"Let your light shine before others"

Some New Testament Texts: Matthew 5-7; Acts 2:43-47;
Ephesians 4:17-6:9; Philippians 1:27-28; 2:12-15; 1 Peter 2:11-4:19.

SOURCES

CLEMENT OF ROME: What visitor among you is there who has not   XVI.1
proved your most excellent and firm faith, who has not marvelled at your
prudent and gentle piety in Christ, who has not proclaimed your
magnificent practice of hospitality, and who has not blessed your perfect
and sure knowledge? For you did all things without respect of persons and
walked in the commandments of God. You were obedient to your rulers
and showed appropriate honor to those who were older. You instructed
the younger to think moderate and reverent thoughts. . . .[1]

You were all humbleminded and in no way arrogant, rather being
subjected than subjecting and giving more gladly than receiving. You
were satisfied with and paid attention to the travel provisions supplied by
Christ, and you were storing up carefully in your hearts his words and
were keeping his sufferings before your eyes. Thus a deep and rich peace
was given to all. There was an insatiable desire to do good, and a full
outpouring of the Holy Spirit came upon all. You were full of holy
counsel. You stretched forth your hands in noble desire with pious
confidence to the Almighty God, beseeching him to be merciful if you
committed any unwilling sin. You had great concern day and night for
the whole brotherhood, in order that the number of God's elect might be
saved with mercy and conscience. You were sincere and innocent and
bore no malice to one another. All rebellion and schism was abominable
to you. You mourned over the transgressions of your neighbors. You
counted their shortcomings your own. You never regretted doing any

XVI.   good, but were "ready for every good work." (1.2-2.7)

2   SECOND CLEMENT: Let us not only call him Lord, for this will not save us. He says, "Not everyone who says to me, 'Lord, Lord' will be saved, but he who does righteousness." Therefore, brethren, let us confess him in deeds, in loving one another, in not committing adultery, nor speaking against one another, nor being jealous, but in being self-controlled, merciful, good. And we ought to sympathize with one another and not to love money. By these deeds we confess him and not by the opposite. And we must not fear people rather than God. (4)

3   ARISTIDES: For they [the Christians] know and trust in God, the Creator of heaven and of earth, in whom and from whom are all things, to whom there is no other god as companion, from whom they received commandments which they engraved upon their minds and observe in hope and expectation of the world which is to come. Wherefore they do not commit adultery nor fornication, nor bear false witness, nor embezzle what is held in pledge, nor covet what is not theirs. They honor father and mother, and show kindness to those near to them; and whenever they are judges, they judge uprightly. They do not worship idols (made) in the image of man; and whatsoever they would not that others should do unto them, they do not do to others; and of the food which is consecrated to idols they do not eat, for they are pure. And their oppressors they appease and make them their friends;[1a] they do good to their enemies. And their women are pure and virgins and do not offer their wombs; and their men exercise self-control from every unlawful union and especially from impurity; and their wives similarly exercise self-control, for they cling to a great hope of the world to come.[2] ... They do not worship strange gods. They are gentle, moderate, modest, and truthful. They love one another.[3] ... They observe carefully the precepts of God and live holily and justly as the Lord their God commanded them. They give thanks to him every morning and every hour for food and drink and other good things. If any righteous person among them dies, they rejoice and offer thanks and pray concerning that one; and they escort the body as if for one setting out on a journey.[4] ... But if any one should die in sins, they weep, since that one goes to punishment. (Apology 15)

4   EPISTLE TO DIOGNETUS: For Christians are distinguished from other people neither by country, language, nor customs. They do not dwell in cities of their own, nor do they use some strange language, nor practice a peculiar kind of life. Their teaching indeed has not been discovered by any speculation or consideration of persons full of curiosity, nor do they busy themselves with human doctrine as some do. While dwelling in Greek or barbarian cities, as each has received his lot, and

following the local customs in dress, food, and the rest of life, they display   XVI.
the marvellous and admittedly unusual constitution of their own
citizenship. They live in their native countries, but as sojourners. They
share all things, as citizens; and they endure all things, as foreigners.
Every foreign land is their fatherland, and every fatherland is a foreign
land to them. They marry as do all others; they bear children; but they do
not abandon their offspring. They furnish a common table, but not a
common bed. Their lot is cast "in the flesh," but they do not live
"according to the flesh." They pass their time upon the earth, but their
citizenship is in heaven. They are obedient to the appointed laws, but
they surpass the laws in their own lives. They love all people and are
persecuted by all. They are not understood, and they are condemned.
They are put to death, and they are made alive. "They are poor, and they
make many rich." They lack all things, and they abound in everything.
They are dishonored, and they are glorified in their dishonor. They are
evil spoken of, and they are justified. "They are reviled, and they bless."
They are insulted, and they give honor. While doing good, they are
punished as evil. Being punished, they rejoice as being made alive. They
are fought against as foreigners by the Jews, and they are persecuted by
Greeks. And those who hate them cannot state a reason for their enmity.

To speak simply, what the soul is in the body, Christians are in the
world. The soul has been dispersed throughout the members of the body,
and Christians are in each of the cities of the world. The soul lives in the
body, but is not of the body. And Christians live in the world but are not
of the world. The invisible soul is imprisoned in a visible body.
Christians, being in the world, are recognized, but the nature of their
godliness remains invisible. The flesh hates the soul and fights against it,
although receiving nothing unjust itself, because it is prevented from
enjoying pleasures. The world, although experiencing nothing unjust,
hates the Christians, because they are opposed to its pleasures. The soul
loves the flesh, which hates it, and the body's members. Christians love
those who hate them. The soul has been shut up in the body, but itself
holds the body together. Christians are held in the world, as in a prison,
but they uphold the world. The immortal soul dwells in a mortal tent,
and Christians sojourn among corruptible things but expect incorruption
in heaven. The soul becomes better when ill-treated with food and drink,
and Christians when punished increase daily. God has appointed them to
such a post which it is not lawful for them to desert. (5-6)

JUSTIN: After being persuaded by the Word we keep far away from the   5
demons and follow the only unbegotten God through his Son. We who
formerly rejoiced in fornication now embrace self-control alone. We who
employed magical arts now have dedicated ourselves to the good and
unbegotten God. We who loved more than anything else ways of
acquiring wealth and possessions now bring what we have into a common

XVI.   treasury and share with everyone who is in need. We who hated and murdered one another and would not show hospitality to those not of the same tribe on account of different customs now after the coming of Christ eat with others, pray for our enemies, and attempt to persuade those who hate us unjustly so that those who live according to the good counsels of Christ may share with us the things hoped for from God the Lord of all. . . .

For not only he who commits adultery in deed is rejected by Christ, but also he who wishes to commit adultery, since not only works but also thoughts are manifest to God. For what do we say of the countless multitude of those who learned these things and changed from licentiousness . . . .

He urged us through forbearance and gentleness to lead everyone out of shame and the desire for evil. This we are able to show in regard to many who were once of your way of thinking. They changed from their violent and tyrannical ways, being overcome when they observed the patient endurance of life by their neighbors or perceived the unusual forbearance of their fellow travellers when defrauded or made proof of those with whom they had business dealings. . . . Let those who are not found living as Christ taught be recognized as not being Christians, even though they profess with the mouth the teachings of Christ. For he says that not those who only say but those who also do will be saved. (*Apology* I, 14-16).

6   THEOPHILUS: We have as our lawgiver the true God who teaches us to practice righteousness, to be pious, and to do good. . . .

Consider then if those who have been taught such things are able to live indifferently and to be joined in unlawful intercourse or most ungodly of all to eat human flesh. . . It would be far from Christians to think about doing any such thing. With them temperance is present, self-control is exercised, monogamy is preserved, chastity is guarded, unrighteousness is cast out, sin is rooted out, righteousness is cared for, law is lived, godliness is practiced, God is confessed, truth arbitrates, grace is maintained, peace shelters, the holy word guides, wisdom teaches, life arbitrates, God rules. (*To Autolycus* 3.9; 3.15)

7   ATHENAGORAS: By means of the teachings themselves to which we adhere we are able to persuade you not to think of us as atheists, since they are not human but spoken and taught by God. What then are the words in which we are trained? "I say to you, love your enemies, bless those who curse you, pray for those who persecute you, in order that you may be children of the Father in heaven who causes his sun to rise on the wicked and the good and sends rain on the righteous and the unrighteous." . . . Who of those [rhetoricians] have so purged their souls that instead of hating their enemies they love them and instead of speaking evil to those who first began to revile them (itself evidence of

the greatest moderation) they bless them and pray for those who plot   XVI.
against their lives? . . . But among us you may find uneducated persons,
workmen, and old women, who if by word are unable to present the
benefit that comes from our doctrine, by deed demonstrate the benefit
that comes from this persuasion. For they do not call to mind the words,
but they exhibit good works. When they are struck, they do not strike
back. When robbed, they do not go to law. They give to those asking and
they love their neighbors as themselves. (*Plea for the Christians* 11)

GALEN: 'Most people are unable to follow any demonstrative   8
argument consecutively; hence they need parables, and benefit from
them'–and he (Galen) understands by parables tales of rewards and
punishments in a future life–'just as now we see the people called
Christians drawing their faith from parables [and miracles], and yet
sometimes acting in the same way [as those who philosophize]. For their
contempt of death [and its sequel] is patent to us every day, and likewise
their restraint in cohabitation. For they include not only men but also
women who refrain from cohabiting all through their lives; and they also
number individuals who, in self-discipline and self-control in matters of
food and drink, and in their keen pursuit of justice, have attained a pitch
not inferior to that of genuine philosophers.'[5]

DISCUSSION

Much early Christian literature presents and interprets Christian moral
teaching. The "Two Ways"–the way of life and the way of death–are
spelled out in the beginning of the *Didache* and at the end of *Barnabas* (cf.
VII.1 for a comparably early report from a pagan of things Christians did
not do). The *Shepherd of Hermas*, especially the *Mandates*, is a treatise on
practical matters of Christian living. The sermon known as *Second
Clement is* an exhortation concerning various aspects of Christian
conduct (XVI.2). The *Letter* of Clement of Rome, in contrasting the
good past with the bad present at Corinth, gives a description of the ideal
Christian community (XVI.1). In another vein, Irenaeus has a beautiful
passage to the effect that Christians do not need the law of Moses because
of the superiority of the Christian way of life, based on the teachings of
Christ.[6]

Such writings were addressed to Christians telling how they ought to
live. Many fine passages could have been selected from them in order to
illustrate the Christian moral standard. Nevertheless, we have chosen to
make most of the selections from writings addressed to non-Christians
telling how Christians did live. The very existence of the former group of
writings shows that not all Christians lived up to the standard. The
preceding chapter shows how the early church dealt with the more
serious offenders. Nonetheless, the standard attained in Christian living

in the second century was notable and contrasted sharply with the standard of conduct current in the pagan world. It was used by the literary advocates of Christianity to show the superiority of Christianity to other ways of life.

The Greek apologists were defending Christianity before a pagan world. An analysis of the context in which the quoted passages occur will be instructive on several counts. Aristides divides mankind into four classes–Barbarians, Greeks, Jews, and Christians.[7] After exposing the shortcomings of the other three, he describes Christians. The greater part of what he says about Christians is included in our quotation (XVI.3). Aristides is willing to rest his case for Christianity on a description of the Christian life. He adds an invitation to read the writings of Christians so that the inquirer may see that his picture of Christian teachings is accurate.

The *Epistle to Diognetus* is similar. After refuting the practices of pagans and Jews, he comes to describe Christians. Life is described first, and then there is a rudimentary statement of doctrine. The author's picture of the Christian life (XVI.4) is one of the most beautiful literary gems from early Christianity. From the standpoint of Biblical doctrine, one can fault the author for his Greek distinction between body and soul. The sharp separation he makes is more in accord with Greek philosophy than it is with the Biblical view of the unity of the whole person. Nevertheless, his readers would certainly have understood what he was saying. If the author's anthropology is faulty, his ethics are superb.

With Justin we come to a more ambitious defense of Christianity, but the argument from the Christian life still comes early in his first *Apology*. Christians are not atheists, Justin declares, for they worship the triune God (ch. 6); moreover, in contrast to idolatrous worship, the worship of Christians is rational (13). Other human beings have been deceived by demons, but Christians follow God. Then comes the passage quoted about the conversions effected by Christian teaching (XVI.5, from ch. 14). Chapters 15-17 cite what Christ himself taught–concerning chastity (part of which is quoted), love to all, sharing with the needy, patience and gentleness (a part of which is quoted), abstinence from swearing, and civil obedience. Most of the quotations made by Justin from the teaching of Jesus come from the "Sermon on the Mount" tradition in Matthew and Luke. The contacts of pagans with Christians who lived according to this teaching led to conversions.

For Theophilus the appeal to the Christian life stands toward the close of his apology. God's teaching has been made known in the Prophets and Gospels (3.12). Theophilus cites the Ten Commandments and other Old Testament teaching in regard to hospitality, repentance, and righteousness (3.9-12). On the subjects of chastity and love for enemies the sayings of Jesus in Matthew 5 and 6 are quoted (3.13-14). What he has given, Theophilus is convinced, is sufficient to lead one to study more about "the Christian manner of life and the ordinances of God."

Athenagoras' literary plan is much more shaped by the philosophical tradition of his time.[8] Hellenistic philosophy gave much attention to ethics, so Athenagoras is able to put the Christian case on this subject in the framework of philosophical discussions with which his readers were familiar. He too begins with theology–Christians worship Father, Son, and Holy Spirit (ch. 10). Then he takes up the moral teachings, citing the "Sermon on the Mount," as the unique or striking feature of the Christian life (XVI.7). Christianity accomplished what philosophy had not been able to do in transforming the lives of even the uneducated. Consequently, Christians could not be atheists; people would not live this way if they did not believe in a supreme being to whom they were answerable. The eschatological motivation for Christian ethics is prominent when Athenagoras returns to talk about the elevated morality of Christians in chapters 31-36.

From this survey it may be noted that the Apologists had to refute the charge of atheism made against Christians. The popular slander was that the Christians were also guilty of incest and cannibalism.[9] Such charges seem incredible to us. Some explanation may make their existence more understandable. Christianity began within Judaism, and so it initially suffered from the anti-Jewish sentiments of the ancient world. Moreover, Christians remained aloof from much of society. They were a secluded, secretive group. The *Epistle to Diognetus*[10] affirms their participation in ordinary life, but admits that they remained "unknown," unrecognized, and misunderstood. A society always thinks the worst of a foreign element in its midst and blames all wrong-doing and misfortunes on that presence.[11] Furthermore, the very growth of the church provoked reaction and opposition.

There was a good reason for Christian non-participation in many features of public life in the Empire. Idolatry thoroughly permeated all phases of life. Drama had originated in pagan cult and continued to be dedicated to the gods. In addition, the stage of the early Empire was characterized by an appeal to the grossest immorality. The games were held in honor of the gods. The public spectacles which provided entertainment for many were exceedingly cruel and violent. Several early Christian writers point out that Christians did not attend the theater, the games, the gladiator shows, and racing contests because of the immoralities and violence associated with them.[12] Meetings of the town councils and assemblies were opened with sacrifice and prayer to the gods. Sacrifices and oaths to the gods touched all phases of life, and the state religion seemed to hold society together. Christians, of course, could not participate in these features of pagan cult. Because of their rejection of the commonly accepted gods of the State, they were considered atheists. Because they held aloof from so much that others participated in, they were considered "haters of humanity."[13] The populace was suspicious of non-conformists.

Christians spoke of themselves as "brothers and sisters" (language for husband and wife in the Egyptian papyri) and had their "love feasts." It was perhaps natural that a suspicious populace should put the worst possible construction on the nocturnal gatherings of Christians. The Apologists ruefully answered that pagans attributed to others the actions they would do themselves under similar circumstances.[14] Christians also spoke of eating the body and drinking the blood of the Son. Is it any wonder that pagans who heard only so much understood this as the ritual killing of an infant and eating it?[15] False confessions were extorted from pagan slaves, and there was enough irregularity in the conduct of some Christian Gnostics to give credence to the worst rumors.[16] Informed pagans soon learned better, but slander dies hard, especially among the uninformed and those who want to believe the worst.

The defenders of Christianity appealed to the actual life lived among Christians in order to rebut the charges of immorality. Furthermore, they argued that the kind of life lived by Christians proves that they are not real atheists. If there were no God and if there were no life after death, any kind of conduct might be expected. But Christians believed in both. It is notable that the Apologists grounded Christian ethics in theology. Christian practice came from the commandments of God (XVI.3, 6, 7 for explicit statements). The next chapter of the *Epistle to Diognetus* after the quotation declares that this manner of life comes from revelation:

> For this, as I said, was not an earthly discovery which was delivered to them ... but truly the almighty, all-creating, and invisible God himself founded the truth from heaven.

He sent it down to human beings by the one through whom he created the world, the author continues. This is the uniform declaration of the Apologists.

The spokesmen for the Christian case go further and argue that the Christian manner of life is a demonstration of the truth of Christian doctrine. The earliest Apologists (XVI.3, 4) make the description of the Christian life the main point in their exposition of Christianity. The later Apologists give more elaborate defenses of Christianity. But the argument from Christian living still holds a prominent place. Justin pays tribute to the converting power of the Christian example (XVI.5).[17]

As defenders of Christianity, the Apologists had every reason to put their best foot forward. They would not talk about the worst Christians, even when recognizing that not all professing Christians lived as they should (XVI.5). A certain idealizing is to be expected in their presentation. But when every allowance is made for the apologetic setting and motives, one must be astonished at the confidence with which the Apologists speak of the way in which Christians lived. There must have been some substance to their claims or they would have been too easily refuted.

The argument from the quality of the Christian life to the truth of Christian doctrine is strongly put, and the description of the Christian life is impressive. Again, it is to be remarked that the case is not simply, "These are Christian teachings" (although that is done too), but "This is the way Christians live" (XVI.7 especially). There was ample room for contrast with life in the pagan world.

What stood out were not the externals, not arbitrary badges of distinctiveness, but the actual moral conduct. The earliest Christians participated as fully as possible in all areas of life that were open to them. Increasingly, they came to take over the borderland areas where the earlier moralists maintained a rigoristic opposition. By the end of the fourth century the line between the church and the world was becoming blurred. But we note here some of the actual differences in matters of moral conduct in earlier times.

It was common practice in the Greco-Roman world to abandon ("expose") unwanted babies.[18] This was an early form of population control in a society threatened by too many mouths to feed. According to the religious practices, a baby was not a part of the family until formally accepted by the father. The exposure of an unwanted baby was, therefore, not looked on in the way it might be now. The newborn was not regarded as a member of the family just by reason of birth. Modern debates about abortion raise the question, too, at what point does terminating a life that has been conceived constitute murder. The ancient world put that time later than Jews and Christians would have. Christians and Jews alone of the peoples in the Mediterranean world protested against the practice.[19] It was especially girl babies who might be exposed, for they were an economic liability.[20] There were many attendant evils to the practice of exposure, for the abandoned babies would be taken and raised for a life of slavery or of prostitution. But Christians did not abandon their offspring and often took children who were abandoned to rear themselves. Such unwanted children furnished many of the "orphans" mentioned in our next chapter.

On sexual ethics Christianity created the greatest revolution. It was not only to refute gossip that the Apologists insisted that Christians did not have a "common bed" (XVI.4).[21] The sexual purity of Christians was a notable contrast to general pagan practice, and Christian teachings on divorce set them above Jews as well. Justin can boast both of those who have lived their lives in the church in a state of sexual purity and of those converted from the licentiousness of paganism to a life of chastity (XVI.5). In reaction against the loose sexual morals of the time, and in accord with a dualistic pessimism which viewed the created world as evil (including sex and reproduction) and a philosophical trend to view suppression of desires as the mark of virtue and wisdom, the ideal of celibacy gained ground in the church, becoming particularly evident in the writings of the third and following centuries.[22] It was common for even those Christians who took a positive view of marriage to consider that the only proper occasion for intercourse was in order to bring children into the world.[23]

What the Apologists considered most distinctive and unique about Christ's ethics was his teaching on love for enemies. The spirit of non-retaliation, and even beyond that of actually blessing those who did evil to one, was considered the most remarkable thing of all. This was so unusual that it could only be divine. This leads us to note how frequently the "Sermon on the Mount" appears in the Apologists' discussion of Christian living. This teaching had thoroughly imprinted itself on the early Christian moral consciousness. Returning good for evil was presented as the distinguishing mark of Christian practice.

According to the Apologists, although the philosophers had some good ethical teachings, Christians actually lived by a philosophical (or more than philosophical) teaching. Here, too, was another great contrast (XVI.7).[24] There was a strong feeling in the ancient philosophical tradition, stemming from Socrates, that if a man knew the right he would do the right. Therefore, the more he knows the better he will be. This was picked up in the rhetorical tradition, and most of the education in the ancient world was dominated by rhetoric. This belief led to the feeling that one could not expect uneducated people to live on a very high plane. They were not capable of the "philosophic life," of high moral conduct. This view was countered by another tenet familiar to Greek thought since Plato's time, namely that common people without intellectual excellence could by religious superstitions be led to conduct themselves virtuously. Galen (XVI.8) made reference to Christians as an illustration of this. Galen himself dislikes their accepting things on faith. But he praises them for possessing the cardinal virtues of Hellenistic philosophy—courage, temperance, and justice—which is why he singles out the aspects of conduct that he does. The Christians attained moral virtue through following a law by faith, not by a theoretical ethical philosophy.[25] Taking up this problem in contemporary ethical discussions,[26] the Christian Apologists made the claim that Christianity was the product of supernatural revelation. Only by divine teaching and divine power could the common people exemplify such an extraordinary manner of life.

Christians lived by the laws of their country, provided such did not conflict with God's laws. By their manner of life they surpassed those laws. Their lives were very distinctive. Clearly "church life" was "daily life," and Christian living extended to all phases of existence.

BIBLIOGRAPHY

Arnold, Eberhard. *The Early Christians After the Death of the Apostles.* Rifton: Plough, 1970.

Cadoux, C. J. *The Early Church and the World.* Edinburgh: T. & T. Clark, 1925.

Davies, J. G. *Daily Life in the Early Church: Studies in the Church Social History of the First Five Centuries.* London: Lutterworth Press, 1952.

Ferguson, Everett, ed. *Christian Life: Ethics, Morality, and Discipline in the Early Church.* Studies in Early Christianity, Vol. XVI. New York: Garland, 1993.

Forell, George. *History of Christian Ethics*, Vol. 1. Minneapolis: Augsburg, 1979.

Meeks, Wayne. *The Origins of Christian Morality: The First Two Centuries.* New Haven: Yale University Press, 1993.

Murphy, F. X. *Moral Teaching in the Primitive Church.* New York: Paulist, 1968.

_____. *The Christian Way of Life.* Collegeville: Liturgical Press, 1986.

Osborn, Eric. *Ethical Patterns in Early Christian Thought.* Cambridge: Cambridge University Press, 1976.

Wormer, J. L. *Morality and Ethics in Early Christianity.* Minneapolis: Fortress, 1987.

NOTES

[1] The omitted section is quoted in XIX.1.

[1a] Translated from the Syriac version by D. M. Kay in *Ante-Nicene Fathers* (Reprint of the American edition; Grand Rapids: Wm. B. Eerdmans, 1951), Vol. X, pp. 276ff., and used by permission. At this point takes up an early papyrus fragment of Aristides, published by H. J. M. Milne in *Journal of Theological Studies*, Vol. 25 (1924), pp.73-77, and from which I have made my own translation of the remainder.

[2] See Chapter V, p. 57 for the omitted sentence.

³ The omitted section is quoted XVII.1.

⁴ The next sentence is quotation V.5.

⁵ Translated from an Arabic quotation of Galen's lost summary of Plato's *Republic*, written about 180, by R. Walzer, *Galen on Jews and Christians* (London: Oxford U. Press, 1949), p. 15. Used by permission of the publisher.

⁶ *Proof of the Apostolic Preaching* 96.

⁷ The later Greek version preserved in *Barlaam and Josaphat* has three races–polytheists (Chaldaeans, Greeks, and Egyptians), Jews, and Christians.

⁸ Abraham J. Malherbe, "The Structure of Athenagoras, 'Supplicatio pro christianis,'" *Vigiliae Christianae*, Vol. 23 (1969), pp. 1-20, and "Athenagoras on Christian Ethics," *Journal of Ecclesiastical History*, Vol. 20 (1969), pp. 1-5; the latter reprinted in Everett Ferguson, ed., *Christian Life: Ethics, Morality, and Discipline in the Early Church*, Studies in Early Christianity, Vol. XVI (New York: Garland, 1993), pp. 37-41.

⁹ Minucius Felix, *Octavius* 9; 30-31; Athenagoras, *Plea for Christians* 3; 31; Tertullian, *Apology* 7. See Chapter XI, at note 8.

¹⁰ XVI.4; cf. Tertullian, *Apology* 42 (quoted XVIII.7)

¹¹ Tertullian, *Apology* 40.

¹² Theophilus, *To Autolycus* 3.15; Athenagoras, *Plea for Christians* 35 (quoted XVIII.4); Tatian, *Oration* 23; Clement of Alexandria, *Instructor* 3.11.76f.; Minucius Felix 30.6; Tertullian, *On the Shows*.

¹³ Tacitus, *Annals* 15.44; also Tertullian, *Apology* 37.

¹⁴ Or, as Athenagoras says, they tell about Christians "such as they tell of their own gods"–*Plea for Christians* 32. Cf. Justin, *Apology* I, 27; II,12.

¹⁵ References in note 9. Irenaeus, *Fragment* 13 makes the connection between the "body and blood" and the charge of cannibalism. Is the fragment based on the passage quoted by Eusebius, *Church History* 5.1.14? Cf. Josephus, *Against Apion* 2.91-96 for a parallel to the charge of cannibalism against Christians.

¹⁶ See the *Letter of the Churches of Lyons and Vienne* in Eusebius, *Church*

History 5.1.14; Justin, *Apology* II,12; and Chapter XI, note 8.

[17] Cf. his *Apology* II, 12 for Christian conduct in martyrdom influencing his own conversion.

[18] W. W. Tarn, *Hellenistic Civilization* (Cleveland: World Publishing Co., 1961 reprint of the third edition, 1951), pp. 100ff.

[19] For Christian statements, see *Didache* 2 and 5; Justin, *Apology* I, 27 and 29; Athenagoras, *Plea for Christians* 35; Clement of Alexandria, *Miscellanies* 2.18.93.1; *Apocalypse of Peter* 1. Certain pagan individuals did protest against the exposure of babies, e.g. the philosopher Musonius Rufus in the first century. The rite for receiving a baby into the family is described in H. J. Rose, *Religion in Greece and Rome* (New York: Harper, 1959 reprint of the 1946 edition), pp. 30ff. A survey of different views on when what is conceived is a soul is given by George Williams, "Religious Residues and Presuppositions in the American Debate on Abortion," *Theological Studies*, Vol. 31 (1970), pp. 14-53.

[20] Famous for its date (1 B.C.) as well as for its instructions is the letter of Hilarion to his wife Alis in *Oxyrhynchus Papyri* IV:744: "If you bear a child, if it is a boy, let it live; if it is a girl, expose it."

[21] Cf. Tertullian in XVII.16 to XVI.4 for all things common "except our wives."

[22] Athenagoras, *Plea for Christians* 33. Cf. C. J. Cadoux, *The Early Church and the World* (Edinburgh: T. & T. Clark, 1925), pp. 281f., 443f., 597f.

[23] Athenagoras, *Plea for Christians* 33; Clement of Alexandria, *Miscellanies* 3.7.58; Justin, *Apology* I, 29.

[24] Origen, *Against Celsus* 1.4 and 2.5 accepts the complaint that Christians had no new *teaching* to offer. That Christian moral teaching was not original is argued by John Whittaker, "Christianity and Morality in the Roman Empire," *Vigiliae Christianae*, Vol. 33 (1979), pp. 209-225; repr. in Everett Ferguson, ed., *Christian Life: Ethics, Morality, and Discipline in the Early Church*, Studies in Early Christianity, Vol. XVI (New York: Garland, 1993), pp. 19-35.

[25] Walzer, *op. cit.*, p. 68. For another pagan view on Christian conduct see XVII.3.

[26] In addition to XVI.7 note Tatian, *Oration* 32-33 and Clement of

Alexandria, *Miscellanies* 4.8.58.3–"It is possible for the person who lives according to our teaching to philosophize even without learning, whether barbarian, Greek, or slave; whether an old man, a child, or a woman." By "philosophize" Clement meant living a life of self-control as the context shows. Cf. Tertullian, *Apology* 46.

XVII

Early Christian Acts of Mercy

"Love in deed and in truth"

Some New Testament Texts: Matthew 25:31-46; Luke 10:29-37;
Acts 4:32-37; Romans 12:6-18; 2 Corinthians 9:12-14; Galatians 6:10;
James 1:27; 2:14-17; 1 Peter 4:8-11; 1 John 3:16-18; 4:20-21.

SOURCES

ARISTIDES: They [Christians] love one another. They do not overlook the widow, and they save the orphan. The one who has ministers ungrudgingly to the one who does not have. When they see strangers, they take him under their own roof and rejoice over him as a true brother, for they do not call themselves brothers according to the flesh but according to the soul. And whenever they see one of their poor has died, each one of them according to his ability contributes ungrudgingly and they bury him. And if they hear that some are condemned or imprisoned on account of the name of their Lord, they contribute for those condemned and send to them what they need, and if it is possible, they redeem them. And if there is any that is a slave or a poor man, they fast two or three days and what they were going to set before themselves they send to them, considering themselves to give good cheer even as they were called to good cheer. (*Apology* 15)[1]

EPISTLE TO DIOGNETUS: By loving you will be an imitator of 2 God's kindness. And do not marvel that a human being is able to be an imitator of God. One is able if willing to be. For happiness is not in ruling over your neighbors, nor wishing to have more than the weak, nor being rich and powerful over those who are in a lower station. Neither is one able to imitate God by doing these things; these things are outside his majesty. But whoever accepts the burden of a neighbor—the one who wills to benefit another who is worse off in respect of those things where this

XVII.   one is better off, who takes the things received from God and distributes them to those who are in need–this one becomes a god to the ones who receive. This person is an imitator of God. (10.4-5)

3   LUCIAN OF SAMOSATA: Then Proteus was apprehended as a Christian and thrown into prison. . . . The Christians, regarding the affair as a great misfortune, set in motion every effort to rescue him. Then, when this was impossible, every other attention was paid him, not cursorily but diligently. At dawn there were to be seen waiting at the prison aged widows and orphan children, and their officials even slept inside with him, having bribed the guards. Varied meals were brought in, and their sacred words were spoken. This excellent Peregrinus, for he was still called this, was named by them "the new Socrates."
    There were some even from the cities in Asia who came, the Christians sending them from their common fund to succour, defend, and encourage the man. They exhibit extraordinary haste whenever one of them becomes such a public victim, for in no time they lavish their all. And also to Peregrinus at that time much money came from them on account of his bonds, and he made of this no little revenue. For these poor devils have altogether convinced themselves that they will be immortal and will live for all time; for which reason they despise death and many of them willingly surrender themselves. Furthermore, their first lawgiver persuaded them that they were all brothers of one another when they transgressed and denied the Greek gods and worship that sophist who was impaled on a stake and live according to his laws. Therefore they despise all things equally and consider them a common possession. They receive such teachings without any rational faith. If any charlatan and clever fellow who is able to profit by his opportunities should come among them he quickly becomes forthwith exceedingly wealthy while scoffing at simple men. (*The Death of Peregrinus* 12-13)

4   CLEMENT OF ROME: Let the strong take care of the weak; let the weak respect the strong. Let the rich minister to the poor; let the poor give thanks to God that he gave him one through whom needs might be satisfied. Let the wise manifest wisdom not in words but in good deeds. (38.2)
    We know many among us who have given themselves into bondage in order that they might ransom others. Many delivered themselves into slavery and taking their price provided food for others. (55.2)

5   IGNATIUS: Widows are not to be neglected. You, after the Lord, be their protector. . . . Do not despise male or female slaves, but neither are they to be puffed up. Rather they are to be even more slaves to the glory of God, in order that they may attain a better freedom from God. They are not to ask to be ransomed from the common treasury lest they be

found slaves of their desires. (*To Polycarp* 4)   XVII.

HERMAS: Bishops and hospitable men gladly received into their own   6
houses without hypocrisy the servants of God. The bishops always by
their ministry ceaselessly sheltered the destitute and the widows and
always conducted their lives in purity. All of these, therefore, will always
be sheltered by the Lord. (*Similitudes* 9.27.2=104.2)

Do not take an excessive share of God's created things for yourselves,   7
but share with those who lack. For some are inducing illness in their flesh
and injuring their flesh from eating too much, and the flesh of others who
do not have food is being injured because of insufficient food and their
body is being destroyed. So this lack of sharing is harmful to you who are
rich and do not share with the needy. (*Visions* 3.9.2-4=17.2-4)

Do good, and give liberally to all who are in need from the wages that   8
God gives you. Do not hesitate about to whom you should give and to
whom you should not give. Give to all. For God wishes gifts to be made
to all out of his bounties. (*Mandates* 2.4=27.4)[2]

On that day in which you fast, you shall taste nothing except bread and   9
water. Of the foods which you were going to eat, reckon how much the
food of that day when you fast was going to cost, and give the amount to
a widow or orphan or one in need. Thus you shall be humble-minded that
by your humblemindedness the soul of the one who has received may be
filled and pray on behalf of you to the Lord. (*Similitudes* 5.3.7=56.7)

Therefore instead of fields, purchase afflicted souls, as each is able. And   10
"visit widows and orphans," and do not neglect them. Spend your wealth
and all your possessions on such "fields and houses" which you received
from God. For the Master made you rich for this purpose that you might
perform these ministries for him. (*Ibid.* 1.8-9=50.8-9)

IRENAEUS: And instead of the tithes which the law commanded, the   11
Lord said to divide everything we have with the poor. And he said to love
not only our neighbors but also our enemies, and to be givers and sharers
not only with the good but also to be liberal givers toward those who take
away our possessions. (*Against Heresies* 4.14.3)

CLEMENT OF ALEXANDRIA: Do not judge who is worthy and who   12
unworthy, for it is possible for you to be mistaken in your opinion. In the
uncertainty of ignorance it is better to do good to the unworthy for the
sake of the worthy than by guarding against those who are less good not
to encounter the good. For by being sparing and trying to test those who
are well-deserving or not, it is possible for you to neglect some who are
loved by God, the penalty for which is the eternal punishment of fire. But
by helping all those in need in turn you must assuredly find some who are
able to save you before God. . . .

Contrary to other people, enlist for yourself an army without weapons,

XVII.   without war, without bloodshed, without wrath, without stain–pious old men, orphans dear to God, widows armed with gentleness, persons adorned with love. Obtain with your wealth as guards of body and soul such as these whose commander is God. (*Who Is the Rich Man that Is Saved?* 33-34)

13   All things therefore are common, and the rich are not to be avaricious. . . . And it is not right for one to live in luxury, while many are in want. How much more glorious is it to do good to many, than to live sumptuously! How much wiser to spend money on human beings than on jewels and gold! (*Instructor* 2.13.20.3 and 6)

14   He impoverishes himself on account of the perfection that is in love in order that he may never overlook a brother who happens to be in affliction, especially if he knows that he himself will bear the condition of need easier than his brother. . . . And, if, by supplying from his own indigence in order to do good, he suffers any hardship, he does not fret at this, but increases his beneficence still more. (*Miscellanies* 7.12.77.6-78.1)

15   SEXTUS: Kindness to others on behalf of God is the only suitable sacrifice to God.
      God does not hear the prayer of the one who does not hear those in need. (*Sentences* 47; 217)[3]

16   TERTULLIAN: These contributions [put into the church's treasury–see VII.3 for the context] are the trust funds of piety. For they are not spent on banquets, drinking parties, or dining clubs; but for feeding and burying the poor, for boys and girls destitute of property and parents; and further for old people confined to the house, and victims of shipwreck; and any who are in the mines, who are exiled to an island, or who are in prison merely on account of God's church–these become the wards of their confession. So great a work of love burns a brand upon us in regard to some. "See," they say, "how they love one another.". . . They are furious that we call ourselves brothers, I think, for no other reason than that among them every name of kinship is a feigning of affection. . . . But possibly we are thought less than real brothers because no tragedy cries aloud about our brotherhood, or because we are brothers in the family possessions, which with regard to you are the very things that dissolve brotherhood. So we who are united in mind and soul have no hesitation about sharing property. All things are common among us except our women. (*Apology* 39.5-11)

17   DIONYSIUS OF CORINTH: This has been your custom from the beginning, to do good to all the brethren in many ways and to send contributions to all the churches in every city, relieving the poverty of those in need and ministering to the brethren who were in the

mines. . . . Your blessed bishop Soter has not only kept up this practice but has even augmented it, ministering to the saints the bounty which has been transmitted and exhorting with blessed words the brethren who come to Rome, like a loving father to his children. (Letter to the church at Rome, quoted in Eusebius, *Church History* 4.23.10)

DISCUSSION

The gifts which Christians offered in their worship were not only the spiritual sacrifices of praise and thanksgiving but also the physical goods necessary to relieve human needs (VII.2, which is important for this chapter, and XVII.16). There are less tangible human needs which may be more important, but this study deals with the alleviation of physical want and distress.

Christians possessed a strong sense of brotherhood (e.g., XVII.1, 3, 16) and therefore a feeling of obligation concerning their mutual needs. The practical expression of the distinctive quality of the Christian life noted in the preceding chapter was to be found in the acts of brotherly love described in this chapter. The setting for the quotation from the *Apology of Aristides* (XVII.1) is the general description of the Christian life (XVI.3).

The description of the Christian life given in the *Epistle to Diognetus* is quoted in the preceding chapter (XVI.4). The passage quoted in this chapter (XVII.2) introduces a new thought–the imitation of God. That action which makes one most god-like is bestowing benefits on human beings.[4] "Philanthropy" (in its literal Greek meaning, "love for humanity") was a widely discussed attribute of God in the popular philosophy of the day. The author thus places the Christian attribute of brotherly love in relation to the divine love for human beings.

The spirit of the author of the *Epistle to Diognetus* is continued in the piety of Clement of Alexandria (XVII.12-14) and the ethical ideals of the compiler of the *Sentences of Sextus* (XVII.15). All three reflect a moderately ascetic piety, a combination of the "best" in Hellenistic philosophy with the Christian revelation, and the ideal of the truly "wise man" within the framework of orthodox Christian doctrine. The otherworldly spirit of these writers, largely drawn from the philosophical tradition and not from Christian eschatology, is not divorced from a concern for the practical needs of others. Indeed the relationship with God is made by Sextus directly dependent on benevolence to those in need (XVII.15). Clement reflects the problem whether to help the undeserving (XVII.12). His inclusive answer shows the same spirit of the instructions in Hermas (XVII.8). Church leaders who had to make the actual decisions on the use of funds could not always respond so generously.[5] Clement's entire homily *Who Is the Rich Man that Is Saved?* deals with the problem raised by Mark 10:17-31 whether a person with wealth can be saved. Clement's answer is that it is not the mere possession of wealth which excludes one from heaven. The important question is what one does with wealth, whether being attached to it or living as if having none. Detachment from the things of the world is the spirit which pervades Clement's other writings, and he has several passages which reflect the same attitude toward wealth as that expressed in this sermon.[6] The indifference and detachment are not complete. People and not things are the proper object of a Christian's concern (XVII.13; cf. 10). The same sentiment had found expression among classical authors.

An important non-Christian testimony has been included–the second-century satirist Lucian (XVII.3). Lucian was not especially well-informed about Christianity. He still associated it very much with Judaism. Proteus (or Peregrinus) is said to have learned the teaching of Christians in Palestine from their "priests and scribes" and to have become a "prophet, cult-leader, and head of the synagogue" among them (ch. 11). After Proteus' release from prison he continued to possess an ample source of income from the Christians until they rejected him for eating some forbidden food (ch. 16). This may have been pagan sacrificial meat, or Lucian may only have been thinking of Jewish food laws. Lucian does know that Christians "worship the man who was impaled in Palestine because he introduced this new mystery into the world" (ch. 11). Lucian does not have a high regard for Christians. They are uneducated and easily deceived; they accept their teachings on faith and not on reason. He introduces them as an example of how Proteus, who loved notoriety, could take them in. Whether Proteus was simply a show-off and charlatan, that is the way Lucian presents him. In so doing, he has given us a valuable picture of the sense of brotherhood among Christians and the generosity with which they rallied to one another's aid. Through his mocking description, the Christian can see an admirable picture of Christian attention to the needs of others. Taking him with the other sources, we find in Lucian an authentic picture of Christian good works. Part of that authenticity is the ease with which men of singleminded purity can be deceived. Lucian shows us the kind of problem which troubled Christian communities in dealing with itinerant teachers. The problem exercised Christians but it did not put an end to their acts of mercy. Tertullian can later testify to the astonishment (or is it the mockery of a Lucian?) with which pagans said, "See, how they love one another" (XVII.16).

Clement of Rome introduces us to the theme of mutuality (XVII.4). It frequently recurs (XVII.7, 9, 10, 12, 13). Benevolence was not a one-way street. The material gifts excited prayers of thanksgiving and intercession on behalf of the benefactors. These prayers from the beneficiaries would help in saving one before God. Hermas expresses the interchange pointedly:

> The poor by interceding on behalf of the rich
> before the Lord supply what is lacking to their wealth,
> and the rich by ministering to the poor in their needs
> aid their souls.[7]

Another kind of mutuality is expressed in the *Didache*:

> You shall not turn away the one in need, but you
> shall share everything with your brother and not say
> that it is your own. For if you are partners in immortal
> things how much more are you in temporal things?[8]

The Christian is to "lay up treasures in heaven" (XVII.10).

The quotation from Irenaeus (XVII.11) comes from a context contrasting commands of the Old Testament with those given by Christ. The emphasis is upon the superior requirements of the new covenant. One is not limited to tithing, but is to share all he has with one in need (cf. XVII.14).[9] The idea of all things being in common finds fairly frequent expression in the texts (XVI.5, XVII.3, 13, 16). This was apparently not absolute. The same passages speak of giving out of what one has; hence the thought must be that all possessions were *regarded* as common and so to be used for others as need required.

There was a common treasury, or common fund, into which contributions were made. And we would like to give emphasis in this study to what was done with these church funds. There were many individual acts of kindness, commended or described in our texts (XVII.2, 4, 7-15).[10] This was one aspect of the personal Christian life which was so distinctive in the ancient world. And, there were other corporate expressions of relief for the needy, notably in the love feasts (Ch. XI). But we want to note here what was done with the contributions to the church.

Justin and Tertullian (VII.2 and XVII.16) speak to this point specifically. Dionysius (XVII.17) speaks of what was done by the Roman church, a church especially famous for its charity.[11] Hermas (XVII.6) and Ignatius (XVII.5) speak concerning the official duties of overseers of the church. Polycarp himself gave official instructions to the elders along the same lines (XIV.6). What was said surely applied to the personal qualities of the elders or bishops, but in their context these statements bear on what they will be doing as pastors, how they will be acting as administrators of church funds. Similarly, many of the passages about personal benefactions speak of things that might be performed through the church (XVII.10, 12, 14).

Not a great deal is said about the use of contributions for other than benevolent purposes–for example, the support of Christian ministers.

The *Didache* has the principal early reference:

> Every true prophet who wishes to settle among you
> is worthy of his food. Likewise the true teacher also is
> worthy, like the workman, of his food. Therefore you
> shall take every first fruit of the winepress and the
> threshing floor, of cattle and sheep, and you shall give
> the first fruits to the prophets, for they are your high
> priests. But if you do not have a prophet, give to the
> poor. (13.1-4)

Lucian's *Death of Peregrinus* (XVII.3) speaks of the support for a Christian teacher in describing the career of such an imposter as the author of the *Didache* warns about (chs. 11-12). In general the second-century sources say little about church funds for the support of the church itself and its leaders.[12] Many church officials had independent sources of income, and the church's own expenses at this stage were small. A major reason why more information is not given may be that our most explicit sources about the use of church funds are the Apologists (VII.2; XVII.1 and 16), and they can make the most favorable impression for Christianity by calling attention to its benevolent activities. This is not to say that their accounts are unreliable but that they are selective.

If one takes a composite look at the texts, an impressive list can be drawn up of the types of individuals who were recipients of Christian assistance. Aid was extended to the following classes: the poor, the aged, widows, the sick,[13] victims of shipwreck, exiles, the imprisoned, laborers in the mines.[14]

The slaves who were condemned to work in the government mines were the most unfortunate of the ancient world's outcasts. Prisoners of war, criminals, and sometimes Christians were sent to the mines.[15] The labor was extremely hard, the hours long, and the working and living conditions incredibly hard. Few lived long under the circumstances.

A notable act of benevolence was burying the dead. One of the great horrors of the ancient world was to die and not receive proper burial. The poor often banded together in burial societies and contributed small sums monthly into a common fund which was used to care for the funeral expenses of members.[16] Many associations of the better off also assumed this duty. Nearly all such associations had some religious character. Membership was a kind of burial insurance. The church early assumed this responsibility for its poorer members.[17]

Although the church took no stand on slavery as an economic institution, it was aware of the circumstances of slaves. Domestic servants might have a rather good life, if the owner was kind. Not all slaves were so fortunate. Sometimes the church (XVII.5) or individual Christians (XVII.4) acted to secure the freedom of slaves.[18] Ignatius cautions against this and wants proper safeguards. But the early church apparently was not totally indifferent to the plight of slaves, even if its social sensitivity about slavery was not so great as it was to become.

Hospitality to travelers is another virtue which finds frequent expression in Christian sources (VII.2; XVII.1, 6). Inns were generally not desirable places–either in quality of accommodations or in moral climate.[19] Christians were often traveling, especially teachers and messengers of the churches. The *Didache* gives explicit instructions about the treatment of traveling Christians who come seeking hospitality (chs. 11-12); apparently many communities had unfortunate experiences of being defrauded. And the problem of false teachers was acute in the first and second centuries. But for all the danger there is an impressive testimony to the way in which Christians cared for their own. The prominence of hospitality in connection with church officers may be related to the practice of meeting in the houses of well-to-do Christians. Such would likely become the bishops of the church–having the education, the leadership experience, and the resources which would be desired in one who was to represent the church. Naturally the homes of such men became also the place of accommodation for fellow-believers who came to town.

Christians had a special concern for their brethren who were imprisoned for their faith (XVII.1, 3, 16). They sought their freedom first of all. Next they cared for their physical needs. The prison system of the ancient world was not designed for the long-term internment of prisoners, as today. If one were to have even the bare necessities of life, he was often dependent on outside help. Finally, Christians encouraged those condemned for their faith to martyrdom.[20]

It is to be expected that the sources would say more about Christian acts of mercy to fellow-Christians. The church would have felt its first obligation here. But there is nothing to indicate an arbitrary limitation and indeed much which implies that non-Christians were aided. The very question concerning aid for the unworthy suggests such an extension. This was of the essence of doing good to one's enemies (XVII.11). It was better to err on the side of liberality (XVII.12).

These acts of benevolence laid the basis for the social legislation of the Christian Empire and kingdoms later. Early Christianity was not so socially uninvolved as it is often pictured.

BIBLIOGRAPHY

Countryman, L. William. *The Rich Christian in the Church of the Early Empire*. New York: Edwin Mellen, 1980.

Grant, Robert M. "The Organization of Alms." *Early Christianity and Society: Seven Studies*. San Francisco: Harper & Row, 1977. Pp. 124-145.

Hamman, A. and Quéré-Jaulmes, F. *Riches et pauvres dans l'église ancienne.* Lettres Chrétiennes, 6. Paris, 1962.

Harnack, Adolf. *The Mission and Expansion of Christianity.* New York: Harper Torchbooks, 1962 reprint of 1908 edition. Pp. 147-198.

Pearson, Birger A. "Philanthropy in the Greco-Roman World and in Early Christianity." *The Emergence of the Christian Religion.* Harrisburg: Trinity Press International, 1997. Pp. 186-213.

Phan, P. C. *Social Thought.* Collegeville: Liturgical Press, 1985.

NOTES

[1] See XVI.3 for the context and Chapter XVI, note 1 for the papyrus from which this is translated.

[2] This passage is quoted in *Didache* 1.5. The further quotation in 1.6, usually translated "Let your alms sweat in your hands until you know to whom you should give," appears to modify the thought; but the passage probably should be understood as saying, "Let your almsgiving bring the sweat of diligent labor to your hands until you know that it is to God to whom you are giving"–Steven L. Bridge, "To Give or Not to Give? Deciphering the Saying of *Didache* 1.6," *Journal of Early Christian Studies,* Vol. 5 (1997), pp. 555-568.

[3] Henry Chadwick, *The Sentences of Sextus,* in *Texts and Studies,* Vol. V (Cambridge, 1959), pp. 107-162, has established that the compiler of these gnomic maxims was a Christian, and he suggests a date of A.D. 180-210.

[4] Closely parallel to the *Epistle to Diognetus* is the quotation ascribed to a *Teaching of Peter* (perhaps the same as the second-century *Preaching of Peter*) cited in W. Schneemelcher, *New Testament Apocrypha,* Vol. II (Louisville: Westminster/John Knox, 1992), p. 37.

[5] Cf. the instructions in *Didache* 11-13.

[6] *Miscellanies* 1.4 and 4.5-6.

[7] *Similitudes* 2.8=51.8, in which the whole passage elaborates the thought. Carolyn Osiek, *Rich and Poor in the Shepherd of Hermas* (Washington: Catholic Biblical Association, 1983). In Greece and Rome the poor man's return to his benefactor was honor–A. R. Hands, *Charities and Social Aid in Greece and Rome* (London: Thames and Hudson, 1968), pp. 35, 49ff.; this book is useful for giving perspective to early Christian

acts of charity.

[8] Chapter 4.8.

[9] Cf. *Against Heresies* 4.18.2 and *Proof of the Apostolic Preaching* 96; see Chapter VII, note 19.

[10] For instructions to perform such good deeds see Hermas, *Mandates* 8.10=38.10; 5 Ezra 2.15-32 (the designation of the Christian addition to the beginning of 4 Ezra, extant only in a Latin version).

[11] Already noted by Ignatius, *Romans*, preface.

[12] The passage quoted by Eusebius in his *Church History* 5.28.10 (reproduced in our XV.10) suggests that Natalius' fixed stipend was an innovation, but the size of it may have been the cause for criticism. Origen, *Against Celsus* 3.9 is relevant, as is the Pseudo-Clementine *Homilies* 3.71.

[13] A notable case was Christian ministry during a third-century plague at Alexandria, reported by Eusebius, *Church History* 7.22. See A. Harnack, *Mission and Expansion* (New York: Harper, 1962), pp. 120ff. for Christian care of the sick.

[14] An extended list of those to whom material assistance was given, and what kind of assistance was to be given, that can be gathered from the Apostolic Fathers alone is given by Wesley Lee Gerig, "The Social Ethics of the Apostolic Fathers" (unpublished doctoral dissertation at the State University of Iowa, 1965), pp. 211ff. Traditional objects of charity are noted in *Acts of Peter* 8 and 17. A striking addition to our list is the provision in *Didache* 12 for the church to provide suitable employment for a person willing to work who settles in its midst.

[15] In addition to XVII.16 and 17 see Hippolytus, *Refutation of All Heresies* 9.7.

[16] George LaPiana, "Foreign Groups in Rome During the First Centuries of the Empire," *Harvard Theological Review*, Vol. 20 (1927), pp. 241ff., 271ff.; Marcus N. Tod, *Sidelights on Greek History* (Oxford: Basil Blackwell, 1932), pp. 92f.; W. R. Halliday, *The Pagan Background of Early Christianity* (London, 1925), chapter II.

[17] XVII.1, 16. Hippolytus, *Refutation of All Heresies* 9.7 refers to a cemetery of the Roman church at the beginning of the third century which Callistus, as a deacon, supervised. One of the Roman catacombs still bears his name. The catacombs were burial sites.

[18]See also Hermas, *Mandates* 8.10=38.10; cf. later the *Apostolic Constitutions* 4.9.2. Carolyn Osiek, "The Ransom of Captives: Evolution of a Tradition," *Harvard Theological Review*, Vol. 74 (1981), pp. 365-386; repr. in Everett Ferguson, ed., *Acts of Piety in the Early Church*, Studies in Early Christianity, Vol. XVII (New York: Garland, 1993), pp. 311-332; J. A. Harrill, *The Manumission of Slaves in Early Christianity* (Tübingen: Mohr/Siebeck, 1995); idem, "Ignatius, *Ad Polycarp* 4.3 and the Corporate Manumission of Christian Slaves," *Journal of Early Christian Studies*, Vol. 1 (1993), pp. 107-142; repr. in Everett Ferguson, ed., *Christianity and Society: The Social World of Early Christianity*, Recent Studies in Early Christianity, Vol. 1 (New York: Garland, 1999), pp. 279-314.

[19] W. C. Firebough, *The Inns of Greece and Rome* (Chicago, 1923); John Bell Matthews, "Hospitality and the New Testament Church" (Princeton Theological Seminary Dissertation, 1964), pp. 21-28; Abraham J. Malherbe, *Social Aspects of Early Christianity*, second ed. (Minneapolis: Fortress, 1983), pp. 92-112.

[20] As a sampling of texts about Christian attention to martyrs in prison, note *Passion of Perpetua and Felicitas* 3 and 9 (1.2 and 3.1); Eusebius, *Church History* 5.1.61; 5.2.1ff.; Tertullian, *To the Martyrs* 1 (2).

XVIII

Christians and Military Service

"Love your enemies"

Some New Testament Texts: Luke 3:14; Acts 10:1-33; Matthew 5:38-48; Romans 12:14 - 13:10.

SOURCES

JUSTIN: We who formerly murdered one another, not only do not war against our enemies but, in order not to lie or deceive our judges, gladly die confessing Christ. (*Apology* I, 39)[1]   XVIII.1

We who were full of war and murder of one another and all wickedness have each changed his warlike instruments–swords into plows and spears into agricultural implements. (*Dialogue* 110)   2

TATIAN: I do not want to rule, I do not wish to be rich, I reject military command, I have hated fornication. (*Oration* 11)   3

ATHENAGORAS: Since we consider that to see a man put to death is next to killing him, we have renounced such spectacles [gladiator contests]. How then can we, who do not look lest we be stained with guilt and defilement, commit murder? (*Plea for Christians* 35; see also 34).   4

TERTULLIAN: Letters of Marcus Aurelius, that most venerable of emperors, testify that the drought in Germany was broken by rain obtained through the prayers of Christians at that time in his army. (*Apology* 5.6)   5

We are but of yesterday, and we have filled everything of yours–cities, islands, forts, towns, marketplaces, the army itself, tribes, councils, the palace, senate, forum. We have left you the temples only! For what war [against Rome] were we not fit and ready even if we were not equal in   6

XVIII.   forces, we who are willing to be slaughtered, were it not that according to our doctrine greater permission is given to be killed than to kill. (*Ibid.* 37.4-5)

7   We live together with you in this world, not apart from the forum, nor meatmarket, nor baths, shops, factories, inns, nor your market days and affairs of business. We sail with you, fight with you in the army, we farm and trade with you. (*Ibid.* 42.2-3)

8   To begin with the real basis of the military crown, I think we must first inquire whether military service is proper at all for Christians. . . . Shall it be held lawful to make an occupation of the sword when the Lord proclaims that he who makes use of the sword shall perish by the sword? And shall the son of peace take part in the battle when it is not proper for him even to go to law? . . . Of course, if faith comes later to those already occupied with military service, the case is different . . . . Yet at the same time, when faith has been acknowledged and sealed [at baptism], there must be either an immediate abandonment of the army, as has been done by many; or there must be all sorts of quibbling in order not to offend against God, and that is not allowed even outside of military service; or, at last, for God there must be the suffering which a citizen-faith has equally accepted. For military service promises neither impunity from wrongs nor exemption from martyrdom. (*On the Crown* 11)

9   But now inquiry is made about this point, whether a believer is able to turn himself to military service, and whether the soldier may be admitted unto the faith, even the ordinary soldier or the lower ranks, to whom there is no necessity for taking part in sacrifices or capital punishments? There is no agreement between the divine and the human oath, the standard of Christ and the standard of the devil, the camp of light and the camp of darkness. One soul cannot be under obligation to two, God and Caesar. . . . But how will a Christian war, indeed how will he serve even in peace without a sword, which the Lord has taken away? . . . The Lord, in disarming Peter, unbelted every soldier. (*On Idolatry* 19)

10   HIPPOLYTUS: A soldier of the government must be told not to execute men; if he should be ordered to do it, he shall not do it. He must be told not to take the military oath. If he will not agree, let him be rejected [from baptism]. A military governor or a magistrate of a city who wears the purple, either let him desist or let him be rejected. If a catechumen or a baptized Christian wishes to become a soldier, let him be cast out. For he has despised God. (*Apostolic Tradition* 16.17-19)[2]

11   CELSUS: If everyone should do the same as you, nothing would prevent the emperor from being left alone and deserted, and the affairs of the earth would come into the hands of the most lawless and the wildest barbarians. (Quoted by Origen, *Against Celsus* 8.68)

ORIGEN: For if, as Celsus says, "everyone should do the same" as I, it   XVIII.12
is evident that even the barbarians, having come to the word of God, will
be most law abiding and civilized, and every religion will be destroyed
except that of the Christians, which will prevail. And it alone some day
will prevail as the word more and more holds sway over human souls.
(Ibid.)
    If all the Romans, according to the supposition of Celsus, are converted,   13
they will by their prayers prevail over their enemies. Rather, they will not
war in the first place, since they will be protected by that divine power
which promised to save five whole cities for the sake of fifty righteous
persons. (Ibid. 8.70)
    We also by our prayers destroy all the demons, the ones who cause wars,   14
violate oaths, and disturb the peace, and we are more help to those who
rule than those who seem to be fighting his battles. . . . We fight better
on behalf of the king. Indeed we do not fight at his side, even if he should
command it, but we fight on his behalf, organizing our own army of piety
through our petitions to God. (Ibid. 8.73)
    Christians benefit their country more than other people because they   15
train up citizens and teach piety toward the God of the universe. (Ibid.
8.74)
    Celsus urges us to take up the rule of the country if this should be   16
necessary for the preservation of law and religion. But we recognize in
each city another native constitution, created by the word of God, and
we exhort those powerful in word and experienced in a wholesome life to
rule over the churches. . . . Christians decline public offices not in order
to escape these duties but in order to keep themselves for a more divine
and necessary service in the church of God for the salvation of human
beings. (Ibid. 8.75)

DISCUSSION

    Early second-century literature gives no direct evidence in regard to
Christian participation in military service. The general statements which
do occur imply a negative attitude. They reflect the Christian abhorrence
of bloodshed[3] and a general Christian affirmation about peace.
    Both of our passages from Justin (XVIII.1, 2) occur in contexts where
he quotes the famous peace passage of Micah 4:14 (=Isaiah 2:1-4).[4]
Peace and not war is the ideal and goal of the Christian dispensation.
Tatian's spirituality was world-denying and his declaration against
military command (XVIII.3) is in a context affirming freedom against
fate, so generalizations cannot be made from it, but military duty is in bad
company. Athenagoras (XVIII.4) is rebutting the charge of ritual murder
committed in Christian gatherings (for which see chapter XVI on the
pagan slanders about Christians). His reply is that Christians so abhor
bloodshed as not even to be allowed to attend the gladiatorial contests.[5]

This shows the typical rigorist Christian attitude on morality, but may or may not be relevant to the actual presence of Christians in the army.

Only in the early 170s do we find the first explicit evidence since apostolic times to the presence of Christians in the military service (XVIII.5). The evidence concerns an incident involving the "Thundering Legion" while on campaign on the Danube frontier. A drought threatened the army, and the soldiers prayed for rain. A thunder storm frightened the barbarians away and brought relief to the Roman troops. The incident is reported by pagan authors, who ascribed the supposed miracle to pagan deities.[6] The earliest Christian reference comes from Claudius Apolinarius, quoted by Eusebius.[7] Apolinarius addressed an apology to the emperor Marcus Aurelius not long after the incident. He is wrong in his details,[8] but he is a witness to the firm conviction of Christians that it was the prayers of Christian soldiers which saved the day for Rome. The legion concerned had been recruited from Melitene, in Armenia, later a strong Christian region. The presence of Christians in the legion, therefore, seems certain. Later the Christians elaborated the story so that the whole legion was reported to have been Christian, but this has no claim to credibility. It was a famous story and the basic incident was historical. Its importance for this study is its indication of the presence of at least some Christians fighting in the Roman army and apparently with the approval or acceptance of their fellow-believers.

Tertullian provides further incidental information about Christians in the army (XVIII.6, 7).[9] His statements occur in the context of an apology addressed to the Roman authorities. These statements are testimonies to the way Christianity had permeated all of society. At this point he registers neither approval nor disapproval but simply records the fact. That was to his apologetic purposes, and there was no need for him to declare his full mind on the matter.

Elsewhere Tertullian shows what his real feelings were (XVIII.8, 9), and the probable chronology of his writings is against there being any change in his attitude. Indeed his very treatises that argue against the possibility of a Christian serving in the army are an evidence that Christians did so, even had joined the army after conversion.

The occasion for the work *On the Crown* was the refusal of a Christian soldier to wear a laurel crown in a procession on the grounds that it was a sign of idolatry. A military tribunal imprisoned him. While he awaited martyrdom, adverse criticisms were made against him (perhaps by Christians) for a headstrong and rash action. Tertullian defends the man as more faithful than his brothers in the army who thought they could serve two masters (ch. 1). The treatise then takes up the question whether it is lawful for a Christian to wear the laurel crown. In the passage quoted Tertullian turns to argue against the lawfulness of warfare at all for Christians. If a Christian cannot even sue in court to defend his rights, how can he take the sword to do so?

In *On Idolatry* Tertullian seems to be engaging in a real debate, answering real arguments which had been put forward. The support for the presence of Christians in the military, cited by Tertullian, came from the Bible: Joshua led a "line of march," Israel engaged in wars, soldiers received from John the Baptist instructions about their conduct, and the centurion Cornelius became a believer (ch. 19). We do not hear elsewhere for the early period other arguments which may have been used. Social and cultural considerations would come later, but the first Christians in the military made a simple and unreflective appeal to Biblical examples without dealing with the Biblical teachings.

Tertullian's reply on the Scriptural level is that Jesus had forbidden the military occupation in his words spoken at his arrest (Matthew 26:52; John 18:10-11). Peter had taken a sword and struck off the ear of the servant of the high priest. Jesus told him to put up his sword. Tertullian interpreted the declaration by Jesus as a denunciation of any use of the sword, a disarming of every soldier. In a more fundamental way Tertullian sees a basic incompatibility between the profession of a soldier and the profession of a Christian. It is a matter of trying to serve two masters. This double allegiance is an impossibility, and Tertullian is at his rhetorical best when he can flourish antitheses (XVIII. 9).[10]

Tertullian's views were often highly individual, but on the question of a Christian serving in the army his thought appears to have been in harmony with that of the other leading thinkers and spokesmen of Christianity at his time.

The weightiest theological case for Christian non-involvement in military service came from Origen. His fullest discussion occurs in his apologetic writing *Against Celsus*. About the same time the "Thundering Legion" was praying for rain, Celsus was criticizing Christians because they held themselves aloof from the state and the necessary tasks of society. Specifically, he reproaches Christians because they will not fight in the emperor's armies and so defend the state from its barbarian enemies. Apparently Celsus did not know of any Christians in the army and understands the rejection of military service to be a matter of principle with them. On most points Celsus, although prejudiced, was reasonably well informed about the Christianity he writes against. Origen, in his answer, gives his own defense of Christianity, but he writes as the defender of the church at large. Although some of the arguments may be original, what he is defending is not original with him. Thus it is notable that he does not answer Celsus by saying, "You are wrong; look, here are the Christians who do fight for the empire." Rather Origen accepts the accuracy of what Celsus says and seeks to justify the Christian abstention from military service. If Origen knows of Christian soldiers, he chooses to ignore the fact. For him, the Christian position is a consistent pacifism.

Origen, like Tertullian, had to reckon with the wars of Israel in the Old Testament. He explains that the Jews had a "land and form of government of their own," which required that they fight their enemies and execute criminals. Now the Gospel of Jesus Christ has supplanted the law, and the Jewish state has been destroyed.[11] Christians cannot slay their enemies. He cites the text, "sell your tunic and buy a sword" (Luke 22:36), if taken literally, as an example of "the letter kills."[12]

Since Celsus was a pagan, Origen's main task was to answer objections which came from the standpoint of a champion of classical civilization. Clearly, one of Celsus' prime criticisms of Christianity was the way it held itself aloof from the affairs of society. Origen's vindication depends on the notion of a divine society, independent of the political state. Origen initially takes Celsus' "everyone" (XVIII.11, 12) literally and shows that there will be no barbarian problem if all have become Christians. And Origen sees the progress of the Gospel as a herald of this time. Further, if all the Romans are Christians (XVIII.13), they will be protected by the divine power that promised to save the five cities of the plain at the intercession of Abraham (Genesis 18:22-23). Christians "will not war" at all. Until such a time as the general acceptance of the Christian faith, Christians "fight" for the emperor in a different way. Instead of fighting for the emperor with physical weapons or leading an army, as Celsus calls on the Christians to do, they fight with the spiritual weapons of prayer and intercessions (XVIII.14). Origen seems to imply a distinction between what Christians may do and what unbelievers may do. Piety is a better help than that rendered by soldiers (ch. 73). Indeed, paganism recognized this principle, for the priests were exempt from military service so that they could serve the gods with unstained hands. For Origen the whole church is this holy priesthood, who by their prayers aid those who are fighting in a righteous cause. The Christians' part in public affairs is fulfilled by prayer and righteous living. In this way they overcome the demonic forces which are behind all wickedness. Christians also benefit their country in disciplining citizens and teaching godliness (XVIII.15). Origen, furthermore, justifies an abstaining from all public office in favor of leadership in the church (XVIII.16). The ministry of the church is a better and more necessary service to human well-being.

The *Apostolic Tradition* of Hippolytus contains a long list of occupations and circumstances in life that were forbidden to Christians. Some of these we would expect: the prostitute and panderer. Some may occasion surprise: the teacher. The reason here was that the basic curriculum for children involved teaching the basic texts of polytheism. The situation was marginal, for one might teach in such a way as to avoid contamination, so the provision is added that if one has no other way to make a living he should be forgiven. The charioteer, the gladiator, and the pagan priest are to be rejected from baptism unless they cease their occupation. The instructions about the magistrate and the military man fall last in this list (XVIII.10).

Hippolytus' instructions suggest the possibility of making certain distinctions. A difference was recognized between converts made out of the army and Christians entering the army. The former, if they can stay in without taking again the military oath and without shedding blood, presumably could remain in the army.[13] The problem with the military oath was that it was sworn by the gods of paganism, particularly by the genius (the life principle) of the emperor. Tertullian (XVIII.8) sees three alternatives before the military convert: (1) immediate abandonment of his profession, (2) compromising of conscience, or (3) martyrdom. He did not see any hope of one staying in the army without compromise on sacrifices, oaths, bloodshed, execution of penalties, and other things. Hippolytus forbids the one already a Christian or undergoing instruction for baptism to volunteer for military service. Since the Roman army under the Empire was largely raised from volunteers,[14] there would not have been many occasions where a Christian was forced to choose between military service and defiance of the government. One might not be able to do much about a situation in which he already found himself, but a Christian was not deliberately to seek trouble.

A second distinction seems to be allowed between what might be called "police duties" and bloodshed. Certain functions now performed by other public servants, such as fire fighting and road building, were the responsibility of military organizations in the Empire. Tertullian implies a difference between peacetime and wartime service, but he rejects both. Hippolytus seems to allow the possibility of a soldier not being called on to perform an execution; otherwise his exception would be meaningless. The military calling as such, then, did not exclude from baptism, but the activities that often went with it did.

Hippolytus, moreover, makes a distinction between officers and common soldiers. Magistrates and officers must resign before being admitted to baptism. Presumably their official capacities did not allow for possible exemptions from tasks considered inconsistent with the Christian calling. They would be responsible for the orders to execution. And their role in public affairs was inextricably bound up with idolatrous sacrifices, oaths, and ceremonies.

These distinctions bring us to the core of the early Christian rejection of military service. The question is closely bound up with the early Christian separation from the world and what was meant by it. How much of that separation was cultural and how much was theological? Various explanations have been offered for the anti-militarism of the ancient church: the idolatry inherent in the army of an Empire held together by the worship of Rome and the emperor; the cultural isolation of the early church; the incompatibility of warfare with Christian ethics. The problem of idolatry was real and was recognized by the authors cited.

However, that does not seem to be the real reason for their objections, and that could at least in some cases be avoided. The cultural isolation again is true for the formative periods of the church. Christianity began within Judaism, and one of the privileges of the Jews was exemption from military duty.[15] As the church reached out into the non-Jewish world, it drew its recruits from the underprivileged and those segments of society which ordinarily were not called on for military service. Thus a pattern of non-involvement was established before there was ever a question of its ethical propriety raised on a large scale. With the growth of the church and its increasing cultural accommodation, converts were won from the military, and some Christians went into the army as a matter of course. This situation raised the ethical and theological issue. The numbers initially were few. The arguments advanced soon touched on most of the points that have since been debated in the history of Christian ethics. In that period, as often since, the leaders of thought and the writers voiced opposition whereas many of the rank and file Christians did in fact serve in the army. The opposition of the theologians was to killing. The sayings of Jesus and the whole of his teaching were felt to be contrary to active participation in warfare. The ones who did serve tended to be the ones confronted with the concrete issue, and they decided on pragmatic rather than theoretical grounds what should be done. The evidence is that initially the numbers of Christians in the army were few. This can be sustained in spite of the fact that most of what we hear is from those who opposed participation. But the numbers grew steadily in the third century, and when Constantine recognized the church in the fourth century the situation altered radically. Finally Theodosius II in 416 decreed that only Christians could be in the army, for he wanted divine favor to rest with the armies of the empire against the barbarian threat.

BIBLIOGRAPHY

Bainton, Roland H. *Christian Attitudes Toward War and Peace*. New York: Abingdon, 1960.

Cadbury, Henry J. "The Basis of Early Christian Anti-Militarism," *Journal of Biblical Literature*, Vol. 37 (1918), pp. 66-94.

Cadoux, C. J. *The Early Christian Attitude to War*. London: Headley Bros., 1919; repr. New York: Seabury, 1982.

Campenhausen, Hans von. "Christians and Military Service in the Early Church." *Tradition and Life in the Church*. London: Collins, 1968. Pp. 160-170.

Harnack, Adolf von. *Militia Christi: The Christian Religion and the Military in the First Three Centuries*. Philadelphia: Fortress, 1981.

Helgelund, John, Robert J. Daly, and J. Patout Burns. *Christians and the Military*. Minneapolis: Fortress, 1985.

Hornus, Jean-Michel. *It Is Not Lawful for Me to Fight*. Scottdale: Herald, 1980.

NOTES

[1] Cf. selection XVI.5.

[2] Quoted from Gregory Dix, *The Treatise on the Apostolic Tradition of St. Hippolytus of Rome* (Reissued with corrections; London: S.P.C.K., 1968), pp. 26f.

[3] Cf. the *Acts of John* 36 for "warmongers" in a list of those who go to eternal torment. Statements against war include Athenagoras, *Resurrection* 19; Tatian, *Oration* 1; 8; 19; Justin, *Apology* II, 5. Cf. Pseudo-Clement, *Recognitions (Ascents of James)* 1.71.1, "Because of their fear of God, they [disciples] allowed themselves to be slain by the few rather than slay others."

[4] The passage is quoted in reference to the peacefulness of Christianity in Irenaeus, *Against Heresies* 4.34.4 and Origen, *Against Celsus* 5.33. Cf. also Justin's statements in *Apology* I, 14 quoted XVI.5.

[5] References to Christian opinion about gladiatorial contests are given in Chapter XVI, note 12.

[6] Dio Cassius 71.8-10 (72.14) gives the story of the battle in detail and attributes the salvation of the Roman army to an Egyptian magician. The *Scriptores Historiae Augustae*, "Marcus Aurelius Antoninus" 24.4 has the emperor's prayers bring a thunderbolt against the enemy and rain for his thirsty men. The Column of Marcus Aurelius in Rome portrays the rain god showering rain on the Roman army.

[7] *Church History* 5.5.4.

[8] The legion had its name "Thundering" before this time and did not acquire it as a result of the incident.

[9] *To the Nations* 1.1 is closely parallel; see also *To Scapula* 4.

[10] *On Patience* 3 parallels the contrasts in *On Idolatry* 19.

[11] *Against Celsus* 7.26. Origen also interpreted the wars of the Old Testament as figures of spiritual wars, since carnal wars are "no longer to be waged by us"–*Homily on Joshua* 15.

[12] *Homily on Leviticus* 7.5.

[13] Clement of Alexandria seems to contemplate a convert remaining in the army–*Exhortation* 10.100; *Instructor* 2.11.117. Elsewhere he speaks negatively of war–*Instructor* 1.12.98, 2.4.42; *Miscellanies* 4.8.61; *Exhortation* 11.116. The Utrecht Coptic papyrus of the *Acts of Andrew* (W. Schneemelcher, *New Testament Apocrypha* Vol. II [Louisville: Westminster/John Knox, 1992], pp. 127-128) has a youth, when he is converted, take off his military uniform. There were in the third and early fourth centuries military martyrs; a notable case is studied against the background of earlier teaching in the church by Peter Brock, "Why Did St. Maximilian Refuse to Serve in the Roman Army?" *Journal of Ecclesiastical History*, Vol. 45 (1994), pp. 195-209.

[14] H. M. D. Parker, *The Roman Legions* (Oxford: Clarendon Press, 1928), pp. 45, 185; R.E. Smith, *Service in the Post-Marian Roman Army* (Manchester University Press, 1958), pp. 44ff., 72. Later there was an obligation on sons of veterans to follow the military profession.

[15] Josephus, *Antiquities* 14.204, 226, and elsewhere.

XIX

Women in the Early Church

"Adorned with good works that are fitting for women who profess godliness"

Some New Testament Texts: Luke 8:1-3; Acts 2:17-18; 21:9; 9:36;
16:15, 40; 18:26; Romans 16:2, 12; 1 Corinthians 11:5; 14:33-40;
Ephesians 5:21-33; Philippians 4:2-3; 1 Timothy 2:1-15; 5:1-16;
Titus 2:3-5; 1 Peter 3:1-6; Revelation 2:20-23.

SOURCES

CLEMENT OF ROME: You gave instructions to the wives to perform   XIX.1
everything in a blameless and pure conscience and to be properly
affectionate to their own husbands. You taught them to fulfill their
household duties honorably and to live by the rule of submission, being
altogether prudent. (1.3)

POLYCARP: Teach your wives to walk in the faith given to them, in   2
love, and in purity, to be altogether truly affectionate to their own
husbands, to love all others equally in all chastity, and to bring up their
children in the discipline of the fear of God. Teach the widows to be
prudent in the faith of the Lord, to pray unceasingly for all, to be far from
all slander, evil speaking, false witness, love of money, and every evil, and
to recognize that they are an altar of God. (*Philippians* 4.2-3)

CLEMENT OF ALEXANDRIA: It is possible for man and woman   3
equally to share in perfection. . . .
  The wise woman then would first choose to persuade her husband to be
a partner with her in the things that lead to true happiness. If that should
be impossible, alone she should be diligent in virtue, being obedient
to her husband so as to do nothing against his will except in regard
to those things that are considered to make a difference to virtue and
salvation. . . .
Marriage then that is fulfilled according to reason is sanctified, if the
union is subjected to God . . . . The truly happy marriage must be judged

by neither wealth nor beauty but by virtue. (*Miscellanies* 4.19, 20)

4   TERTULLIAN: What a marriage is that between two believers! They have one hope, one desire, one way of life, the same religion. They are brother and sister, both fellow servants, not divided in flesh or in spirit — truly "two in one flesh," for where there is one flesh there is also one spirit. They pray together; they prostrate themselves together; they carry out fasts together. They instruct one another and exhort one another. Side by side they are present in the church of God and at the banquet of God; they are side by side in difficulties and in consolations. Neither ever hides things from the other; neither avoids the other; neither is a grief to the other. Freely the sick are visited and the poor are sustained. Without anxiety, misgiving, or hindrance from the other, they give alms, attend the sacrifices [of the church], perform their daily duties [of piety]. They are not secretive about making the sign of the cross; they are not fearful in greetings; they are not silent in giving benedictions. They sing psalms and hymns one to the other; they challenge each other as to who better sings to God. When Christ sees and hears such things, he rejoices. (*To His Wife* 2.8)

5   JUSTIN: Many men and sixty- and seventy-year old women, who were disciples of Christ from childhood, remain (sexually) pure. And I vow to show such from every race of humanity.

We do not marry initially except for the bringing up of children, or if we renounce marriage, we live in complete chastity. (*Apology* I, 15; 29)

6   ATHENAGORAS: You would find among us many men and women who have lived to old age unmarried in the hope rather of living together with God. (*Plea for the Christians* 33)

7   ACTS OF PAUL AND THECLA: Thecla said to Paul, "I will cut my hair short and follow you wherever you go.". . .

Thecla entered with [Tryphaena] and rested in her house for eight days, instructing her in the word of God, so that many of her maidservants believed; and there was great joy in the house.

Thecla said to Paul, "I am going to Iconium." And Paul said, "Go and teach the word of God." So Tryphaena sent with her much clothing and gold, so that she could leave it for the ministry of the poor. . . .

Having testified to these things [to Theokleia], she departed for Seleucia, and after enlightening many with the word of God she died with a good sleep. (25; 39; 41; 43)

8   MARTYRS OF LYONS: Blandina was filled with such power that those who took turns torturing her in every way from morning to evening became weary and tired. They acknowledged that they were defeated,

since they had nothing further that they could do to her. They marvelled that she was still breathing, for her entire body was broken and torn open, and they testified that one kind of torture was sufficient to take her life, without so many and such grievous tortures. Nevertheless, this blessed woman, like a noble athlete, gained renewed strength in her confession. Her recovery, refreshment, and insensibility to her sufferings came from saying, "I am a Christian, and among us there is nothing wicked." . . .

Blandina was hung on a stake and exposed as food for the wild beasts that were released. Her hanging in the form of a cross, by being seen and by her intense prayer, inspired great enthusiasm in her fellow combatants, for in the contest and with their own eyes they saw by means of their sister the One who was crucified for them, so that Christ might convince those who believe in him that all who suffer for Christ's glory will have everlasting fellowship with the living God. When none of the wild beasts touched her, she was taken down from the stake and brought back to the prison. . . .

The blessed Blandina was last of all. Like a noble mother encouraging her children, she sent them victorious before her to the King. Filling up the measure of all the struggles of her children, she hastened to them with rejoicing and gladness at her death, as if invited to a bridal banquet and not as thrown to the wild beasts. After the scourges, the wild beasts, the hot frying pan, at last she was thrown into a net and was exposed to a bull. After being much tossed about by the animal, she no longer had any feeling of what was happening, because she had hope, held on to the things believed, and had communion with Christ. She too was sacrificed, while the pagans themselves acknowledged that no woman among them had suffered so many and such terrible things. (Eusebius, *Church History* 5.1.18-19, 41-42, 55-56)

PASSION OF PERPETUA AND FELICITAS: [Perpetua writes:] **9**
While we were still in official custody, my father out of his affection for me would have desired with words to turn me around and have prevailed upon me to change my purpose. "Father," I said, "do you see, for example, this utensil lying here, a waterpot or something else?" And he said, "I see it." And I said to him, "It could not be called by any other name than what it is, could it?" And he said, "No." "Even so I cannot call myself by any other name than what I am, a Christian.". . .

After a few days, we were placed in the prison. I was terrified, because I had never experienced such darkness. O day of despair! Terrible heat because of the crowding. Extortion by the soldiers. Worst of all I was tormented by anxiety for my baby. . . . I claimed the right for the baby to remain with me in prison. At once I recovered my health, and I was relieved of my worry and anxiety for my baby. The prison suddenly became a palace for me, so that I preferred to be there rather than anywhere else. . . .

XIX.   [The compiler continues:] As for Felicitas, she too experienced the Lord's grace in this manner. She was now in the eighth month with child (for she was pregnant when arrested). As the day of the games approached, she was in great sorrow lest her martyrdom be postponed because of her pregnancy (since it was not lawful for a pregnant woman to be exhibited for punishment) and she should shed her holy, innocent blood later with heinous criminals. Her fellow martyrs were also greatly saddened that they would leave behind alone such a good companion and fellow traveler in the same road of hope. On the third day before the games they poured forth prayer to the Lord in united and common grief. Soon after the prayer her birth pains came upon her . . . . One of the assistants of the prison guards said to her, If you suffer so much in this, what will you do when you are tossed to the wild beasts, whom you despised when you refused to sacrifice?" She responded, "What I suffer now, I suffer myself. But at that time another will be in me who will suffer for me, since I will suffer for him." Thus she gave birth to a girl, whom one of the sisters brought up as her own daughter. . . . .

The day of their victory dawned, and they went joyfully in procession from the prison to the amphitheater as if to heaven. Their appearance was composed, and they trembled, if at all, with joy and not fear. Perpetua followed with shining appearance and calm step, as a wife of Christ, as beloved of God, putting down everyone's stare with the intensity of her own eyes. . . .

The martyrs kissed one another so that they might accomplish their martyrdom with the customary rites of the kiss of peace. . . . Perpetua, having yet more pain to taste, was struck to the bone and cried out. She herself guided the wavering right hand of the inexperienced gladiator to her throat. It was as if so great a woman, who was feared by the unclean spirit, could not die unless she herself willed it. (3; 15; 18; 21)[1]

10   MONTANISTS: The Phrygians received the beginning of their heresy from a certain Montanus, Priscilla, and Maximilla. They considered these women to be prophetesses and Montanus to be a prophet. (Hippolytus, *Refutation of All Heresies* 10.25)

11   The devil . . . raised up and filled with a spurious spirit two other women so that like [Montanus] they spoke in ecstasy, unsuitably and abnormally. (An anonymous opponent, quoted by Eusebius, *Church History* 5.16.9)

12   There suddenly came forth a certain woman prone to ecstacy who presented herself as a prophetess and acted as if she were filled with the Holy Spirit. . . . That woman, who previously by deceptions and tricks of the demon attempted many things to deceive the faithful, among other things by which she deceived many dared frequently even this, that by an invocation not to be despised she pretended to sanctify the bread itself and to celebrate the eucharist and she offered the sacrifice to the Lord by the sacrament of the usual prayer. She also baptized many, employing the

customary and proper words of interrogation so that nothing might seem different from the ecclesiastical rule. (Firmilian in Cyprian, *Epistles* 75 [74].10)

TERTULLIAN: A certain female viper of the Cainite heresy, who recently spent some time here, carried away many with her most venomous doctrine, giving first importance to destroying baptism. . . . That most atrocious woman, to whom it was not lawful to teach correctly, knew very well how to kill the little fishes [Christians] by taking them away from the water. . . .

The impudence of that woman who assumed the right to teach [against baptism] of course did not seize for herself also the right of baptizing. . . . For how would it seem worthy of belief that Paul would give to a female the power to teach and to baptize who did not permit a woman boldly to learn. (*On Baptism* 1; 17)

The very women among the heretics — what impudence! For they dare to teach, to dispute, to do exorcisms, to promise healings, perhaps also to baptize. (*Prescription Against Heretics* 41)

HIPPOLYTUS: When a widow is appointed she is not ordained but she shall be chosen by name. . . . Let the widow be instituted by word only and (then) let her be reckoned among the (enrolled) widows. But she shall not be ordained, because she does not offer the oblation nor has she a (liturgical) ministry. But ordination is for the clergy on account of their (liturgical) ministry. But the widow is appointed for prayer, and this is (a function) of all (Christians). (*Apostolic Tradition* 11.1, 4-5)[2]

APOSTOLIC CHURCH ORDER: Three widows shall be appointed, two to persevere in prayer for all those who are in temptation, and for the reception of revelations where such are necessary, but one to assist the women visited with sicknesses, she must be ready for service, discrete, communicating what is necessary to the presbyters, not avaricious, not given to much love of wine, so that she may be sober and capable of performing the night services, and other loving service if she will; for these are the chief good treasures of the Lord. (5)[3]

DIDASCALIA: Wherefore, O bishop, . . . those that please thee out of all the people thou shalt choose and appoint as deacons: a man for the performance of the most things that are required, but a woman for the ministry of women. For there are houses whither thou canst not send a deacon to the women, on account of the heathen, but mayest send a deaconess. Also, because in many other matters the office of a woman deacon is required. In the first place, when women go down into the water, those who go down into the water ought to be anointed by a deaconess with the oil of anointing. . . . But let a man pronounce over

13

14

15

16

17

XIX.   them the invocation of the divine Names in the water.
And when she who is being baptized has come up from the water, let
the deaconess receive her, and teach and instruct her how the seal of
baptism ought to be (kept) unbroken in purity and holiness. . . . And
thou hast need of the ministry of a deaconess for many things; for a
deaconess is required to go into the houses of the heathen where there are
believing women, and to visit those who are sick, and to minister to them
in that of which they have need, and to bathe those who have begun to
recover from sickness. (16)[4]

DISCUSSION

Women most often appear in early Christian literature in their
traditional roles of wives and mothers. The quotations from Clement of
Rome and Polycarp (XIX.1, 2) are similar to the "Household Codes" of
the New Testament, which in turn reflect the norms of Jewish, Greek,
and Roman society about the functions and duties of different classes in
society. The husband was the head of the family, but in the sphere of the
home the wife had the management of affairs, although with ultimate
responsibility to his authority. Clement uses the verb form of the noun in
Titus 2:5, "good managers of the household," and both passages use the
same language of submission that characterized the "Household Codes."[5]
Clement and Polycarp share the word for family love or affection (stergō;
cf. the related noun in 2 Tim. 3:3), and Polycarp distinguishes this love
for the husband from the agapē love (active good will) that the wife has
for all others.

Clement of Alexandria has descriptions of a woman's household duties
that are traditional.[6] He is notable among early Christian authors,
however, for his emphasis on the spiritual equality of men and women
(XIX.3).[7] "The virtue of man and woman is the same," "Marriage is an
equal yoke" and "The name human being is common to men and
women."[8] The bodily anatomy of men and women differs, but "in respect
to the soul, there is sameness."[9] Clement's concern in discussing male-
female relations and marriage, as in dealing with other topics, is virtue.
He nonetheless accepts the societal norms about family structure: The
woman ordinarily is submissive to her husband. When it comes to matters
of "virtue and salvation," however, there is a superior calling to which the
wife adheres.

Clement of Alexandria and Tertullian of Carthage are usually
contrasted in temperament and in views on philosophy and culture, but
it is remarkable how they agree on many matters of morality. Tertullian is
usually castigated for some harsh words about women.[10] Nevertheless, he
penned one of the most beautiful tributes to Christian marriage in early
Christian literature (XIX.4). Tertullian in this context was offering a
contrast to the problems caused by a mixed marriage for a Christian

woman married to a pagan husband. Her Christian activities (keeping fasts and vigils, visiting the poor, going to evening love feasts, exchanging the kiss of peace, showing hospitality) would either be resisted or be occasions of suspicion by a pagan husband, not to mention the pagan customs in which he would wish his wife to participate.[11] Tertullian, furthermore, as a Montanist wrote of the superior value of chastity over marital relations[12] and opposed second marriages, even in the case of the death of a spouse.[13] These attitudes, however, do not detract from his attractive picture of the shared religious life of two believers united in marriage.

On the other hand, many Christian women (and men) lived a single life, whether from choice or failure to find a suitable mate (XIX.5, 6). The apologists pointed to this as proof that Christians did not engage in sexually promiscuous rituals. In fact, they repeat the common philosophical viewpoint of the time that marriage was only for bringing children into the world. This limitation reduces the Biblical teaching about sexuality in marriage (e.g. 1 Cor. 7:2-5), but it is understandable in a time when the common options were the extremes of sexual indulgence or the revulsion against sex promoted in the ascetic movements of the time. Even those Christian authors who defended marriage against heretical groups (Marcionites and some Gnostics) often regarded virginity as a higher form of life. Asceticism had a powerful appeal in the world of late antiquity. Early Christians felt that appeal and while affirming the goodness of creation and marriage recognized that a person could forego a good in the interests of (for them) a higher calling (XIX.6).

The great respect for virginity in the mainstream of the church and the statements that refer favorably to those women and men who lived their lives faithfully without entering into marriage were the orthodox counterpart to those teachings that required abstinence altogether from sexual activity. We find this viewpoint not only in clearly heterodox circles (Marcionites and Gnostics) but in the apocryphal acts, whose orthodoxy is often suspect, but many of which flourished in a borderland between the mainstream of the church and other currents of thought.

The *Acts of Paul and Thecla* (a major surviving part of the *Acts of Paul*) are typical of the ascetic emphasis in the apocryphal acts, although more orthodox in doctrine than some of the others. Thecla's refusal of marriage in order to live a life of continence reflects the ascetic tendencies so prominent in the apocryphal acts. For these documents the gospel message became, "Fear one single God only, and live chastely."[14] The *Acts of Paul and Thecla* were used to support the right of women to teach and to baptize (since she baptized herself).[15] Regardless of the accuracy of the narratives, and there are a number of problematic features of her story, she is a reminder of the importance of women in spreading the Christian message. There evidently was a real person named Thecla who made quite an impact in southeastern Asia Minor, for her cult became widespread. Her desire to accompany Paul in his missionary travels evidently involved difficulties of which she was aware, hence her offer to cut her hair, presumably so she could pass as a man. The statements about Thecla's missionary activities (XIX.7) do not specify the setting in which she did her teaching other than in homes. The second-century pagan critic of Christianity, Celsus, complained that the women's quarters of houses were among the places where the Christian message spread.[16] The persecutions experienced by Thecla for refusing the life expected of her and following Paul and his teachings (not included in the quotations) parallel in some respects the stories of women martyrs.

Martyrdom was an equal opportunity employer, and some of the most notable names in the early history of Christian martyrdom were women. Two of the earliest and two of the most impressive martyrs of either sex were Blandina and Perpetua.[17] We are fortunate to possess a detailed contemporary account of the persecution that occurred in 177 in Lyons, Gaul (modern France), contained in a letter written by the churches of Vienne and Lyons to fellow believers in the provinces of Asia and Phrygia and preserved by Eusebius (*Church History* 5.1-4). The letter offers much data for a theology of martyrdom as well as many insights into beliefs and customs at a crucial time in early Christian history.[18] The persecution was particularly severe, and many interesting stories involving a number of heroic individuals (and others not so heroic) came out of the experience. Although many persons were involved in martyrdom, the individual who emerged as the emotional inspiration for the Christians, the marvel of the unbelievers, and the heroine to modern readers is the young slave Blandina (XIX.8). The fire of persecution was fanned by reports of immorality among the Christians such as the apologists had to refute (Ch. XVI). Hence, Blandina added to the usual confession of the martyrs, "I am a Christian" (cf. XIX.9),[19] that Christians did not do the things of which they were accused. Although young, physically not appearing to be strong, and as a woman not expected to be so indomitable, she demonstrated the appropriateness of the title "martyr," that is "witness," and represented the way in which the martyrs won attention and admiration for the Christian faith.[20] Blandina not only imitated Christ in her passion but she and others also were sustained by the presence of Christ. In their suffering was manifested "Christ's glory" and "everlasting fellowship with the living God."

The *Passion of Perpetua and Felicitas* makes explicit the point that Christ suffers in and with his people (XIX.9). The document incorporates the diary of Perpetua, making it notable as one of the rare writings of a woman from the early church. The compiler identifies Vibia Perpetua as "nobly born, well educated, a married woman, . . . with an infant son at the breast, and about twenty-two years of age" (2). She and five other catechumens (including two slaves, Revocatus and Felicitas) were arrested. The portion that is quoted records the first of repeated efforts by

Perpetua's father to dissuade her from her Christian confession. Between her arrest and imprisonment she was baptized. A striking feature of Perpetua's diary is the number of visions (dreams) she had while in prison, one of the features that has caused some scholars to associate the document in some way with Montanism. Perpetua's courage in many tribulations, her modesty, and her victorious confession, placing Christ above family and position in society, made an indelible impression on North African Christianity.

Tertullian did not like women in any teaching or leadership position (XIX.13, 14), but he is not the whole story. However, it is mainly in schismatic and heretical bodies that we hear of women taking teaching and leadership roles.[21] They were especially prominent in the Montanist movement.[22] Montanism gets its name from Montanus, one of the leaders in a movement that revived prophecy and called for stricter Christian living.[23] The Montanists called themselves the "New Prophecy," but their opponents called them the "Phrygian heresy." Beginning in central Asia Minor, the movement spread to Rome and North Africa. Women, especially the prophetesses Priscilla and Maximilla, were prominent in the beginning and continued to exercise a leadership in the movement far greater than women did in the great church and to an extent that disturbed orthodox churchmen. At least this was so in Asia Minor (XIX.12). It may not have been true everywhere, for Tertullian in North Africa (after he identified with Montanism) refers to a woman who received visions during church but reported their contents only after the conclusion of the services.[24]

The principal objection of their opponents to Montanism (XIX.9) was the practice of ecstatic prophecy. A fourth-century literary debate between a Montanist and an orthodox Christian clarifies that the orthodox did not object to women prophesying and cites biblical examples — Miriam, Mary, daughters of Philip. Making an unwarranted extension of the Scripture, however, the orthodox champion claims that for women to write books under their own names was to "prophesy without a veil" (1 Cor. 11:5); but he seems to speak for the church at large when he says, "we do not permit women to speak in the assemblies nor to have authority over men" (1 Tim. 2:12).[25]

Polycarp's instructions to widows (XIX.2) to pray unceasingly is reminiscent of 1 Timothy 5:5. The language of the widow as an "altar of God" was fairly common in the early centuries.[26] Two strands of thought are reflected in the imagery. The gifts offered for the support of widows were viewed as a sacrifice, hence to give to widows was like bringing a sacrifice to the altar. The ministry performed by widows was especially prayer, and prayer was viewed as a spiritual sacrifice; hence widows were the place where sacrifice was offered to God.

Widows as an order of ministry (1 Tim. 5:9-12) were not always clearly distinguished from widows as an object of charity, but the church orders

(XIX.15, 16) make clear that some widows were set aside as a distinct class. There seems to have been a continuity in their presence, along with bishops and deacons, in at least some of the churches from New Testament times. It is assumed that many of them will not be physically capable of much activity. Their ministry is the very important ministry of prayer. A notable residue from early times, now in an orthodox setting, is that in answer to prayer the widows may receive revelations. Those widows still able to do so were supported by the church for benevolent activities, especially in the care of the sick. The twofold ministry of prayer and benevolence by widows harkens back to 1 Timothy 5:5, 10. It appears that in some instances a place for virgins in the ministry of the church was found by including them in the order of widows.[27]

Another class of women servants in the church, not always distinguished from widows, were female deacons, or deaconesses. Apart from possible New Testament references (perhaps Rom. 16:1; more likely but not certainly 1 Tim. 3:11), the earliest reference to women deacons may be from the pagan author Pliny (VII.1). He speaks of those called *ministrae*, "female servants." His manner of expression suggests a technical usage, but this is not certain, and the word did not continue as the Latin term for a deaconess (Latin used the feminine form of a borrowed Greek word, *diakona*). These women referred to by Pliny may have had an official designation in the church, but there are other possibilities. They may only have been known as devoted to Christ (a usual meaning of the word is a devotee of a deity) or as especially active in Christian service, or Christians may have preferred this term over "slaves" (which these women were) to describe valued slaves who were also believers.

The earliest certain reference to deaconesses is in the third-century Syriac *Didascalia*. Here they are paired with male deacons and assigned duties in the baptism of women and in visiting women at home where a woman's services were more appropriate than a man's. Although Tertullian took particular offense to women baptizing (XIX.13, 14),[28] the *Didascalia* shows them assisting at baptism while a male clergyman presided. The deaconesses' responsibilities included teaching the new female converts.

Christian literature reflects the circumstances of the time in having less to say about women than men. Fewer women than men are known by name. Since the activities of women to which objection was taken pertained especially to false teachers, this is understandable, for there was a convention not to dignify opponents (men or women) by giving their name. In certain notable cases it was impossible to avoid this, so it is a recognition of the importance of Priscilla and Maximilla in Montanism that they are often mentioned along with the male leader (XIX.10). Thecla, too, made enough of an impact that her name was preserved, for the orthodox had to make accommodation for her. Otherwise, martyrs were the main class of women from the early period whose names are preserved–there are others besides the ones mentioned in these selections.[29] In spite of their virtual anonymity, women were clearly important to the life and growth of early Christianity. In orthodox, mainstream circles the same situation prevailed as that reflected in the New Testament documents: a very full involvement of women in every aspect of the church's life except speaking in the public liturgical assemblies and serving as elders/bishops.

BIBLIOGRAPHY

Clark, Elizabeth A. *Women in the Early Church*. Message of the Fathers of the Church 13. Collegeville: Liturgical Press, 1983.

Ferguson, Everett. "Women in the Post-Apostolic Church." Carroll D. Osburn, ed. *Essays on Women in Earliest Christianity*, Vol. I. Joplin: College Press, 1993. Pp. 493-513.

LaPorte, Jean. *The Role of Women in Early Christianity*. Studies in Women and Religion 7. New York: Edwin Mellen Press, 1982.

Scholer, David M., ed. *Women in Early Christianity*. Everett Ferguson, ed., Studies in Early Christianity, Vol. XIV. New York: Garland, 1993.

NOTES

[1] I have used the chapter numbers and translated from the text of Herbert Musurillo, *The Acts of the Christian Martyrs*, Oxford Early Christian Texts (Oxford: Clarendon, 1972).

[2] Gregory Dix, *The Apostolic Tradition of St. Hippolytus* (Reissued with Corrections; London: SPCK, 1968), pp. 20-21.

[3] A. Harnack, *Sources of the Apostolic Canons* (London: Adam and Charles Black, 1895), pp. 19-21.

[4] R. Hugh Connolly, *Didascalia Apostolorum: The Syriac Version Translated and Accompanied by the Verona Latin Fragments* (Oxford: Clarendon Press, 1929), pp. 146-148.

[5] P. H. Towner, "Household Codes," *Dictionary of the Later New Testament & Its Developments*, ed. Ralph P. Martin and Peter H. Davids (Downers Grove: InterVarsity Press, 1997), pp. 513-520 with further bibliography. *First Clement* 21.6-7 gives further moral advice to wives.

[6] For example, *Instructor* 3.10.

[7] Donald Kinder, "Clement of Alexandria: Conflicting Views on Women," *The Second Century*, Vol. 7 (1989-90), pp. 213-220; repr. in Everett Ferguson, ed., *Christianity and Society: The Social World of Early Christianity*, Recent Studies in Early Christianity, Vol. I (New York: Garland, 1999), pp.55-62.

[8] *Instructor* 1.4.

[9] *Miscellanies* 4.8.

[10] Notably, *On the Apparel of Women* 1.1.

[11] *To His Wife* 2.4-6.

[12] *Exhortation to Chastity* 1.

[13] *On Monogamy*.

[14] *Acts of Paul and Thecla* 9.

[15] Tertullian, *On Baptism* 17.

[16] Origen, *Against Celsus* 3.49, 55-56.

[17] W. H. C. Frend, "Blandina and Perpetua: Two Early Christian Heroines," *Les Martyrs de Lyon (177): Colloque à Lyon 20-23 Septembre 1977* (Paris: Centre National de la Recherche Scientifique, 1978), pp. 167-177; repr. in David Scholer, ed., *Women in Early Christianity*, in Everett Ferguson, ed., *Studies in Early Christianity*, Vol. XIV (New York: Garland, 1993), pp. 87-97; Stuart Hall, "Women among the Early Martyrs," *Studies in Church History*, Vol. 30 (1993), pp. 1-21; repr. in Everett Ferguson, ed., *Christianity in Relation to Jews, Greeks, and Romans*, Recent Studies in Early Christianity, Vol. II (New York: Garland, 1999), pp. 301-321.

[18] Denis Farkasfalvy, "Christological Content and Its Biblical Basis in the Letter of the Martyrs of Gaul," *The Second Century*, Vol. 9 (1992), pp. 5-25; repr. in Everett Ferguson, ed., *Christianity in Relation to Jews, Greeks,and Romans*, Recent Studies in Early Christianity, Vol. II (New York: Garland, 1999), pp. 279-299.

[19] For example, *Acts of the Scillitan Martyrs*; *Acts of Justin and Companions* 3-4; *Martyrdom of Saints Carpus, Papylus, and Agathonice*.

[20] Everett Ferguson, "Early Christian Martyrdom and Civil Disobedience," *Journal of Early Christian Studies*, Vol. 1 (1993), pp. 73-83;

repr. in idem, *Christianity in Relation to Jews, Greeks, and Romans*, Recent Studies in Early Christianity, Vol. II (New York: Garland, 1999), pp. 267-277.

[21] That women were significantly better off in Montanist and Gnostic sects is effectively challenged by Paul McKechnie, "'Women's Religion' and Second Century Christianity," *Journal of Ecclesiastical History*, Vol. 47 (1996), pp. 409-431; repr. Everett Ferguson, ed., *Christianity and Society: The Social World of Early Christianity*, Recent Studies in Early Christianity, Vol. I (New York: Garland, 1999), pp. 31-53.

[22] Christine Trevett, *Montanism: Gender, Authority, and the New Prophecy* (Cambridge: Cambridge University Press, 1996), pp. 151-197, concludes that although we know of some women who took exceptional leadership positions in Montanism, the evidence is lacking that women in general had different circumstances in Montanism from what they experienced elsewhere.

[23] The sources are conveniently collected in English translation in Ronald E. Heine, *The Montanist Oracles and Testimonia*, Patristic Monograph Series 14 (Macon: Mercer University Press, 1989) and William Tabbernee, *Montanist Inscriptions and Testimonia: Epigraphic Sources Illustrating the History of Montanism*, Patristic Monograph Series 16 (Macon: Mercer University Press, 1996).

[24] *On the Soul* 9.

[25] The whole dialogue is translated in Ronald E. Heine, *The Montanist Oracles and Testimonia*, pp. 113-127 (the passage referred to is on p. 125).

[26] Carolyn Osiek, "The Widow as Altar: The Rise and Fall of a Symbol," *The Second Century*, Vol. 3 (1983), pp. 159-169.

[27] Tertullian, *On the Veiling of Virgins* 9; this may be the meaning of Ignatius, *Smyrnaeans* 13. Charlotte Methuen, "The 'Virgin Widow': A Problematic Social Role for the Early Church?" *Harvard Theological Review*, Vol. 90 (1997), pp. 285-298; repr. in Everett Ferguson, ed., *Christianity and Society: The Social World of Early Christianity*, Recent Studies in Early Christianity, Vol. I (New York: Garland, 1999), pp. 63-76.

[28] Epiphanius, *Against Heresies* 42.3.4 says Marcionites authorized women to baptize.

[29] For example, Agathonice among the saints of Pergamum and Donata, Vestia, Secunda, Sperata, Januaria, and Generosa among the martyrs of Scilli.

Glossary

Adoptionism. The view that Jesus Christ was a good man whom God adopted as his son but who was not in nature divine.

Ante-Nicene. The period before the Council of Nicaea which met in A.D. 325.

Apocrypha. Books written in imitation of biblical books or claiming to preserve material from biblical times but not accepted by the church as genuine.

Apologists. Defenders of the Christian faith who wrote against paganism and Judaism.

Catechumenate. The period of instruction preparatory to baptism.

Church Orders. A class of documents giving instructions about the life, worship, and organization of the church.

Codex. The book form of binding leaves of a manuscript together in contrast to rolls.

Docetism. The view that Jesus Christ only seemed to be a real human being (the Greek dokeō means "to seem" or "appear") but was a wholly spiritual being.

Doctor. A teacher; the title is restricted to the outstanding, authoritative teachers of the ancient church.

Doxology. A word of praise offered to the Deity.

Eastern Church. The church in the eastern part of the Mediterranean world and further east, which in the early period developed mainly in areas of Greek cultural influence.

Ecumenical. Universal or world-wide.

Encratite. The tendency to extremes of self-control in abstention from marriage and animal food.

Eucharist. From "thanksgiving," and used in the early church for the whole service of the Lord's supper.

Fathers. The spiritual leaders of the early church.

Gnosticism. The movement which emphasized salvation by revealed "knowledge" and de-emphasized the historical and material aspects of Christian doctrine.

Heresy. From the meaning of a self-chosen viewpoint held to the point of making a division, it came to refer to false doctrine.

Homily. A popular or familiar form of address; a sermon.

Liturgy. Divine service, especially used of the fixed forms of worship which emerged through traditional usage.

Metropolitans. Bishops of the major cities accorded a higher rank than other bishops.

Modalism. The view that there is only one person in the Godhead who assumes different modes of self-revelation (Father, Son, and Holy Spirit) in the history of salvation.

Monepiscopacy. The form of organization in the church where there is only one bishop in a congregation presiding over the presbyters and deacons.

Montanism. A movement originating in Asia Minor in the later second century which sought to revive prophecy in the church and practiced rigorous moral standards.

Papyrus. A writing material similar to paper made from the papyrus plant which flourished in the Nile valley of Egypt.

Patriarchs. The title which came to be accorded to the bishops of five principal churches–Rome, Constantinople, Alexandria, Antioch, and Jerusalem.

Post-Nicene. The period after the first ecumenical council at Nicaea in A.D. 325.

Presbyter. The spelling in English letters of the Greek word for elder.

Quartodeciman. The observance of the resurrection of Christ on the fourteenth of the month Nisan, regardless of what day of the week it fell on; this accommodation to Jewish Passover reckoning was repudiated by the church at large which insisted that the annual commemoration of the resurrection should be on the nearest Sunday.

Schism. A division over matters of practice where the basic doctrines were the same.

Western Church. The church in the western part of the Mediterranean world which developed under Roman (or Latin) cultural influences.

Alphabetical List
of Sources Cited

Abercius. Bishop of Hieropolis who died before 216.

Acts of John. Probably the earliest of the apocryphal acts, composed in Asia Minor shortly after the middle of the second century, and showing Docetic and Gnostic tendencies.

Acts of Paul and Thecla. Part of the apocryphal *Acts of Paul*, which was compiled in Asia Minor in the late second century.

Acts of Peter. Written late in the second century, they show the ascetic tendency characteristic of the apocryphal acts.

Ambrose. Bishop of Milan, 374-397; one of the great doctors of the Latin Church; influential ecclesiastical statesman and preacher.

Apostolic Church Order. Compiled in Egypt around 300 from earlier sources, some of which may be second-century.

Apostolic Constitutions. Eight books of legislative and liturgical material compiled and rewritten from earlier sources in the late fourth century, claiming to come from the apostles through Clement of Rome.

Aristides. A Christian from Athens who composed the earliest surviving apology for Christianity, addressed to the emperor Hadrian about A.D. 125.

Athenagoras. An apologist from Athens, who addressed a *Plea* on behalf of the Christians to Marcus Aurelius about 177.

Bardesanes. A Syrian Christian who died in 222/23; an influential religious teacher whose views were remembered in the church as tainted with Gnostic ideas.

Barnabas. The name given in tradition to an anonymous epistle, or treatise, written probably in Egypt early in the second century, claiming the old covenant (spiritually interpreted) for Christians instead of Jews, who are said to have misunderstood it by taking its prescriptions literally.

Basil of Caesarea. Bishop of Caesarea in Cappadocia, died 379, great church administrator, statesman, and theologian.

Celsus. A Middle Platonist philosopher who about 178 wrote the *True Discourse* setting forth pagan objections to Christianity.

Clement of Alexandria. A Christian teacher who attempted to harmonize the best in pagan culture with the Christian view; died before 215.

Clement of Rome. One of the bishops of Rome, who in the name of the church at Rome wrote a letter about A.D. 96 to the church at Corinth; later other works were ascribed to him.

Cyprian. Elected bishop of Carthage in 248 after he had been a Christian for only two years; martyred in 258; his extensive correspondence gives a good picture of North African church life.

Cyril of Jerusalem. Bishop of Jerusalem from 348 to 386, whose *Catechetical Lectures* are a major source for doctrinal and liturgical matters in the fourth century.

Didache. "The Teaching of the Twelve Apostles," the first church order, written in Syria in the late first or early second century.

Didascalia. Church order from Syria in the third century, preserved complete only in Syriac.

Dionysius of Corinth. Bishop of Corinth around 170 who carried on correspondence with churches over a wide area.

Epistle of the Apostles. An apocryphal document from around 150 claiming to report revelations made by Christ after his resurrection.

Epistle to Diognetus. An anonymous apology for Christianity of uncertain date but usually placed in the second century.

Eusebius. Bishop of Caesarea in Palestine from 313 to 339; his *Church History* contains an important collection of quotations from, and information about, earlier Christian writings.

Galen. A non-Christian medical writer from Pergamum who spent the last thirty years of his life in Rome, where he died in 199.

Gospel of Peter. An apocryphal Gospel written before 190 and expressing Docetic ideas.

Gregory of Nazianzus. Orator, theologian, friend of Basil of Caesarea; for a brief time bishop of Constantinople; lived 330 to 390.

Gregory of Nyssa. Philosophical theologian; brother of Basil of Caesarea; bishop of Nyssa in Cappadocia from 371 until about 394.

Hermas. A prophet at Rome in the early second century whose book the *Shepherd* is a collection of Visions, Mandates (Commands), and Similitudes (Parables) perhaps compiled over a period of several years.

Hippolytus. A presbyter at Rome in the early third century who wrote extensively in Greek and opposed the theology and disciplinary practices of the bishop Callistus; some scholars think more than one person wrote the works commonly attributed to him.

Ignatius. Bishop of Antioch who was taken about 110 to Rome for martyrdom and on the way addressed seven letters to churches and individuals about the pressing problems of the time.

Irenaeus. Bishop of Lyons in Gaul who about 180 wrote in defense of the orthodox Christian faith against Gnosticism.

Jerome. Prolific writer; great scholar; doctor of the Latin church; lived approximately 347 to 420.

John Chrysostom. As presbyter at Antioch, 386 to 397, he established a reputation as the greatest preacher of the Greek church; became bishop of Constantinople until his banishment in 404.

Justin. Born a pagan in Samaria, converted at Ephesus (perhaps), and a Christian teacher in Rome; the most important of the second-century Apologists; known as "Martyr" from the manner of his death.

Lucian of Samosata. Pagan author of satires, born about 120 and died after 180.

Martyrs of Lyons. The churches of Vienne and Lyons in southern Gaul (France) described the persecution of 177 in a letter (preserved by Eusebius) sent to fellow believers in the provinces of Asia and Phrygia.

Melito. Bishop of Sardis who flourished about 170, most of whose extensive writings have not survived.

Odes of Solomon. A collection of religious hymns having no connection with King Solomon, usually dated to the early second century but perhaps later.

Origen. Perhaps the greatest scholar and most prodigious writer of the ante-Nicene church; lived in Alexandria from 185 to 232 and thereafter at Caesarea until his death at Tyre in 253 from tortures inflicted during a persecution.

Papias. Bishop of Hierapolis in Phrygia, about 130, whose works are known only in fragments quoted by later writers.

Passion of Perpetua and Felicitas. Account of persecution and martyrdoms in Carthage in 203 that included the first-hand reports of Perpetua and Saturus.

Pliny. Known as the Younger to distinguish him from his uncle; Roman governor of Bithynia about 112.

Polycarp. Bishop of Smyrna in the early second century and reputed to have been a disciple of John; the date of his martyrdom is disputed, being placed between 155 and 178.

Second Clement. The oldest extant sermon, from the mid-second century, wrongly ascribed to Clement of Rome.

Sextus. The author of a Christianized version of *Sentences* or maxims drawn from Hellenistic popular philosophy and compiled toward the end of the second century.

Tatian. Author of an apology, about 170; a Syrian who became a leader of the Encratite movement in Christianity.

Tertullian. First major Christian author in Latin; from Carthage, lived about 155 to 222; in his later years associated with the Montanists.

Theophilus. Bishop of Antioch who about 180 wrote an apology on behalf of Christianity.

Time Chart

(Some of the dates are only approximately correct)

Dates	Christian Authors	Non-Christian Authors	Selected Roman Emperors	Events
90			Domitian	
	Didache (?)			Emergence of Monepiscopacy
	Clement of Rome			
			Trajan	
100				
110				
		Pliny the Younger		
	Ignatius Polycarp		Hadrian	
120	*Odes of Solomon* (?)			
	Aristides Papias			

Dates	Christian Authors	Non-Christian Authors	Selected Roman Emperors	Events
130				
	Epistle of Barnabas			
	Hermas			
140			Antoninus Pius	Gnostic crisis becomes acute
	Epistle to Diognetus (?)			Marcion dis-fellowshipped
150				
	Justin Martyr Epistle of the Apostles			
	Acts of John			
160	Second Clement		Marcus Aurelius	
		Lucian of Samosata		
170	Dionysius of Corinth Tatian			Montanist movement
	Melito			"Thundering Legion"
	Athenagoras	Celsus		
180	Theophilus		Commodus	Beginnings of Infant Baptism
	Irenaeus			
	Gospel of Peter Acts of Peter			
		Galen		

Dates	Christian Authors	Non-Christian Authors	Selected Roman Emperors	Events
190				Christological Controversy
	Clement of Alexandria		Septimius Severus	
	Abercius			
	Sextus			
200	"Apostles' Creed" Bardesanes			Beginnings of Christian art
	Tertullian			Hippolytus- Callistus Controversy
	Hippolytus			
225	Origen			Dura Europos "House Church"
	Gregory Thaumaturgus			
			Decius	"Clinical Baptism"
250				Novatian- Cornelius Controversy
	Cyprian		Valerian	
275				
			Diocletian	
300	*Apostolic Church Order*		Constantine	Edict of Toleration
	Eusebius of Caesarea			Council of Nicaea

Dates	Christian Authors	Non-Christian Authors	Selected Roman Emperors	Events
350				
	Cyril of Jerusalem			
	Basil of Caesarea			
375	Ambrose *Apostolic Constitutions* Gregory of Nazianzus Gregory of Nyssa			
	John Chrysostom Jerome		Theodosius I	
400				

Index of References

[Note that numbers in brackets are numbers of passages translated in the sources at the beginning of each chapter in this book.]

OLD TESTAMENT

NEW TESTAMENT

APOSTOLIC FATHERS

APOLOGISTS

MISCELLANEOUS WORKS

NON-CHRISTIAN SOURCES

General Index